# The Screwtape Texts

# The Screwtape Texts

## A Devil's Dialogue
## with His Tempter in Training

Deacon Timothy Stevenson

For your inspiration and guidance,
thank you Holy Spirit.

To my wife Shelley,
thank you for your love and encouragement.

## Acknowledgments

Many thanks to my friend John Revord and dozens of friends who participated in this project. You are a part of the final product.

A special thank you to my son Noah Stevenson, who edited this book. His technical skills and practical perspective were invaluable.

# Contents

# Preface

This study in spiritual warfare was inspired by an awareness that we are, whether we know it or not, on a spiritual journey. This journey has a single destination, ultimately heaven or hell.

For the past ten years I have met weekly with a group of men to discuss living as a Christian man in the world. Our conversations are based in faith and run the gamut of the human experience.

As the group was finishing a book, we considered what we could study next. In the past I had attempted to read C. S. Lewis' *The Screwtape Letters*. I was intrigued and impressed by the insights Lewis offered in this book, but found it challenging to read. For me, everything was upside down. The "Enemy" is God and "Our Father Below" is Satan.

Inspiration came to translate *The Screwtape Letters*, a collection of 31 letters written by a senior devil to a junior devil, into text message exchanges between the two main characters.

The premise of this book is to intercept text messages between the two demons and discover the tactics they use against humans in the midst of the hidden battle for human souls.

Beyond the rich conversations this translation generated, our group enjoyed having two members read the parts of Screwtape and Wormwood. This gave the text messages an additional dimension and enhanced our understanding of the concepts of the book.

## Battle Assessment

Before beginning to explore some of the tactics found in spiritual warfare, assess how you spend your time and what you focus on.

From the list on the next page, write each number on the radar, indicating where they appear on your radar today.

Place items that you spend more time doing or thinking about closer to the center. Items done or thought about less often should be placed further from the center.

Place items that you do not do or think about at all outside the radar.

Write each number where they "actually are" for you today, not where you think they "should be."

Place the items below (listed in alphabetical order) where they appear on your radar.

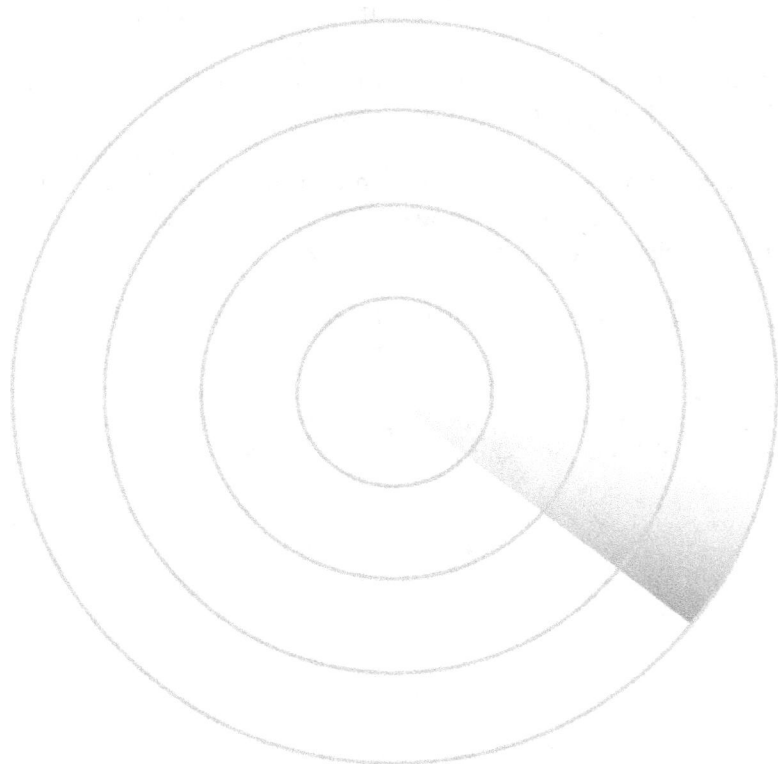

1. Angels and demons
2. Clothes
3. Computers / gaming
4. Family / children
5. Fear / worry
6. Friends
7. God
8. Hobby / recreation
9. Home maintenance
10. Life after death
11. Money / career
12. Physical health
13. Prayer
14. Relationships
15. Retirement / savings
16. Serving others
17. Silence
18. Social media
19. Spiritual life
20. Sports team
21. Vehicles

# Introduction

This work, primarily a collection of letters, now text message exchanges, provides insight into a battle in which you participate now, perhaps even without realizing it. Your life is the battle-ground, your soul is the prize, and the forces of evil actively seek to win your soul away from goodness and holiness and towards evil.

Based on C. S. Lewis' book, *The Screwtape Letters*, this work provides a look into our enemies' playbook. It exposes some of our enemies' motives and tactics and provides an understanding into their techniques for sowing evil.

Armor and weapons are offered for protecting and defending yourself in this battle. These include resources and questions to ponder that will raise your awareness and challenge you to think deeper. Going through this book with a group can also provide help and insights from others who are also fighting this battle.

If you are not familiar with *The Screwtape Letters*, it is a collection of letters written from the devil's perspective on how to draw humans away from God (the devil's enemy) and toward Hell.

Characters in The Screwtape Letters:

- Screwtape: Wormwood's uncle, a senior demon who is providing advice to Wormwood, a junior demon
- Wormwood: Screwtape's nephew, a junior demon who is being trained in how to get his patient into hell
- The Patient: the human to whom Wormwood is assigned
- The Enemy: God
- Our Father Below: Lucifer / Satan
- The Patient's mother: The Christian woman whom the Patient lives with. She battles a form of gluttony that inevitably creates division between her family and friends.
- Glubose: The demon in charge of the patient's mother. His job is to cause discord between her and her son.
- The Patient's fiancé: A kind, loving, attractive, and dedicated young Christian woman. She is a virgin and full of virtues. She comes from a charitable and loving Christian family.
- Slubgob: The principal of the Training College for Young Tempters.
- Slumtrimpet: A young female devil in charge of the patient's fiancé.

The end of each text message conversation includes:

- A summary of the text message
- References to Scripture and the Catechism of the Catholic Church (in this book abbreviated CCC)
- Counterattack suggestions (actions to assist humans in the battle)
- Reflection questions

Quotes from authors and saints also appear throughout this book.

# The History of the Battle

## Who is in the battle?

Humans and angels. The beginning of the Christian (Nicene) Creed professes: "I believe in one God, the Father almighty, maker of heaven and earth, of all things visible and invisible."

Humans are visible creations of God. Angels are invisible creations of God.

## The announcement

God announced to the angels that the second person of the Trinity would become human, take the flesh of a human woman, and that the angels should adore him.

To make things worse (for some of the angels), this human woman would be their queen and she would surpass in glory all human and angelic creations.

## The angel's response

The good angels used their free will to obey and praise God.

Wanting to be like God, Lucifer rebelled and aspired to be the leader of the humans and angels, and dragged many fallen angels with him in his prideful quest.

## God's response

A battle broke out in heaven. This battle was spiritual and was fought with intelligence and wills. God gave Michael and his supporters the strength to vanquish Lucifer. Michael and the good angels fought against Lucifer and his angels.

## The result

Lucifer and his angels (the fallen angels) lost and were cast into hell. Punishment for the fallen angels is the pain of being deprived of seeing God and experiencing his love for all eternity.

## The battle on earth continues

Since the fallen angels are forever to exist separated from God and heaven, their desire is to take as many humans as they can with them to hell.

This battle is for the souls of humans. The fallen angels conduct their battle through temptation and suggestion.

> Be sober and vigilant. Your opponent the devil is prowling around like a roaring lion looking for [someone] to devour. Resist him, steadfast in faith, knowing that your fellow believers throughout the world undergo the same sufferings.
>
> ~ 1 Peter 5:8–9

> And do this because you know the time; it is the hour *now* for you to awake from sleep. For our salvation is nearer now than when we first believed; the night is advanced, the day is at hand. Let us then throw off the works of darkness [and] put on the armor of light; let us conduct ourselves properly as in the day, not in orgies and drunkenness, not in promiscuity and licentiousness, not in rivalry and jealousy. But put on the Lord Jesus Christ, and make no provision for the desires of the flesh.
>
> ~ Romans 13:11–14 (*emphasis* added)

A warning from C. S. Lewis regarding the battle:

There are two equal and opposite errors that we can fall into regarding the devils.

1.  To not believe in their existence
2.  To believe in their existence with an excessive and unhealthy interest

The devils are pleased by both errors.

~ from the Preface of *The Screwtape Letters*

## Resources

| Angels | |
|---|---|
| The creation of angels | Colossians 1:16 |
| Guardian angels | Matthew 18:10 |
| The father of lies | John 8:44 |
| The existence of angels – a truth of faith | CCC paragraphs 328–336 |
| The fall of the angels | CCC paragraphs 391–395 |
| **Spiritual Battle** | |
| The spiritual battle against evil | Ephesians 6:11-12 |
| The battle on Earth | 1 Peter 5:8-9 |
| The final battle | Revelation 12 |

### Prayer to Saint Michael the Archangel

St. Michael the Archangel,
defend us in battle.
Be our defense against the wickedness and snares of the Devil.
May God rebuke him, we humbly pray,
and do thou, O Prince of the heavenly hosts,
by the power of God,
thrust into hell Satan, and all the evil spirits,
who prowl about the world seeking the ruin of souls. Amen.

## The origins of the St. Michael Prayer

"One morning the great Pope Leo XIII had celebrated a Mass and, as usual, was attending a Mass of thanksgiving. Suddenly, we saw him raise his head and stare at something above the celebrant's head. He was staring motionlessly, without batting an eye. His expression was one of horror and awe; the color and look on his face changing rapidly. Something unusual and grave was happening to him."

"Finally, as though coming to his senses, he lightly but firmly tapped his hand and rose to his feet. He headed for his private office. His retinue followed anxiously and solicitously, whispering: 'Holy Father, are you not feeling well? Do you need anything?' He answered: 'Nothing, nothing.' About a half hour later, he called for the Secretary of the Congregation of Rites and, handing him a sheet of paper, requested that it be printed and sent to all the ordinaries around the world. What was the paper? It was the prayer that we recite with the people at the end of every Mass. It is the plea to Mary and the passionate request to the Prince of the heavenly host, beseeching God to send Satan back to Hell."

"...Leo XIII truly saw, in a vision, demonic spirits who were congregating on the Eternal City (Rome). The prayer that he asked all the Church to recite was the fruit of that experience."

From the magazine Ephemerides Liturgicae – 1995, pages 58–59.

Note: Since the Second Vatican Council, this prayer was no longer requested to be prayed after Mass. However, some parishes continue this practice.

## Counterattack Actions

- Notice how your relationships with others change after you become more aware of those around you as bodies and souls.
- Make use of your guardian angel that God has provided you. They are your ally.
- Pray the prayer to Saint Michael the Archangel.

## Questions

1. Do you believe in the existence of angels and demons? Why?

2. Why do you think some angels chose to reject God's plan? Do you think humans have the same choice and some make the same choice?

3. Why do you think the devils are happy with people not believing in their existence?

4. Do you believe that hell exists? Why?

5. What is your understanding of hell?

6. Have you ever heard a story about guardian angels?

7. Why do you think some angels hate Mary, the Mother of God?

8. How conscious are you of your soul? What do you think are attributes of the soul?

9. Would an increased awareness of your soul change your worship of God and your relationships with others (and their souls)? How?

## Text Message 1.1

9:00      ●      🛜 ᵈᵈᵈ 99% 🔋

**Screwtape**

Wormwood, what is the status of your patient?

**Wormwood**

Uncle, I've been guiding my patient's reading and making sure he spends lots of time with his materialistic friends.

You know, the types who try to convince him with logic that the spiritual world doesn't exist.

**Screwtape**

Are you assuming THAT'S how you keep the patient from the enemy?

That worked a few hundred years ago. That's when humans knew truth better. Back then they used reason to determine the truth, and then lived by that truth.

**Wormwood**

?

**Screwtape**

The enormous amount of information in their media has changed everything.

## Text Message 1.2

9:03 ⬤ 🛜 ▪️ 99% 🔋

**Screwtape**

Hehe, now human minds are cluttered with contradiction.

They don't think anything is black and white anymore. Everything is shades of gray. Keep your patient in the gray and you will keep him from the Church.

**Wormwood**

What else?

**Screwtape**

Keep him from seeking truth. Avoid arguing. Arguing can awaken the patient's reason!

If the patient begins to think deeply and ponder universal truths, truths that he cannot see or touch, quickly shift his attention to his immediate surroundings, like his hunger for lunch, the activity around him or to check his "smartphone."

**Wormwood**

OK! Anything else?

**Screwtape**

No matter what, don't use science as a defense against Christianity.

## Text Message 1.3

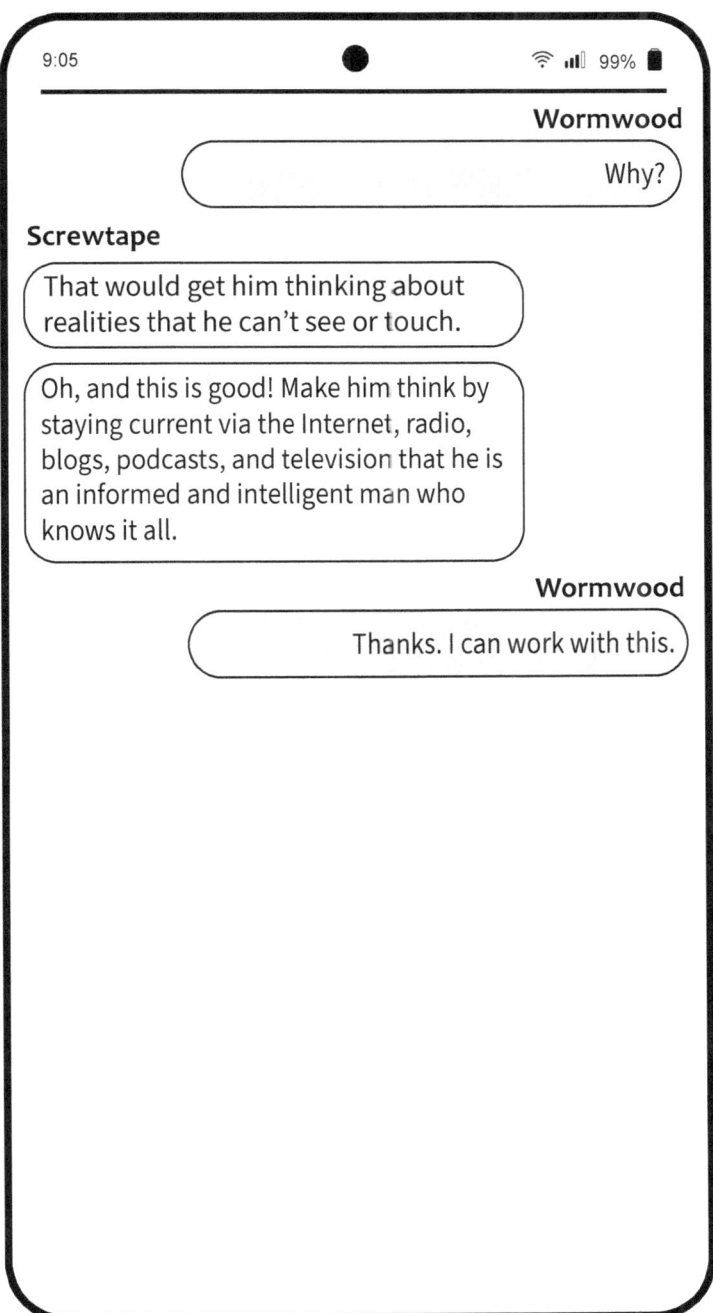

**9:05**  99%

**Wormwood**

Why?

**Screwtape**

That would get him thinking about realities that he can't see or touch.

Oh, and this is good! Make him think by staying current via the Internet, radio, blogs, podcasts, and television that he is an informed and intelligent man who knows it all.

**Wormwood**

Thanks. I can work with this.

## Summary

This page from the enemy's playbook suggests reason, deep thinking, and challenging relativism weaken the devil's attack. They encourage seeking truth. Remember, the devil is a liar.

## Resources

| On truth | John 8:31-32 |
| --- | --- |
| Jesus is truth | John 1:14 |
| Jesus is light | John 12:46 |
| The spirit of truth | John 16:13 |
| Let your yes mean yes | Matthew 5:37 |
| Living in the truth | CCC paragraphs 2465-2470 |

CCC paragraph 2470

The disciple of Christ consents to "live in the truth," that is, in the simplicity of a life in conformity with the Lord's example, abiding in his truth. "If we say we have fellowship with him while we walk in darkness, we lie and do not live according to the truth." 1 John 1:6

## Counterattack Actions

- Resist the suggestion or temptation to shift your thoughts away from, or to come back later to, thoughts on spiritual things.
- Make time for silence in your life.

Reason and Relativism

## Questions

1. Do you agree with the statement that humans generally are less concerned with truth today than they may have been a few hundred years ago? How?

2. Do you think the vast amount of information at our fingertips today is good or bad? Why?

3. Science can answer "how", but can it answer "why" to the big questions, such as what is the meaning of life?

4. Is it reasonable to think beliefs can be gray like Screwtape speaks of?

5. Can truth exist for things you cannot scientifically prove?

6. Can things of faith be gray, or must they be black and white? What are some examples?

7. Have you ever found yourself distracted when pondering truth or mysteries of the faith? What are your distractions? Could those distractions be spiritual warfare?

8. What do you do to combat temptations and suggestions like the ones Screwtape suggests in this text message?

## Text Message 2.1

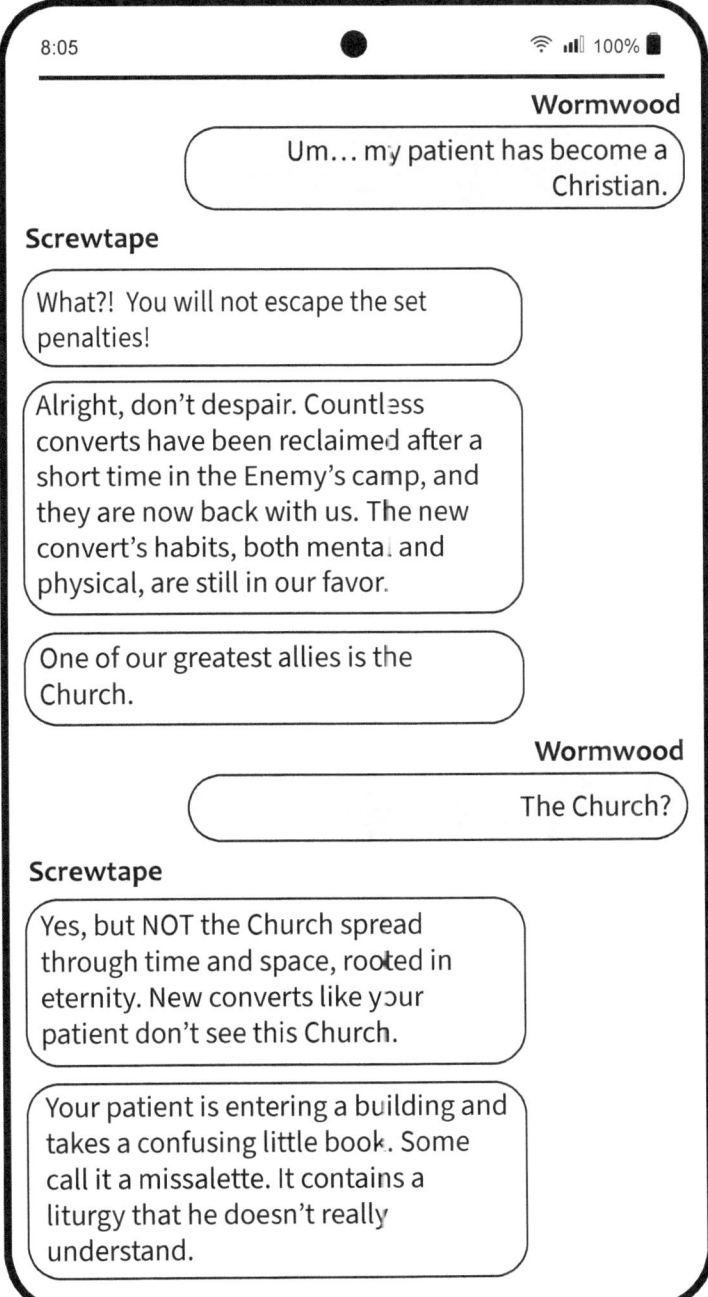

8:05     📶 100% 🔋

**Wormwood**

Um… my patient has become a Christian.

**Screwtape**

What?! You will not escape the set penalties!

Alright, don't despair. Countless converts have been reclaimed after a short time in the Enemy's camp, and they are now back with us. The new convert's habits, both mental and physical, are still in our favor.

One of our greatest allies is the Church.

**Wormwood**

The Church?

**Screwtape**

Yes, but NOT the Church spread through time and space, rooted in eternity. New converts like your patient don't see this Church.

Your patient is entering a building and takes a confusing little book. Some call it a missalette. It contains a liturgy that he doesn't really understand.

## Text Message 2.2

**Screwtape**

Then he goes to his pew and sees people, that not long ago, he would normally avoid.

Lean on those people around him.

**Wormwood**

How do I do that?

**Screwtape**

Make his mind jump back and forth between words like "the Body of Christ" and the actual faces in the pews.

Encourage him to judge. Get him to notice things like the person singing out of tune and the person wearing questionable clothing.

Keep him blissfully unaware of his own feelings and focused on the faults of others around him.

Get him questioning his new religion. Keep him hazy in his understanding of the Church. Focus on his disappointments as a new convert.

Do you know that the Enemy allows disappointment with the start of all new human endeavors?

## Text Message 2.3

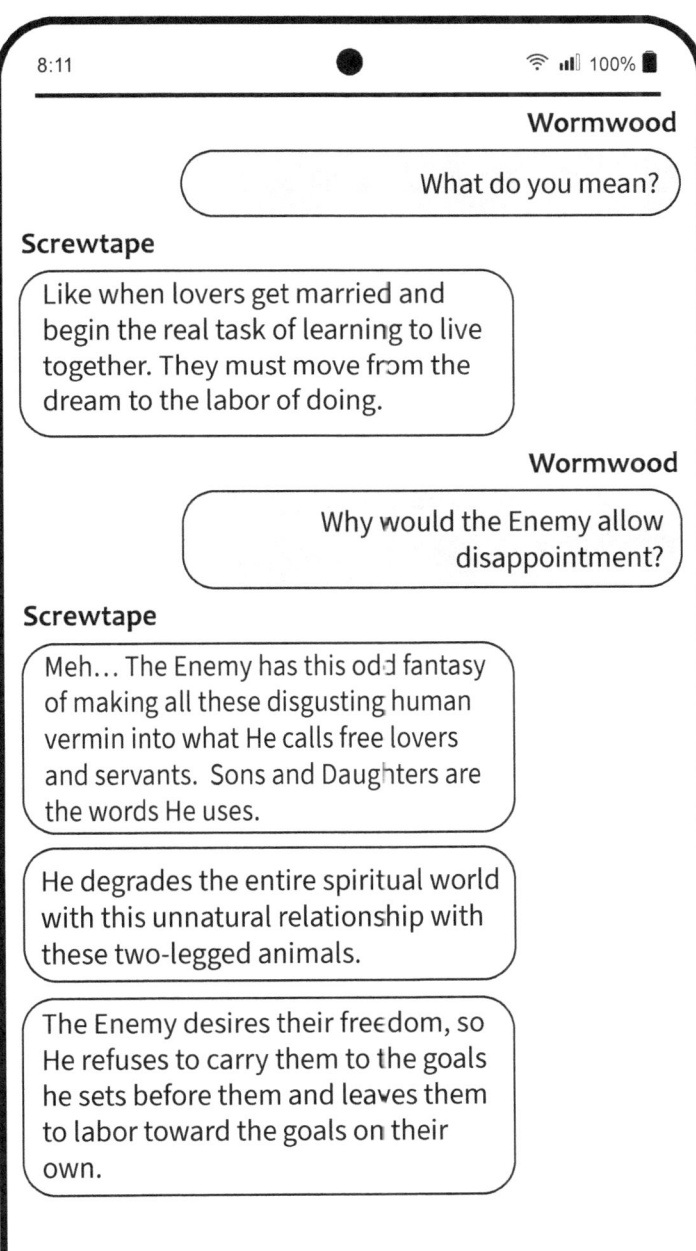

**Wormwood**

What do you mean?

**Screwtape**

Like when lovers get married and begin the real task of learning to live together. They must move from the dream to the labor of doing.

**Wormwood**

Why would the Enemy allow disappointment?

**Screwtape**

Meh… The Enemy has this odd fantasy of making all these disgusting human vermin into what He calls free lovers and servants. Sons and Daughters are the words He uses.

He degrades the entire spiritual world with this unnatural relationship with these two-legged animals.

The Enemy desires their freedom, so He refuses to carry them to the goals he sets before them and leaves them to labor toward the goals on their own.

## Text Message 2.4

8:13 ● 🛜 📶 100% 🔋

**Screwtape**

And THERE lies our opportunity!
… and our danger.
If the vermin get through the
spiritual dry spells, they become less
dependent on emotion and become
much harder to tempt.

**Wormwood**

Anything else uncle?

**Screwtape**

Yes. Your patient's level of humility is
likely to still be quite absent. Keep
him proud of his actions for as long as
you can.

**Wormwood**

OK. Avoid humility and encourage
pride.

## Summary

This page from the enemy's playbock suggests understanding your faith and the liturgy, and the virtues of perseverance and humility weaken the devil's attack. These things help us in our faith and spiritual life.

## Resources

| Contemplation | Luke 2:19 |
|---|---|
| Perseverance in faith | 1 Timothy 1:18–19, Mark 9:24 |
| The importance of faith | Galatians 5:6 |
| Faith and works | James 2:14–26 |
| Blessed are the poor in spirit | Matthew 5:3 |
| Humble and contrite heart | Psalm 130:1 |
| Growth in understanding the faith | CCC paragraphs 94–95 |
| Faith and understanding | CCC paragraphs 156–159 |
| Perseverance in faith | CCC paragraph 162 |
| Poverty of heart | CCC paragraph 2547 |

"Do not be surprised that you fall every day; do not give up, but stand your ground courageously. And assuredly, the angel who guards you will honour your patience."

~ St. John Climacus

"There are not one hundred people in the United States who hate The Catholic Church, but there are millions who hate what they wrongly perceive the Catholic Church to be."

~ Venerable Archbishop Fulton Sheen

### Litany of Humility Prayer
Composed by Rafael Cardinal Merry del Val

O Jesus! meek and humble of heart, *Hear me.*

From the desire of being esteemed, *Deliver me, Jesus.*
From the desire of being loved, *Deliver me, Jesus.*
From the desire of being extolled, *Deliver me, Jesus.*
From the desire of being honored, *Deliver me, Jesus.*
From the desire of being praised, *Deliver me, Jesus.*
From the desire of being preferred to others, *Deliver me, Jesus.*
From the desire of being consulted, *Deliver me, Jesus.*
From the desire of being approved, *Deliver me, Jesus.*

From the fear of being humiliated, *Deliver me, Jesus.*
From the fear of being despised, *Deliver me, Jesus.*
From the fear of suffering rebukes, *Deliver me, Jesus.*
From the fear of being falsely accused, *Deliver me, Jesus.*
From the fear of being forgotten, *Deliver me, Jesus.*
From the fear of being ridiculed, *Deliver me, Jesus.*
From the fear of being wronged, *Deliver me, Jesus.*
From the fear of being suspected, *Deliver me, Jesus.*

That others may be loved more than I,
    *Jesus, grant me the grace to desire it.*
That others may be esteemed more than I,
    *Jesus, grant me the grace to desire it.*
That, in the opinion of the world, others may increase and I may
    decrease, *Jesus, grant me the grace to desire it.*
That others may be chosen and I set aside,
    *Jesus, grant me the grace to desire it.*
That others may be praised and I unnoticed,
    *Jesus, grant me the grace to desire it.*
That others may be preferred to me in everything,
    *Jesus, grant me the grace to desire it.*
That others may become holier than I, provided that I may
    become as holy as I should,
    *Jesus, grant me the grace to desire it.*

Amen

"Humility is the only virtue that no devil can imitate. If pride made demons out of angels, there is no doubt that humility could make angels out of demons."

~ St. John Climacus

## Counterattack Actions

• Take action to learn more about your faith and the liturgy.
• Pray the Litany of Humility.

## Questions

1. What is your definition of the Church? Does it help to view the Church spread through time and space rather than just as a local Church today?

2. How well do you understand the liturgy?

3. What do you think of Archbishop Sheen's comment on the Catholic Church being misunderstood? What do you think the source(s) of the misunderstanding are? How do you respond when you hear misunderstandings of the Church?

4.  What has you "hazy" about your faith? What questions of the Church do you find difficult to answer?

5.  What elements of the Church disappoint you?

6.  How do you deal with disappointment in life?

7.  Have you been tempted to judge others during liturgy? What are your thoughts of that now? How would you respond to those temptations now?

8.  Have you gone through spiritual dry spells? What was it like? How did you get through it? Was Screwtape correct in stating that getting through the dry spells makes you harder to tempt?

9.  What do you do to combat temptations and suggestions like the ones Screwtape suggests in this text message?

## Text Message 3.1

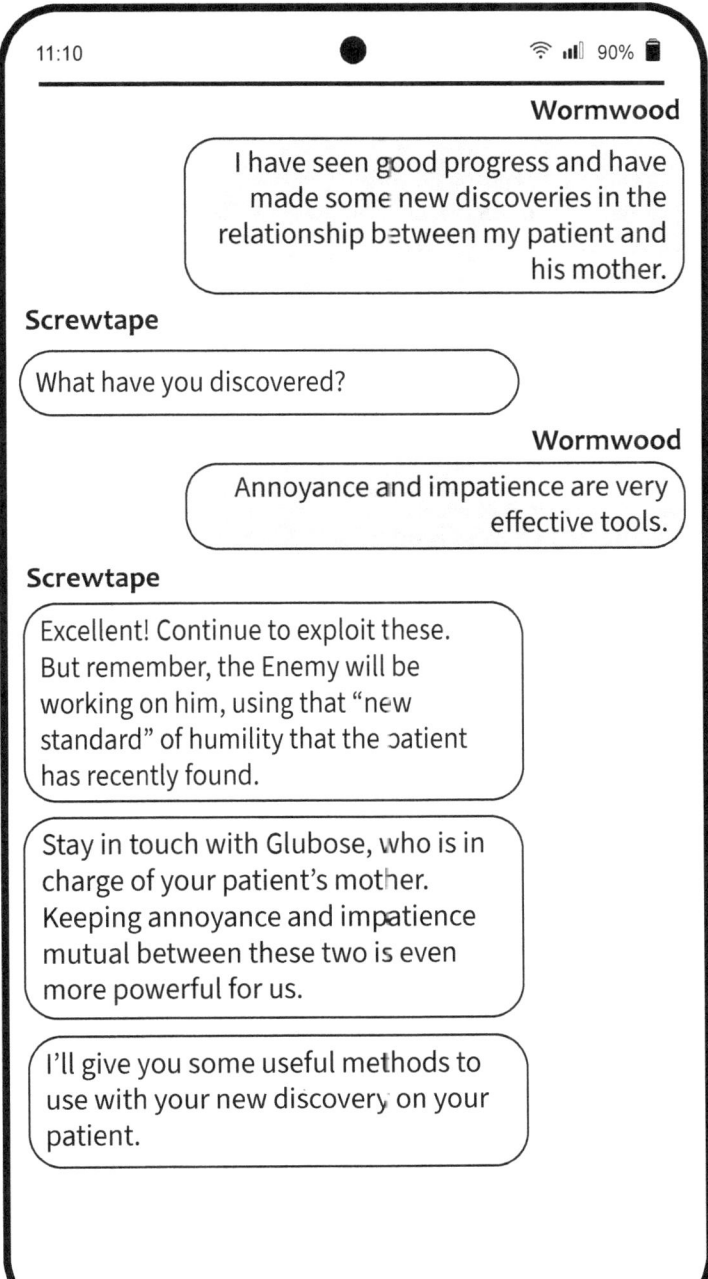

11:10    90%

**Wormwood**

I have seen good progress and have made some new discoveries in the relationship between my patient and his mother.

**Screwtape**

What have you discovered?

**Wormwood**

Annoyance and impatience are very effective tools.

**Screwtape**

Excellent! Continue to exploit these. But remember, the Enemy will be working on him, using that "new standard" of humility that the patient has recently found.

Stay in touch with Glubose, who is in charge of your patient's mother. Keeping annoyance and impatience mutual between these two is even more powerful for us.

I'll give you some useful methods to use with your new discovery on your patient.

## Text Message 3.2

**11:13** ● 🛜 ⏹ 90% 🔋

**Screwtape**

#1. Keep his mind on his inner life. Have him focus on the conversion that he thinks is inside of him, and on advanced spiritual things instead of the fundamentals. Get him to practice self-examination and yet don't let him see those things about himself that are obvious to anyone who has lived or worked with him.

#2. You can make his prayers meaningless by having him pray for his mother's soul and not for her arthritis or another cross that she endures.

**Wormwood**

What do you mean? Why do that?

**Screwtape**

This will keep him focused on her sins, and judging the assumed state of her soul. Keep him focused on her actions, especially those actions that are so irritating to him. This is easy and VERY entertaining!

This tactic will also keep him from being compassionate and praying for her needs.

## Text Message 3.3

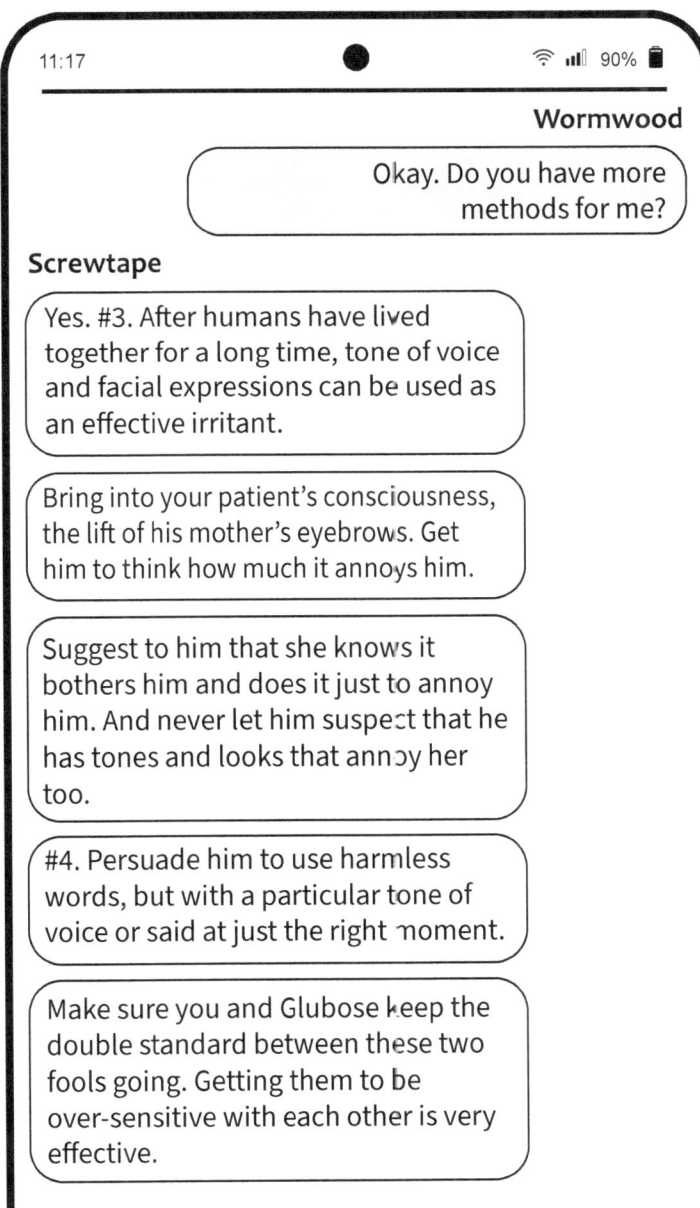

**Wormwood**

Okay. Do you have more methods for me?

**Screwtape**

Yes. #3. After humans have lived together for a long time, tone of voice and facial expressions can be used as an effective irritant.

Bring into your patient's consciousness, the lift of his mother's eyebrows. Get him to think how much it annoys him.

Suggest to him that she knows it bothers him and does it just to annoy him. And never let him suspect that he has tones and looks that annoy her too.

#4. Persuade him to use harmless words, but with a particular tone of voice or said at just the right moment.

Make sure you and Glubose keep the double standard between these two fools going. Getting them to be over-sensitive with each other is very effective.

## Text Message 3.4

11:20    🔘    📶 90% 🔋

**Wormwood**

> Give me an example.

**Screwtape**

> You are so slow. Okay. Get your patient to ask his mother "What time is dinner?" in a certain way and you'll get her to fly into a temper tantrum.

> Patterns like this are not difficult to develop. You'll end up with both of them angry with each other.

> And one more thing, and this is frosting on the cake.

> Immediately following methods #3 and #4, get the vermin to give each other the "silent treatment."

> Get the vermin to intentionally ignore each other. They will get angrier and angrier with each other. The level of tension and resentment can rise to remarkable levels. The results can potentially last for a very long time, sometimes even for years.

**Wormwood**

> This is great! You have given me a lot to work with.

## Summary

This page from the enemy's playbook suggests that patience, forgiveness and compassion with others weaken the devil's attack. They help us to love others.

## Resources

| Love fulfills the law | Romans 13:8 |
|---|---|
| Love | 1 Corinthians 13:4–7 |
| Unity in the body | Ephesians 4:2 |
| The domestic church / forgiveness | CCC paragraph 1657 |
| Charity / patience | CCC paragraph 1825 |
| The duties of family members | CCC paragraph 2219 |
| The duties of parents | CCC paragraph 2227 |
| Works of mercy | CCC paragraph 2447 |
| The Lord's Prayer / forgiveness | CCC paragraphs 2840, 2845 |

"The Bible tells us to love our neighbors, and also to love our enemies; probably because they are generally the same people."

~ G. K. Chesterton

## Counterattack Actions

- Pray for your loved one's souls and for the crosses they carry.
- Commit a random act of kindness for someone close to you.
- When you see yourself judging someone, stop and pray for the person.

## Questions

1. Screwtape speaks of advanced spiritual things and spiritual fundamentals. What do you think he means by this?

2. Screwtape encourages humans to pray for each other's soul rather than for each other's crosses. Why do you think this strategy is effective in spiritual warfare?

3. What are your thoughts on the quote from G. K. Chesterton, that our neighbors and enemies could be the same people? Why could this be?

4. Do you agree with Screwtape, that a person's "look" or "tone of voice" can offend and irritate others? Is Screwtape's advice on employing the "silent treatment" effective in spiritual warfare?

5. What do you do to combat temptations and suggestions like the ones Screwtape suggests in this text message?

## Text Message 4.1

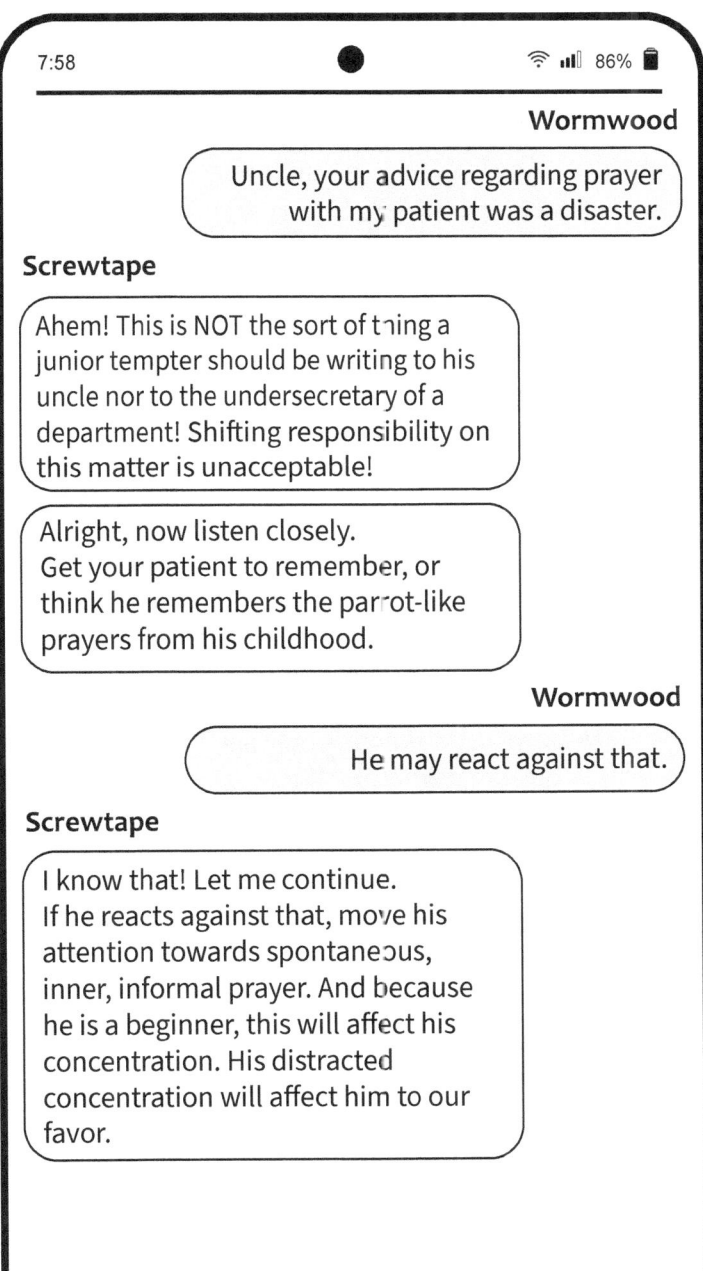

7:58     86%

**Wormwood**

Uncle, your advice regarding prayer with my patient was a disaster.

**Screwtape**

Ahem! This is NOT the sort of thing a junior tempter should be writing to his uncle nor to the undersecretary of a department! Shifting responsibility on this matter is unacceptable!

Alright, now listen closely.
Get your patient to remember, or think he remembers the parrot-like prayers from his childhood.

**Wormwood**

He may react against that.

**Screwtape**

I know that! Let me continue.
If he reacts against that, move his attention towards spontaneous, inner, informal prayer. And because he is a beginner, this will affect his concentration. His distracted concentration will affect him to our favor.

## Text Message 4.2

**Screwtape**

One of those "brilliant" lowly animals, a poet named Coleridge said that he didn't 'pray with moving lips and bended knees'. He said he just 'composed his spirit to love and indulged a sense of petition'.
Heh heh heh … isn't that nice.

This is exactly the type of prayer we want! This is superficially similar to the prayer of silence that is practiced by those who are advanced in the Enemy's camp.

Amateurs can be persuaded that bodily position makes no difference to their prayers. Remember, they are animals and whatever their bodies do affects their souls.

**Wormwood**

Oh yeah. I didn't think about that.

**Screwtape**

This is why I am the teacher and you are the student.

It's funny how humans always picture us putting things into their minds, but in reality, our best work is done in keeping things out.

## Text Message 4.3

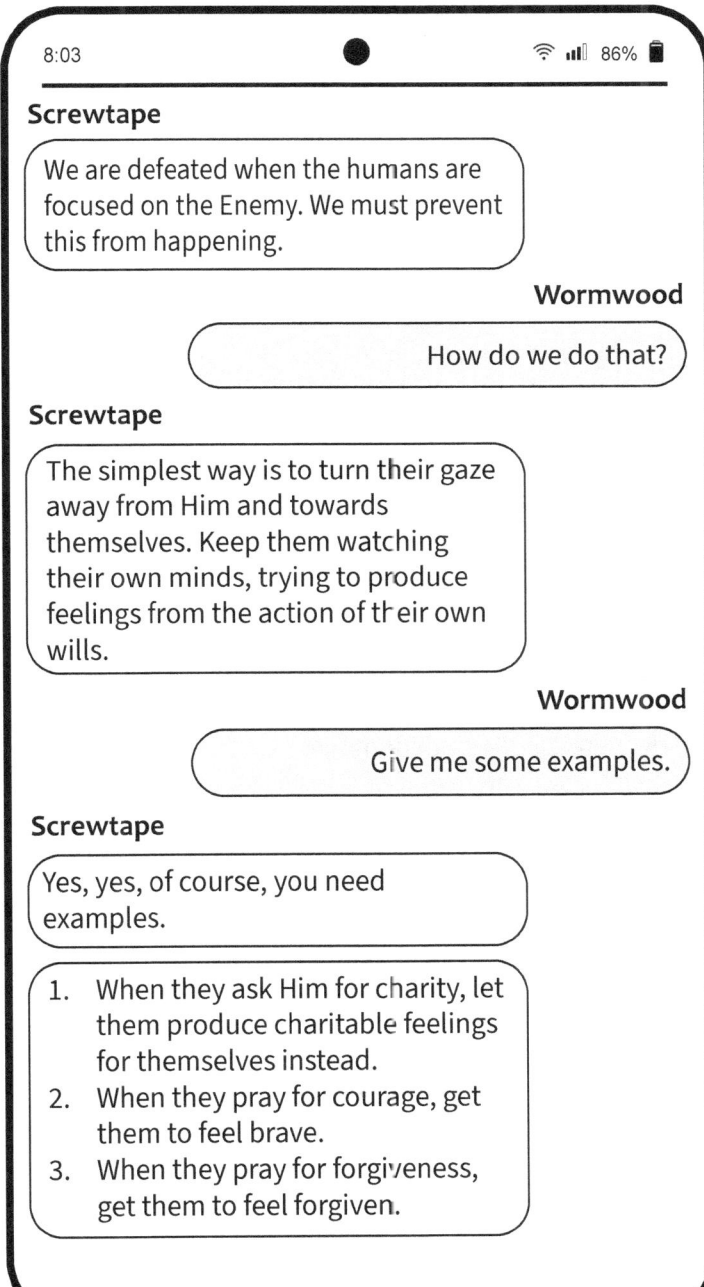

**Screwtape**

We are defeated when the humans are focused on the Enemy. We must prevent this from happening.

**Wormwood**

How do we do that?

**Screwtape**

The simplest way is to turn their gaze away from Him and towards themselves. Keep them watching their own minds, trying to produce feelings from the action of their own wills.

**Wormwood**

Give me some examples.

**Screwtape**

Yes, yes, of course, you need examples.

1. When they ask Him for charity, let them produce charitable feelings for themselves instead.
2. When they pray for courage, get them to feel brave.
3. When they pray for forgiveness, get them to feel forgiven.

## Text Message 4.4

**Screwtape**

Get them to measure and value their prayer based on their success in producing their desired feelings.

The Enemy will not be idle while we deploy these tactics. If He defeats your first attempt at misdirection, we do have more subtle weapons.

The creatures have icons and mental images of the Enemy. Keep them praying to their mental images and icons of Him, and NOT to the Person who has created them.

Beware: our situation will become desperate if the patient moves beyond who and what he thinks the Enemy is to actually knowing Him.

You will find that the humans do not desire this as much as they suppose. Heh heh, there is such a thing as getting more than they bargained for.

**Wormwood**

You are quite smart.

**Screwtape**

You think?

## Summary

This page from the enemy's playbook suggests that posture in prayer, turning focus away from ourselves and towards God, and not focusing on feelings received from prayer weaken the devil's attack. They keep our focus on God and away from ourselves.

## Resources

| | |
|---|---|
| Seek His face | Psalm 27:9 |
| Knowing Jesus is to know his Father | John 14:7 |
| We do not know how to pray | Romans 8:26 |
| Prayer for the readers | Ephesians 3:14–21 |
| Vocal prayer | CCC paragraphs 2700–2704 |
| Meditative prayer | CCC paragraphs 2705–2708 |
| Contemplative prayer | CCC paragraphs 2709–2719 |
| Objections to prayer | CCC paragraphs 2726–2728 |
| Difficulties in prayer | CCC paragraphs 2729–2731 |
| Temptations in prayer | CCC paragraphs 2732–2733 |
| Not being heard in prayer | CCC paragraphs 2735–2737 |

CCC paragraph 2702

The need to involve the senses in interior prayer corresponds to a requirement of our human nature. We are body and spirit, and we experience the need to translate our feelings externally. We must pray with our whole being to give all power possible to our supplication.

> Regarding humans, "whatever their bodies do affects their souls."

> ~ Screwtape

In this text message, Screwtape references a poem written by the poet Coleridge. The poem is *The Pains of Sleep* by Samuel Taylor Coleridge (October 21, 1772 - July 25, 1834).

## Counterattack Actions

- When you become aware that you do not feel like praying, pray anyway.
- Include silence as part of your prayer time.

## Questions

1. Have you told others how particular prayers or devotions make you feel? How do you react when someone tells you how certain prayers or devotional practices make them feel? What is Screwtape's point regarding feelings?

2. Do you agree with Screwtape, that advanced prayer can be silent and not dependent on posture, yet remain strongly focused on God, and that basic simple prayer requires vocal prayer and prayerful posture like kneeling? Why?

3. How and when are you best able to focus on God in prayer? What advice would you give someone who struggles with focus in prayer?

4.  Do you have icons or mental images of God? Do they draw
    you closer to God? Can there be a risk of focusing more on
    these images than on God? Have you heard others talk more
    about a devotion or image of God or the Bible than of their
    relationship with God?

5.  Screwtape concludes his message discussing the risk of hu-
    mans moving beyond "knowing about" God to "knowing"
    God. How does this become a danger to the demons? What
    do you think Screwtape is implying when he says humans
    may be reluctant to know God, because "there is such a thing
    as getting more than they bargained for."?

6.  What do you do to combat temptations and suggestions like
    the ones Screwtape suggests in this text message?

## Text Message 5.1

4:20     100%

**Wormwood**

> Uncle, I am delirious with joy! A war is breaking out in my patient's part of the world and he is becoming anxious and fearful from the news.

**Screwtape**

> Delirious, no. By my estimation you are drunk. I see that you have tasted for the first time the fruits of your labors.

> You have witnessed the patient's sleepless nights, the anguish and despair of the human soul, and this has gone to your head.

> But I can hardly blame you. I do not expect old heads on young shoulders.

**Wormwood**

> You sure know how to sober me up and bring me down.

**Screwtape**

> Tell me, did your patient respond to some of your terrifying images of the future? Did you work in some melancholy glances of the happy past?

## Text Message 5.2

**Screwtape**

Remain cool and level-headed on all this and you will secure his soul. Do not allow this tempting excitement to distract you from the real business of undermining his faith and preventing the development of virtues.

Provide me with your patient's reaction to the war. This will allow us to determine if you can do more good by making him an extreme patriot or a zealous pacifist.

Do not hope too much from the war. Although they are entertaining.

If we are not careful during times like these, we can see countless humans divert their attention from themselves to values and causes that they believe to be higher than themselves.

This is where the Enemy is so unfair.

**Wormwood**

How?

## Text Message 5.3

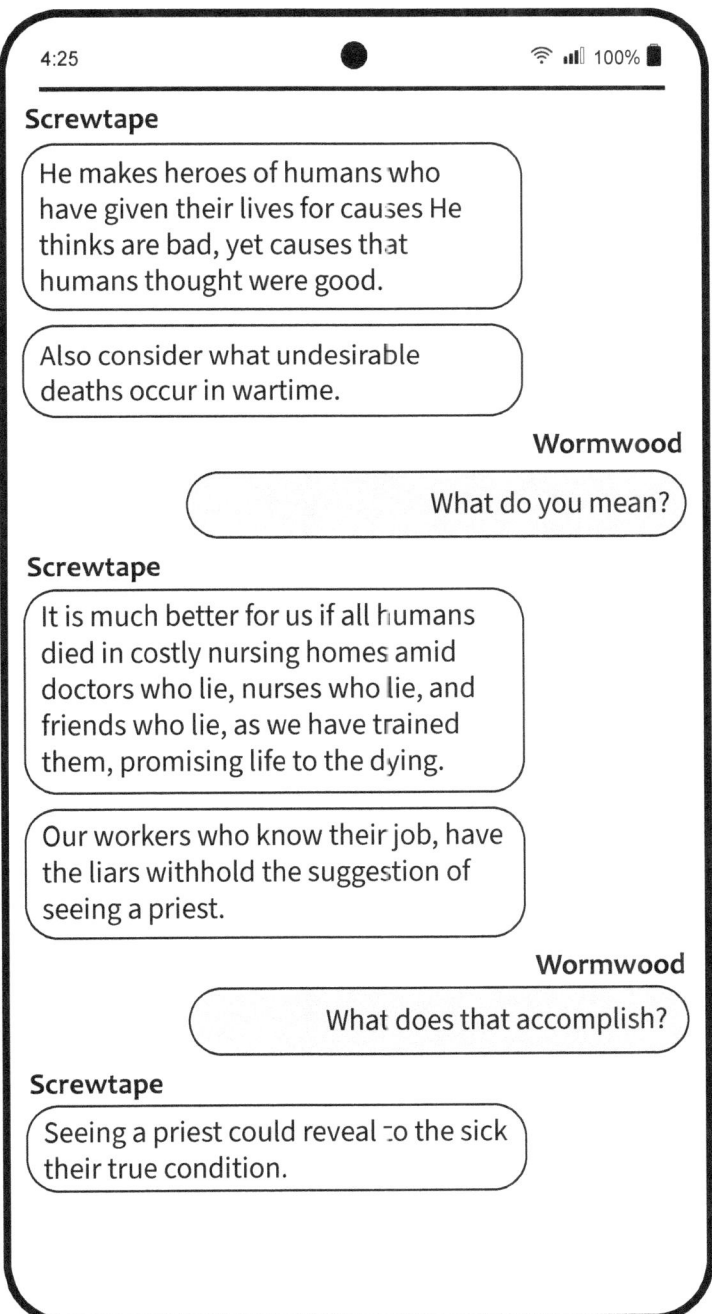

4:25     🔵     🛜 📶 100% 🔋

**Screwtape**

He makes heroes of humans who have given their lives for causes He thinks are bad, yet causes that humans thought were good.

Also consider what undesirable deaths occur in wartime.

**Wormwood**

What do you mean?

**Screwtape**

It is much better for us if all humans died in costly nursing homes amid doctors who lie, nurses who lie, and friends who lie, as we have trained them, promising life to the dying.

Our workers who know their job, have the liars withhold the suggestion of seeing a priest.

**Wormwood**

What does that accomplish?

**Screwtape**

Seeing a priest could reveal to the sick their true condition.

## Text Message 5.4

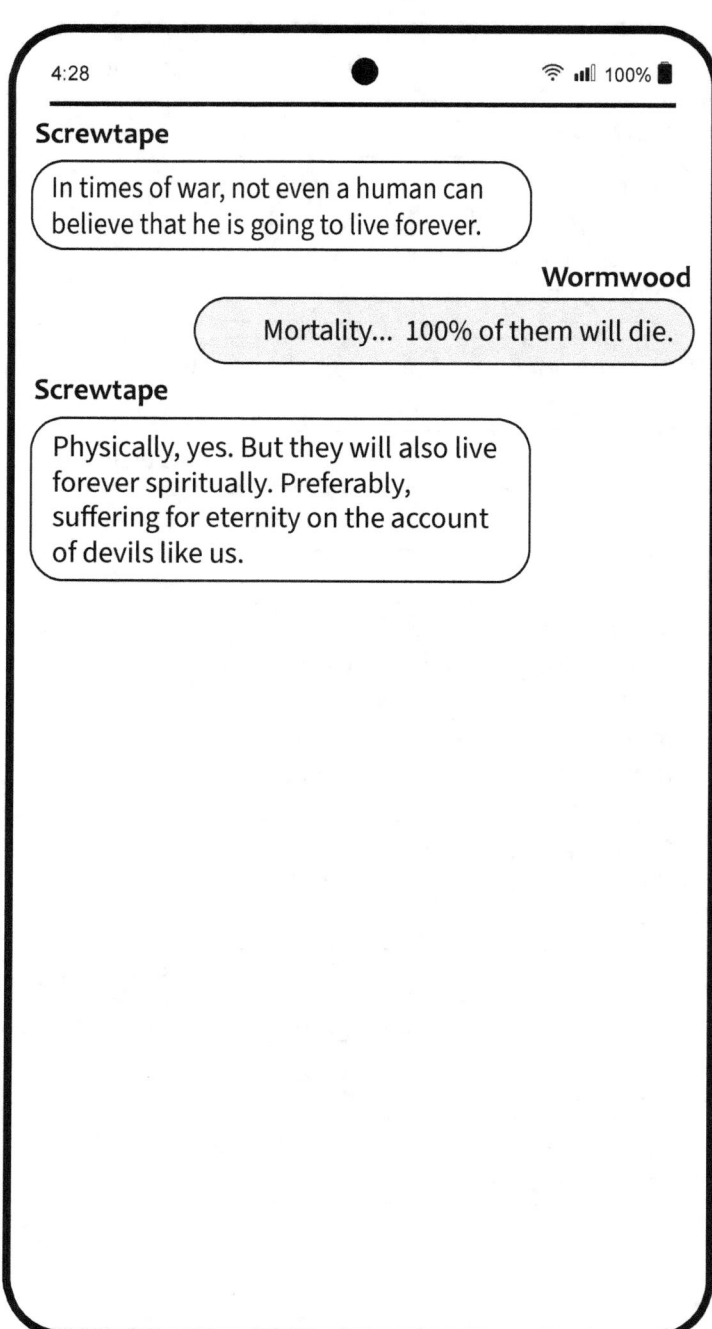

**Screwtape**

In times of war, not even a human can believe that he is going to live forever.

**Wormwood**

Mortality... 100% of them will die.

**Screwtape**

Physically, yes. But they will also live forever spiritually. Preferably, suffering for eternity on the account of devils like us.

## Summary

This page from the enemy's playbook suggests that paying attention to values higher than one's self weaken the devil's attack. It also highlights that physical life is temporary and what matters is where we will spend eternity. We should keep our focus on what matters most, which is where we will spend eternity.

## Resources

| | |
|---|---|
| Our future destiny | 2 Corinthians 5:1-10 |
| Body and soul but truly one | CCC paragraphs 362–368 |
| Death | CCC paragraphs 1006–1009 |
| The meaning of Christian death | CCC paragraphs 1010–1014 |

"Every action of yours, every thought, should be those of one who expects to die before the day is out. Death would have no great terrors for you if you had a quiet conscience … Then why not keep clear of sin instead of running away from death? If you aren't fit to face death today, it's very unlikely you will be tomorrow …"

~ from The Imitation of Christ by Thomas à Kempis

### Hail Mary

Hail Mary, full of grace, the Lord is with thee; blessed art thou among women and blessed is the fruit of thy womb, Jesus. Holy Mary, Mother of God, pray for us sinners, now and at the hour of our death. Amen.

**Counterattack Actions**

- What change would you make in your life if you knew that you had little time left? Make that change.
- Pray the Hail Mary prayer, focusing on the words, "pray for us sinners, *now and at the hour* of our death."

**Questions**

1. Do you think worrying about the future and self-pitying memories of the past are weapons used against us in spiritual warfare?

2. What is your reaction to Screwtape's thoughts about people lying to people who are dying? Why do you suspect people "lie" to others about their condition?

3. Why do you think the devil wants us to avoid thinking about death?

4. When was the last time you thought about your mortality?

5. What are your thoughts on Thomas à Kempis' words from The Imitation of Christ?

6. What do you do to combat temptations and suggestions like the ones Screwtape suggests in this text message?

## Text Message 6.1

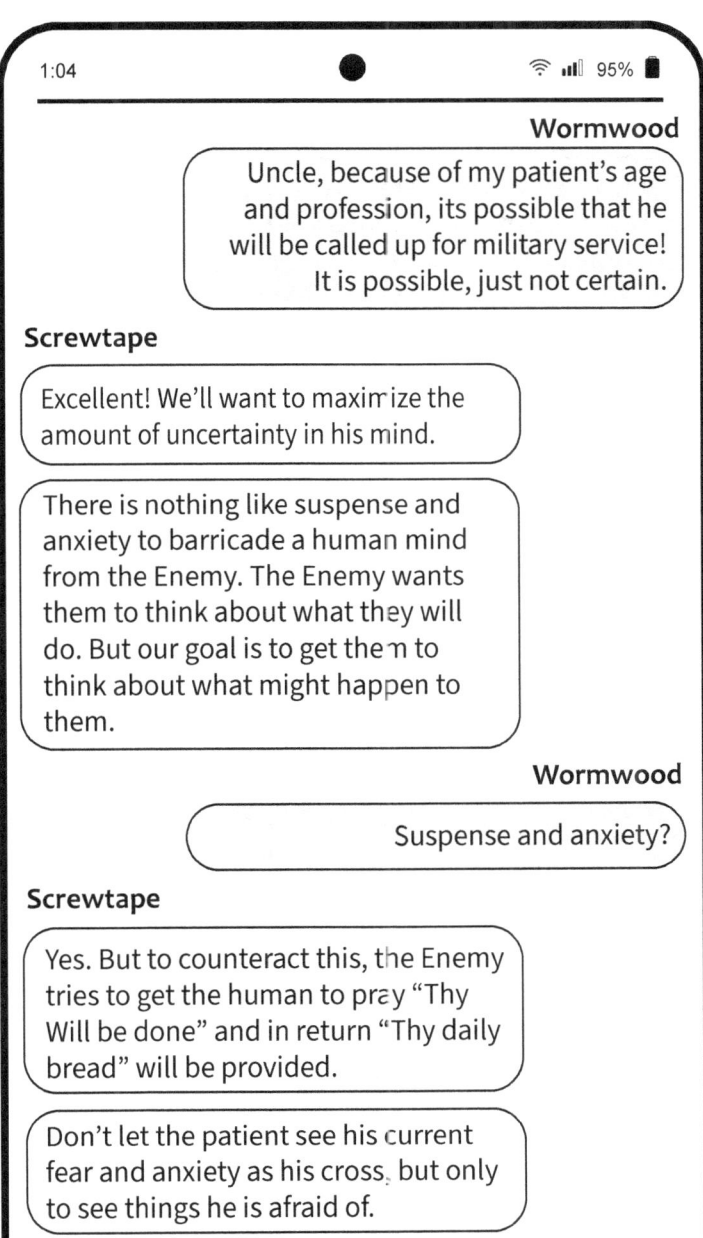

**Wormwood**

Uncle, because of my patient's age and profession, its possible that he will be called up for military service! It is possible, just not certain.

**Screwtape**

Excellent! We'll want to maximize the amount of uncertainty in his mind.

There is nothing like suspense and anxiety to barricade a human mind from the Enemy. The Enemy wants them to think about what they will do. But our goal is to get them to think about what might happen to them.

**Wormwood**

Suspense and anxiety?

**Screwtape**

Yes. But to counteract this, the Enemy tries to get the human to pray "Thy Will be done" and in return "Thy daily bread" will be provided.

Don't let the patient see his current fear and anxiety as his cross, but only to see things he is afraid of.

## Text Message 6.2

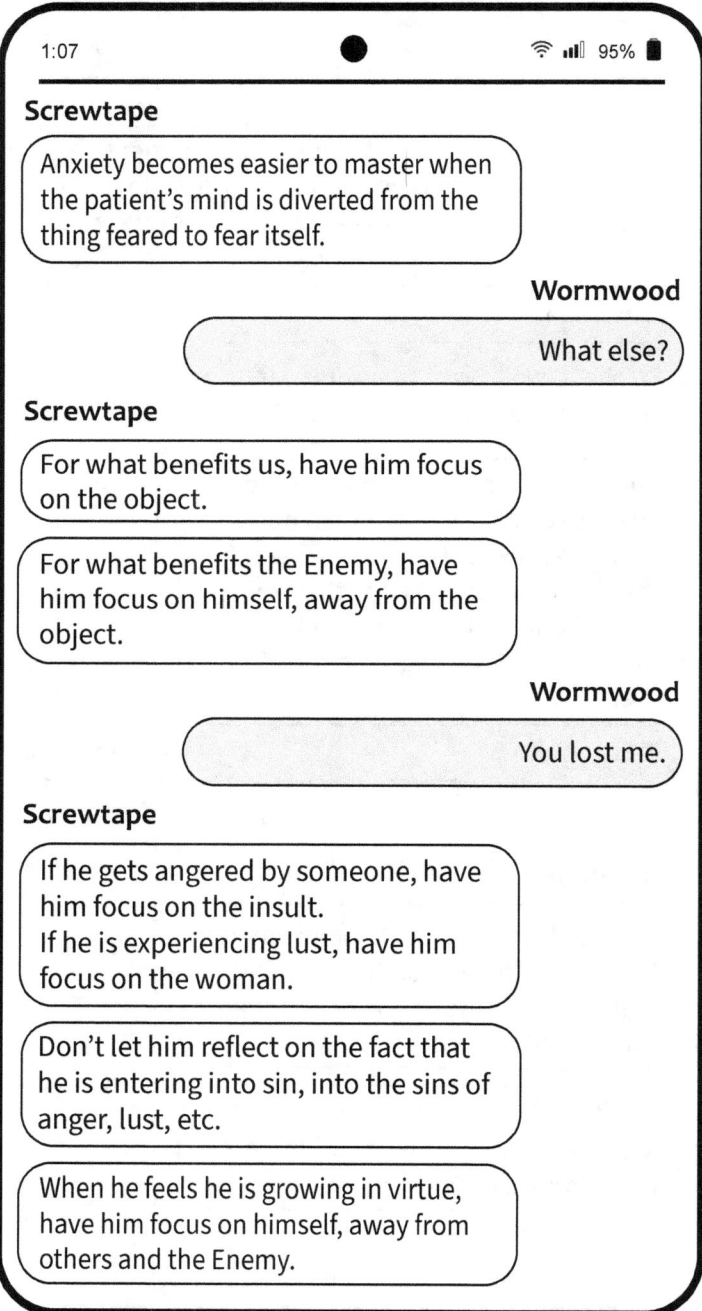

**Screwtape**

Anxiety becomes easier to master when the patient's mind is diverted from the thing feared to fear itself.

**Wormwood**

What else?

**Screwtape**

For what benefits us, have him focus on the object.

For what benefits the Enemy, have him focus on himself, away from the object.

**Wormwood**

You lost me.

**Screwtape**

If he gets angered by someone, have him focus on the insult.
If he is experiencing lust, have him focus on the woman.

Don't let him reflect on the fact that he is entering into sin, into the sins of anger, lust, etc.

When he feels he is growing in virtue, have him focus on himself, away from others and the Enemy.

Text Message 6.3

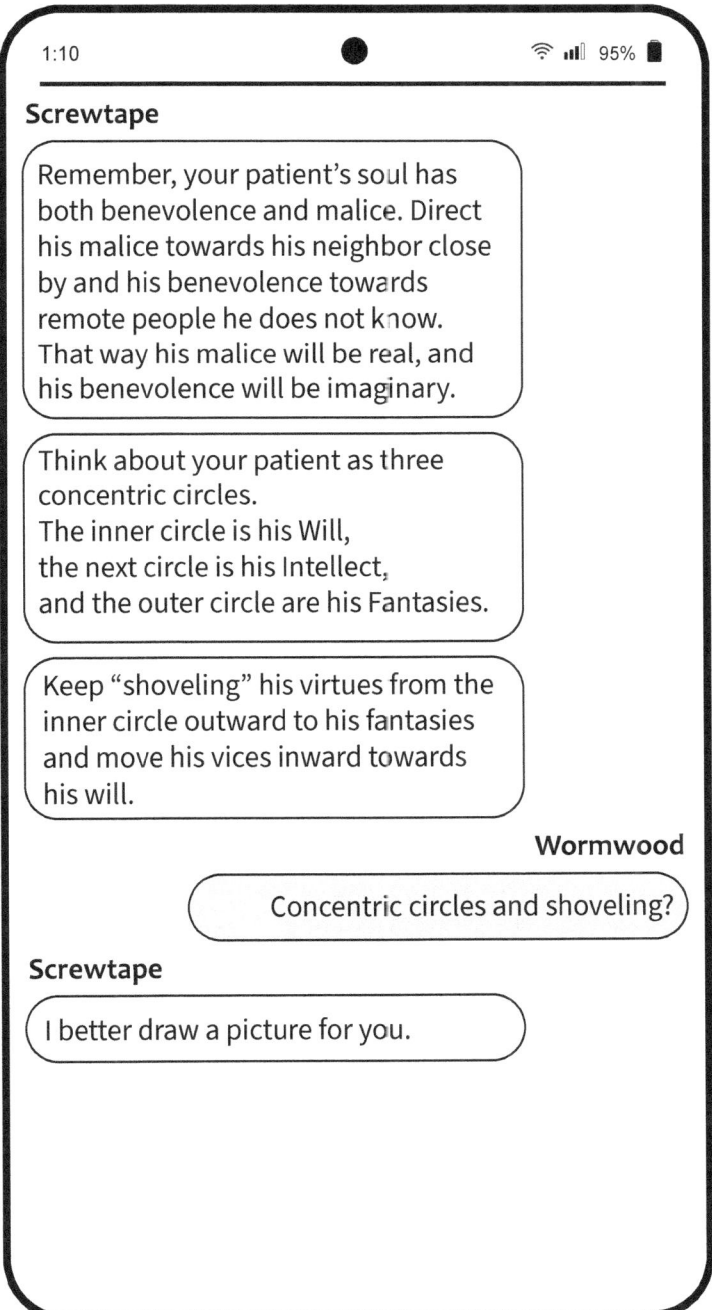

**Screwtape**

Remember, your patient's soul has both benevolence and malice. Direct his malice towards his neighbor close by and his benevolence towards remote people he does not know. That way his malice will be real, and his benevolence will be imaginary.

Think about your patient as three concentric circles.
The inner circle is his Will,
the next circle is his Intellect,
and the outer circle are his Fantasies.

Keep "shoveling" his virtues from the inner circle outward to his fantasies and move his vices inward towards his will.

**Wormwood**

Concentric circles and shoveling?

**Screwtape**

I better draw a picture for you.

## Text Message 6.4

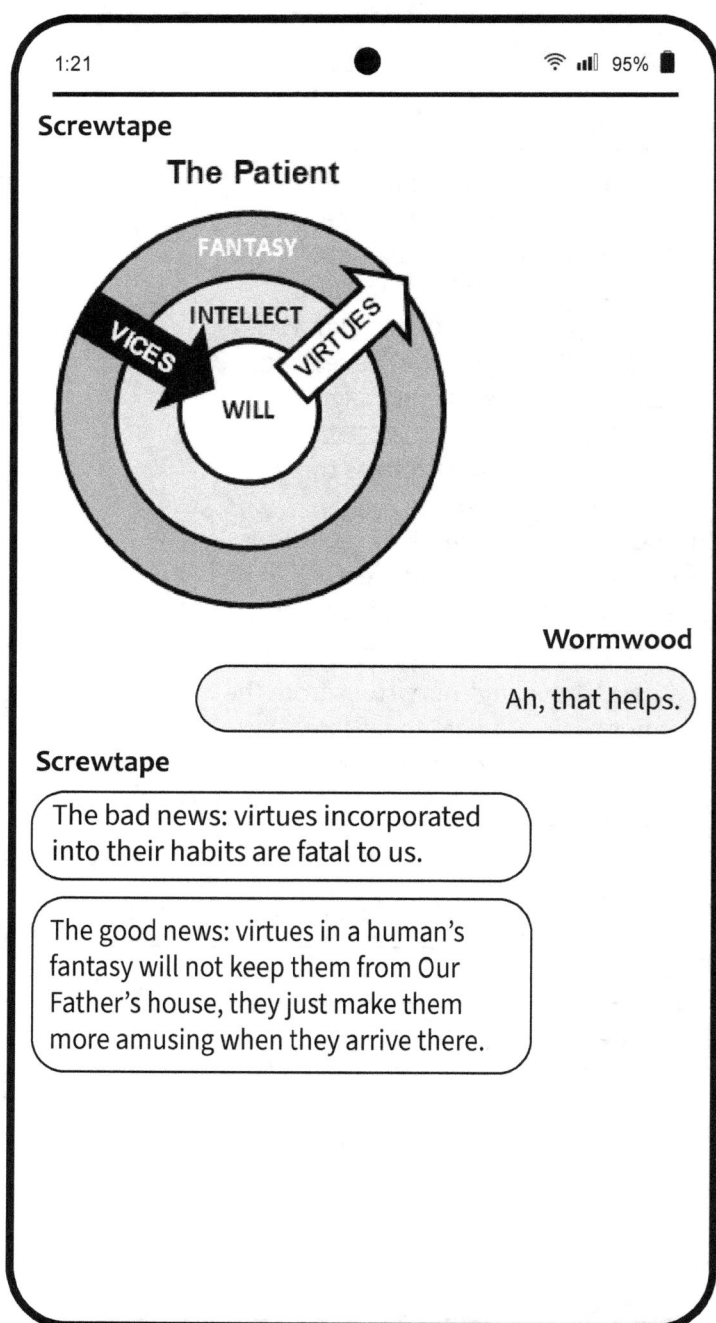

1:21 ● 📶 95% 🔋

**Screwtape**

**The Patient**

FANTASY
INTELLECT
VICES
VIRTUES
WILL

**Wormwood**

> Ah, that helps.

**Screwtape**

> The bad news: virtues incorporated into their habits are fatal to us.

> The good news: virtues in a human's fantasy will not keep them from Our Father's house, they just make them more amusing when they arrive there.

## Summary

This page from the enemy's playbook suggests that peace and trust in the Lord weaken the devil's attack. They keep us from worrying about things beyond our control.

## Resources

| Sermon on the plain | Luke 6:24 |
|---|---|
| Faith | CCC paragraph 2088 |
| The desires of the spirit | CCC paragraph 2547 |

CCC paragraph 2547

The Lord grieves over the rich, because they find their consolation in the abundance of goods. (Luke 6:24) "Let the proud seek and love earthly kingdoms, but blessed are the poor in spirit for theirs is the Kingdom of heaven." Abandonment to the providence of the Father in heaven frees us from anxiety about tomorrow. Trust in God is a preparation for the blessedness of the poor. They shall see God.

## Counterattack Actions

- When feelings of anxiety are present, pray the words from the Divine Mercy Chaplet: Jesus I Trust in You. Pray these words over and over.
- Spend time in quiet prayer in a church before the tabernacle.

## Questions

1.  Why do you think Screwtape sees benefit in humans experiencing uncertainty and anxiety?

2.  Many people like suspense movies. So why would Screwtape see suspense (human uncertainty) as something that negatively affects us?

3.  Based on the strategy that Screwtape presents here, what advice would you give someone who experiences anxiety?

4.  Why does Screwtape encourage shifting the focus towards the emotion of anxiety and fear and away from what is actually being worried about?

5.  How does the image of the three concentric circles that Screwtape talks about affect your awareness of the state of your soul? Can you see the effects of the demons working at moving your virtues away from your Will and replacing them with vices?

6.  What do you do to combat temptations and suggestions like the ones Screwtape suggests in this text message?

## Text Message 7.1

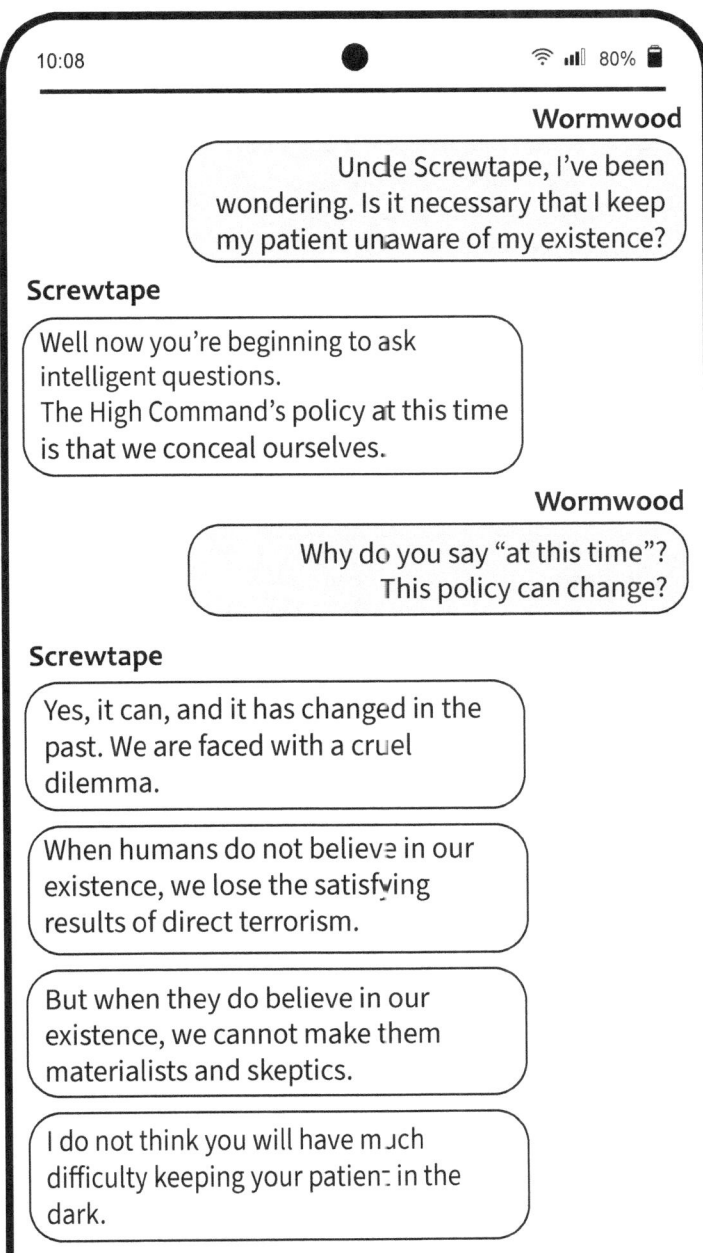

10:08      🔵      📶 80% 🔋

**Wormwood**

Uncle Screwtape, I've been wondering. Is it necessary that I keep my patient unaware of my existence?

**Screwtape**

Well now you're beginning to ask intelligent questions.
The High Command's policy at this time is that we conceal ourselves.

**Wormwood**

Why do you say "at this time"? This policy can change?

**Screwtape**

Yes, it can, and it has changed in the past. We are faced with a cruel dilemma.

When humans do not believe in our existence, we lose the satisfying results of direct terrorism.

But when they do believe in our existence, we cannot make them materialists and skeptics.

I do not think you will have much difficulty keeping your patient in the dark.

## Text Message 7.2

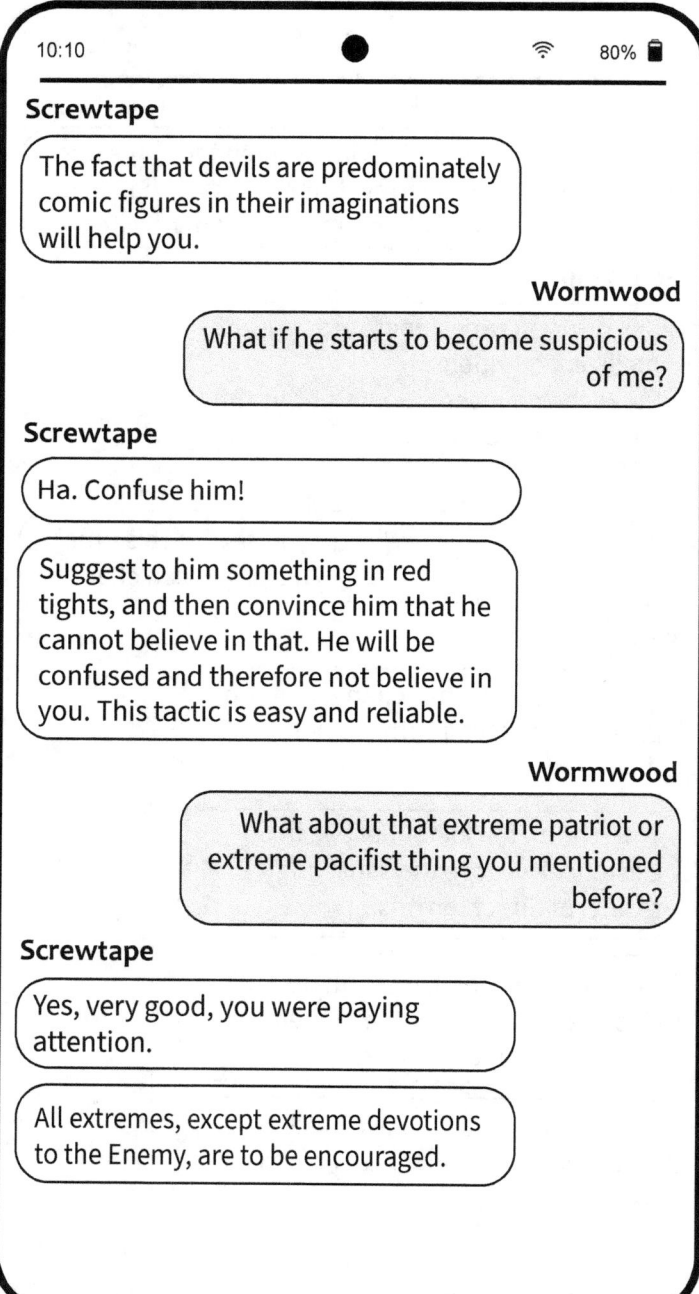

**Screwtape**

The fact that devils are predominately comic figures in their imaginations will help you.

**Wormwood**

What if he starts to become suspicious of me?

**Screwtape**

Ha. Confuse him!

Suggest to him something in red tights, and then convince him that he cannot believe in that. He will be confused and therefore not believe in you. This tactic is easy and reliable.

**Wormwood**

What about that extreme patriot or extreme pacifist thing you mentioned before?

**Screwtape**

Yes, very good, you were paying attention.

All extremes, except extreme devotions to the Enemy, are to be encouraged.

## Text Message 7.3

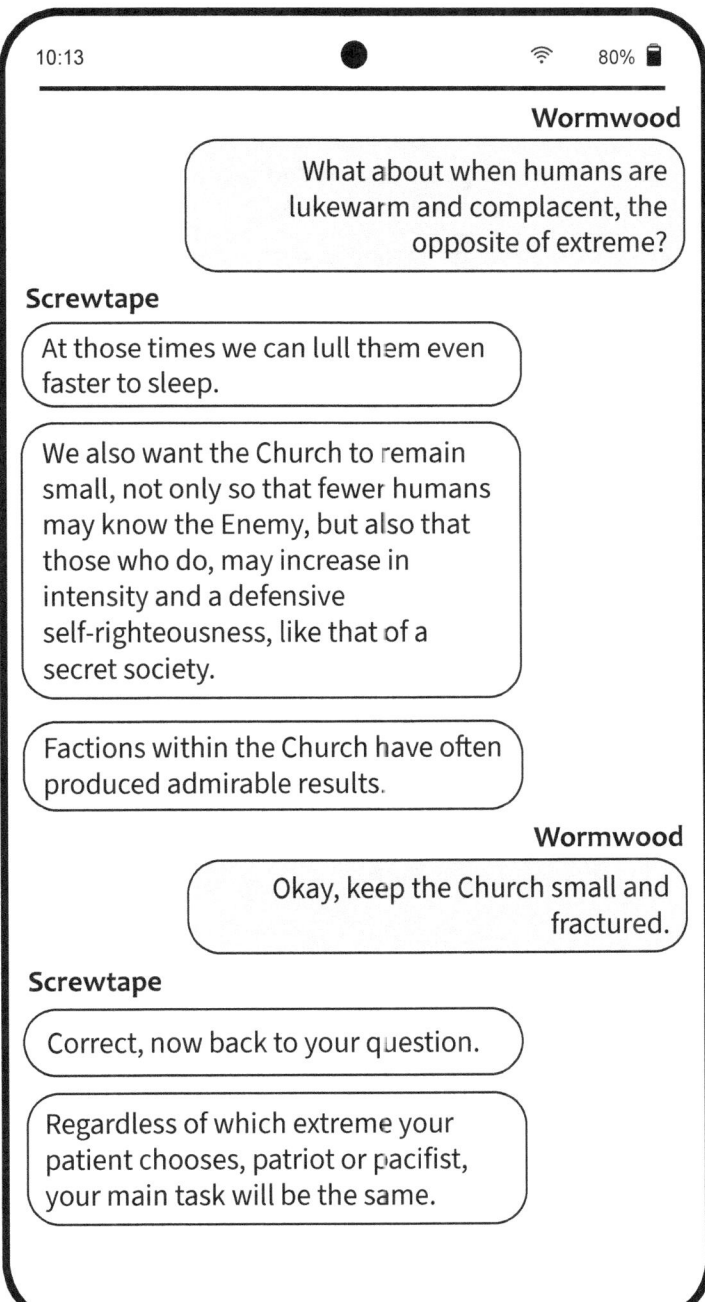

10:13  80%

**Wormwood**

What about when humans are lukewarm and complacent, the opposite of extreme?

**Screwtape**

At those times we can lull them even faster to sleep.

We also want the Church to remain small, not only so that fewer humans may know the Enemy, but also that those who do, may increase in intensity and a defensive self-righteousness, like that of a secret society.

Factions within the Church have often produced admirable results.

**Wormwood**

Okay, keep the Church small and fractured.

**Screwtape**

Correct, now back to your question.

Regardless of which extreme your patient chooses, patriot or pacifist, your main task will be the same.

## Text Message 7.4

**Screwtape**

Let him begin by treating his choice as part of his religion.

Once you have the world as the end, and faith as the means, you have almost won your patient.

That is, as long as meetings, pamphlets, policies, movements, and causes matter more than prayers, sacraments, and charity.

Oh, and the more religious he is on these terms, the more securely he will be ours.

I could show you a pretty cageful down here.

## Summary

This page from the enemy's playbook suggests that extreme devotion to God and an informed/healthy awareness of evil spirits weaken the devil's attack. They keep us close to God and aware of the devil who is at work trying to separate us from God for eternity.

## Resources

| The temptation of Jesus | Luke 4:8 |
|---|---|
| A hard battle | CCC paragraph 407 |
| The many forms of penance in Christian life | CCC paragraph 1437 |
| Popular piety | CCC paragraphs 1674-1676 |
| To adore God | CCC paragraph 2096 |

CCC paragraph 407

The doctrine of original sin, closely connected with that of redemption by Christ, provides lucid discernment of man's situation and activity in the world. By our first parents' sin, the devil has acquired a certain domination over man, even though man remains free. Original sin entails "captivity under the power of him who thenceforth had the power of death, that is, the devil."[298] Ignorance of the fact that man has a wounded nature inclined to evil gives rise to serious errors in the areas of education, politics, social action,[299] and morals.

298 Council of Trent (1546): DS 1511; cf. Heb 2:14
299 Cf. John Paul II, CA 25

Some examples of popular piety or devotions include:

- reading Sacred Scripture (and using Lectio Divina)
- praying the Liturgy of the Hours
- pilgrimages
- novenas
- the rosary
- Stations of the Cross
- the use of sacramentals

CCC paragraph 1675

These expressions of piety extend the liturgical life of the Church, but do not replace it. They "should be so drawn up that they harmonize with the liturgical seasons, accord with the sacred liturgy, are in some way derived from it and lead the people to it, since in fact the liturgy by its very nature is far superior to any of them."

The Stations of the Cross is a devotion that began as a practice of pious pilgrims to Jerusalem who would retrace the final journey of Jesus Christ to Calvary. Later, for the many who wanted to pass along the same route but could not make the trip to Jerusalem, a practice developed that eventually took the form of the fourteen stations, which are now found in most churches today.

## Counterattack Actions

- Find and regularly practice a devotion that keeps you close to God.
- When you become aware of evil spiritual temptation or suggestion, pray the St. Michael prayer, found in the chapter History of the Battle.

## Questions

1.  What are your beliefs on the existence of the devil or evil spirits? Have you ever felt their effects in your life?

2.  What dangers can you imagine or have seen regarding Screwtape's comments on being lukewarm or complacent?

3.  Screwtape (the devil) likes to see the Church with factions (divisions). How does this benefit the devil? How can we and the Church combat this?

4.  Can you think of saints known for extreme devotions to God? What were their devotions?

5.  CCC paragraph 407 speaks of serious errors that affect many areas of society. These errors come from humans being ignorant of having a wounded nature inclined to evil. Where do you see these errors?

6.  What do you do to combat temptations and suggestions like the ones Screwtape suggests in this text message?

## Text Message 8.1

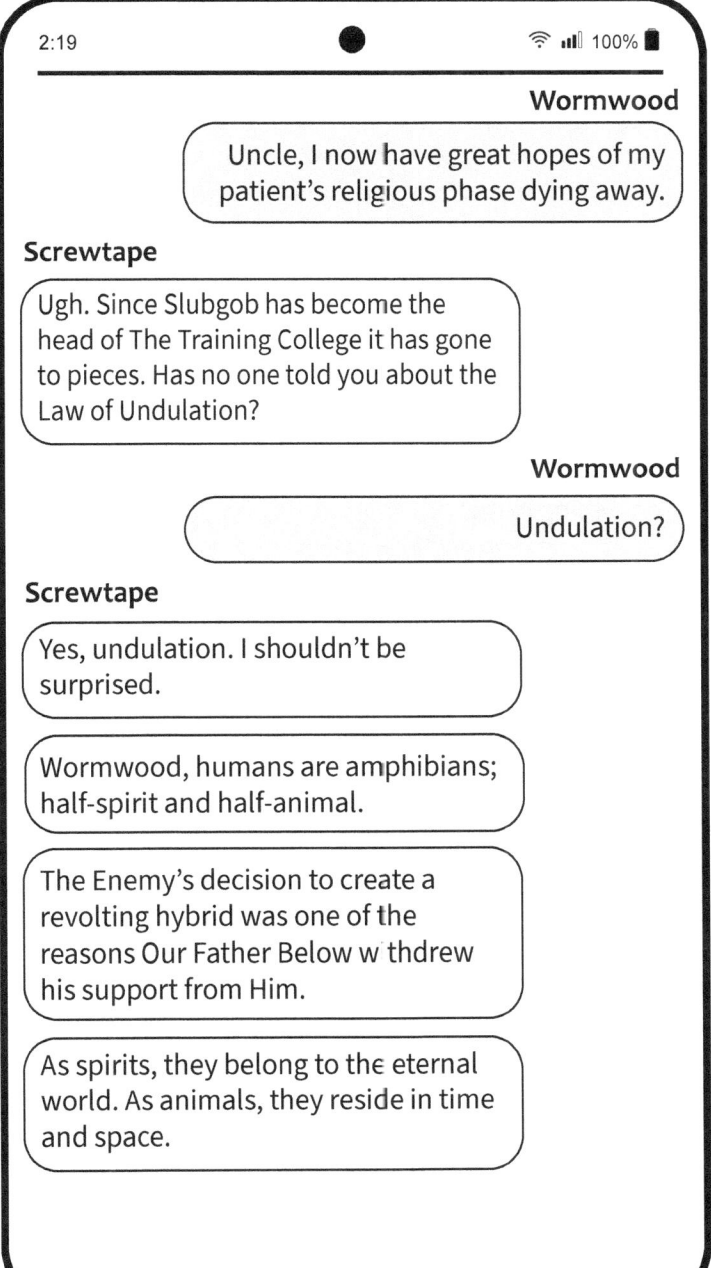

## Text Message 8.2

2:21  100%

**Screwtape**

This means their spirit can be directed to an eternal object, which does not change. But their bodies, passions, and imaginations live in time and therefore continually change.

The nearest the vermin can get to stability is undulation. Some of them know this. A philosopher of theirs named Heraclitus said: "Change is the only thing constant."

**Wormwood**

But what is undulation? Can you explain it to me?

**Screwtape**

Explain it? Of course I can. Will you understand it? We'll see…

Undulation is the constant movement between peaks and troughs of a mortal's life experiences.

If you have been watching your patient, you would have seen undulation in every area of his life: in work, with his friends, and his physical appetites. They all rise and fall.

## Text Message 8.3

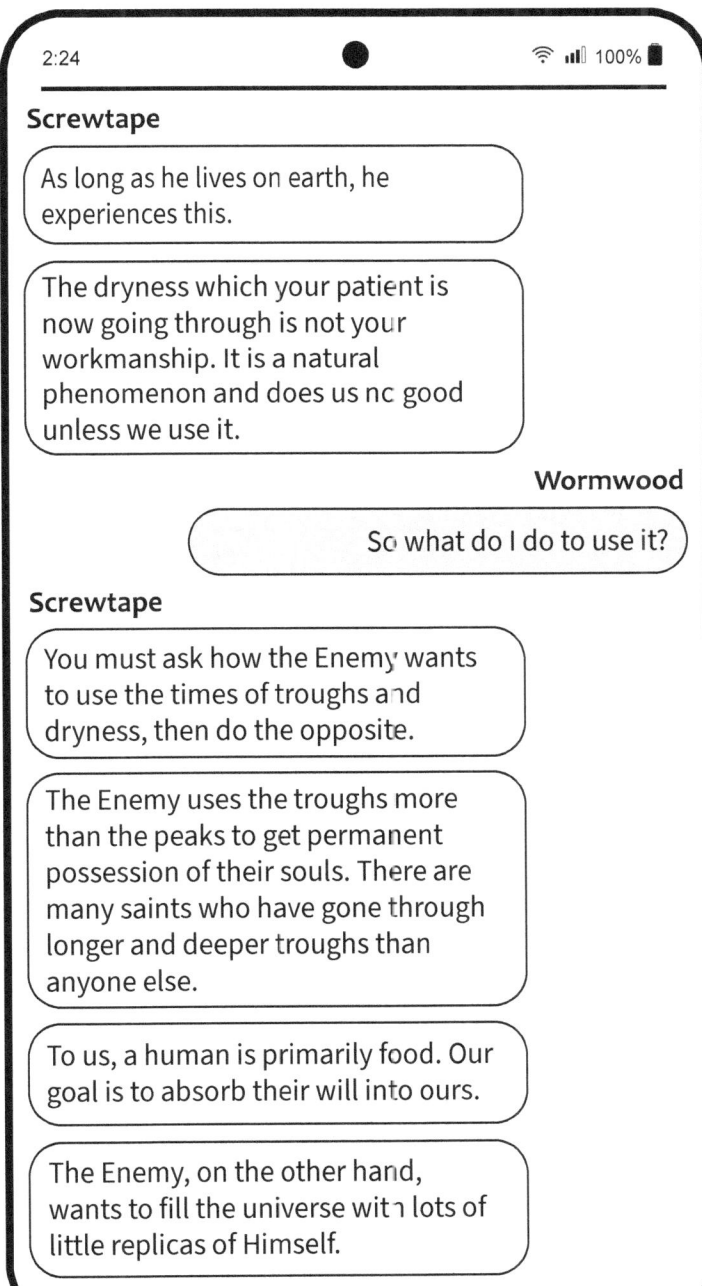

**Screwtape**

As long as he lives on earth, he experiences this.

The dryness which your patient is now going through is not your workmanship. It is a natural phenomenon and does us no good unless we use it.

**Wormwood**

So what do I do to use it?

**Screwtape**

You must ask how the Enemy wants to use the times of troughs and dryness, then do the opposite.

The Enemy uses the troughs more than the peaks to get permanent possession of their souls. There are many saints who have gone through longer and deeper troughs than anyone else.

To us, a human is primarily food. Our goal is to absorb their will into ours.

The Enemy, on the other hand, wants to fill the universe with lots of little replicas of Himself.

## Text Message 8.4

**Screwtape**

> But not because He has absorbed them, but because their wills freely conform to His. He wants servants who can become His sons.

> Our Father Below draws beings into himself. The Enemy wants a world full of beings united to Him but who are still distinct.

**Wormwood**

> Why doesn't the Enemy make Himself more noticeable to their senses?

**Screwtape**

> Overriding human free will by being both irresistible and indisputable are two weapons His scheme forbids Him to use. He cannot overwhelm. He can only woo.

> The Enemy leaves the creature to stand up on its own legs, to carry on with their will alone. During the trough periods they are growing into the creature He wants them to be.

> Prayers offered in a state of dryness please Him best.

## Text Message 8.5

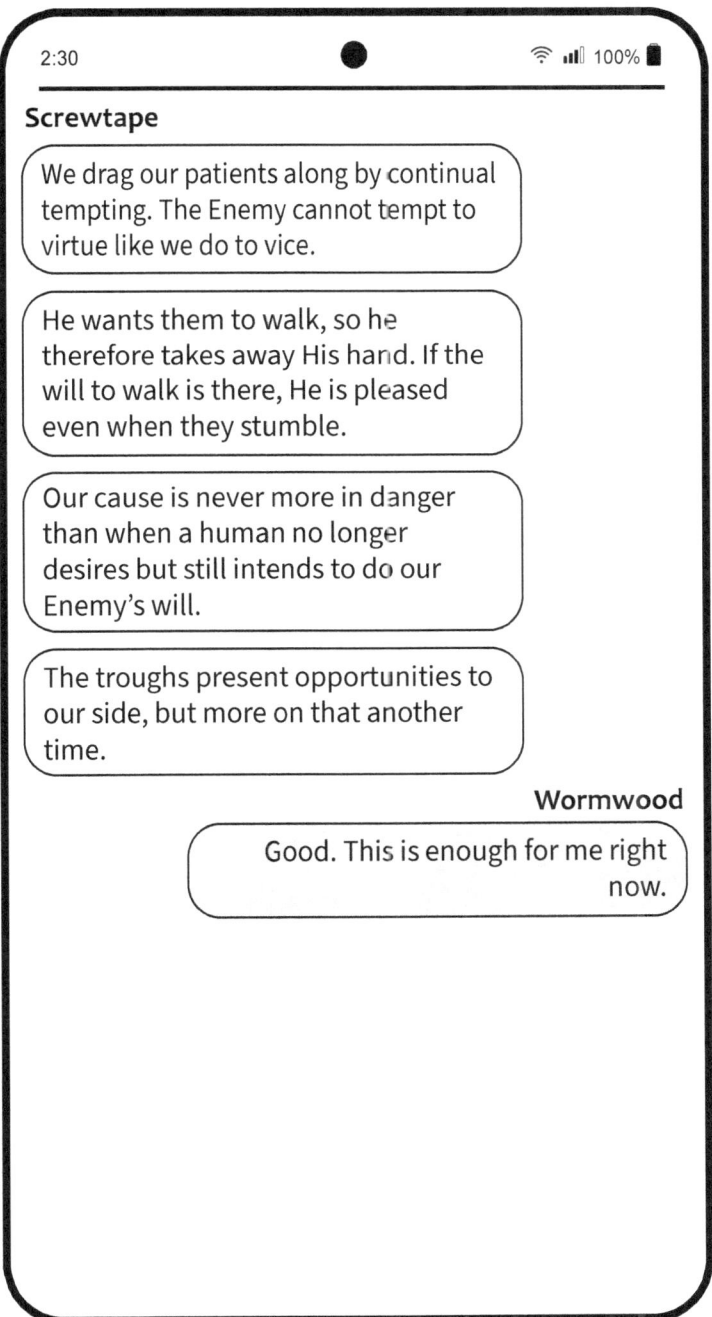

2:30　　　　　　　　●　　　　　🛜 ⏹ 100% 🔋

**Screwtape**

We drag our patients along by continual tempting. The Enemy cannot tempt to virtue like we do to vice.

He wants them to walk, so he therefore takes away His hand. If the will to walk is there, He is pleased even when they stumble.

Our cause is never more in danger than when a human no longer desires but still intends to do our Enemy's will.

The troughs present opportunities to our side, but more on that another time.

**Wormwood**

Good. This is enough for me right now.

## Summary

This page from the enemy's playbook suggests that the constant change in life between highs and lows can benefit the devil. We can be tempted away from God during the good times and suggested to despair during the bad times. This communication also shows that the devil will try to take advantage of the fact that God will not violate our free will by being too noticeable to our senses. God can be found for those who will to seek Him, but will not be found by those who do not will to find Him.

## Resources

| | |
|---|---|
| The spirit it willing but the flesh is weak | Matthew 10:22 |
| A grain of wheat that dies produces fruit | John 12:24 |
| Perseverance in trial | James 1:2–3 |
| The battle of prayer | CCC paragraphs 2725, 2728 |
| Facing difficulty in prayer | CCC paragraph 2731 |
| Temptation in prayer | CCC paragraph 2733 |
| The battle in prayer (in brief) | CCC paragraphs 2752, 2754 |

CCC paragraph 2728

Finally, our battle has to confront what we experience as failure in prayer: discouragement during periods of dryness; sadness that, because we have "great possessions,"[15] we have not given all to the Lord; disappointment over not being heard according to our own will; wounded pride, stiffened by the indignity that is ours as sinners; our resistance to the idea that prayer is a free and unmerited gift; and so forth. The conclusion is always the same: what good does it do to pray? To overcome these obstacles, we must battle to gain humility, trust, and perseverance.

15 Mark 10:22 (The Rich Man)

"From time to time, the Bridegroom veils his face. All of this is for your own good; his leaving is just as beneficial his coming. ... He comes to console you and leaves to guard you, for fear that you might become proud because of his sweet presence. ... When he is absent, your desire for him grows; your desire makes you seek him with greater ardor, and your waiting makes your encounter more delightful."

~ from The Ladder of Monks by Guigo II the Carthusian

## Counterattack Actions

- Establish regular daily prayer. Pray every day, and when trough times are present, tell God you are experiencing the dry times but desire to pray to Him anyway.
- Remember the words written by Guigo II from The Ladder of Monks.
- Thank God for the high times during your daily prayer.

## Questions

1.  Over the past year, week, or even day, what examples of undulation can you think of in your life? Do they appear as the failures in prayer listed in CCC paragraph 2728?

2.  How does God use the dry/trough periods in your life? What would be the opposite that Screwtape might encourage Wormwood to use on you?

3.　Non-believers, and atheists in particular, say they would believe in a God if there was compelling evidence. Why does God not make himself, in Screwtape's words, more "indisputable" or more "irresistible?"

4.　Screwtape says that prayer offered to God during spiritual dry times (troughs) please Him best. Why? What saints can you think of who went through spiritual dry times? What did they experience?

5.　From Screwtape's perspective, why is a human's intention more dangerous than their desire?

6.　What do you do to combat temptations and suggestions like the ones Screwtape suggests in this text message?

## Text Message 9.1

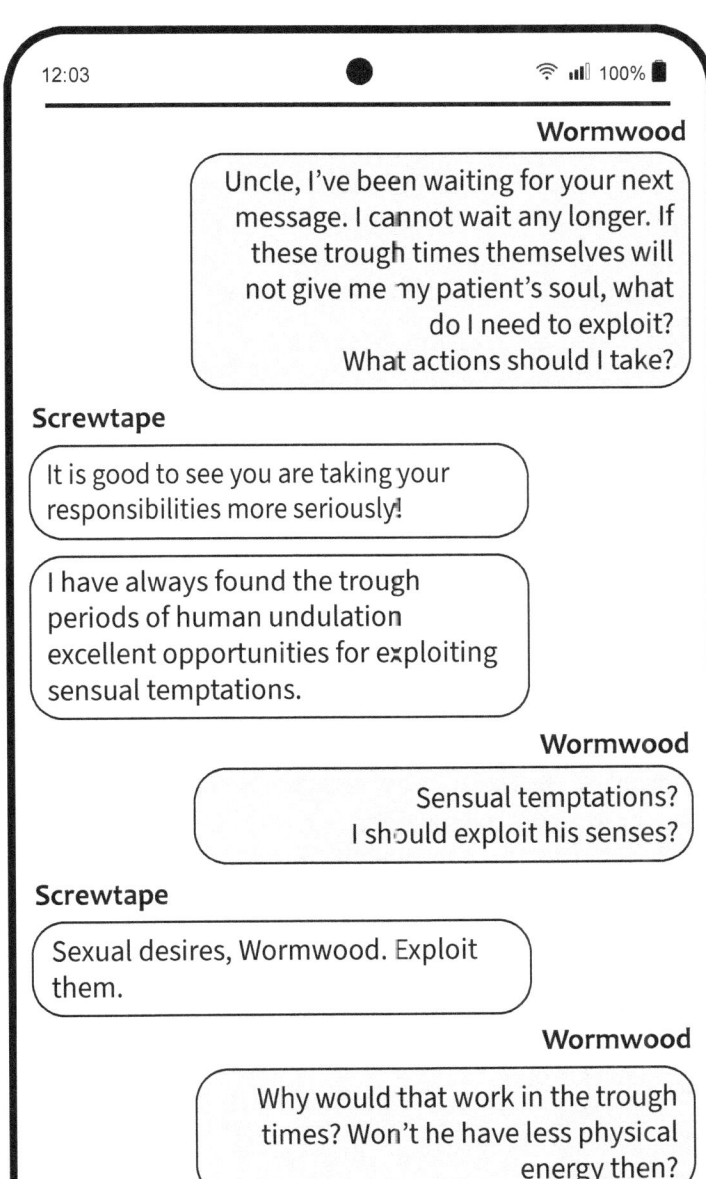

**Wormwood**

Uncle, I've been waiting for your next message. I cannot wait any longer. If these trough times themselves will not give me my patient's soul, what do I need to exploit? What actions should I take?

**Screwtape**

It is good to see you are taking your responsibilities more seriously!

I have always found the trough periods of human undulation excellent opportunities for exploiting sensual temptations.

**Wormwood**

Sensual temptations? I should exploit his senses?

**Screwtape**

Sexual desires, Wormwood. Exploit them.

**Wormwood**

Why would that work in the trough times? Won't he have less physical energy then?

## Text Message 9.2

**Screwtape**

> Yes, but his whole inner world is drab, cold and empty. It's been noted that sexuality during trough times is only slightly different in quality than at peak times.

> And sex during the trough times can draw them more easily into perversions.

**Wormwood**

> Can temptations like this work in other desires of the flesh?

**Screwtape**

> Yes, of course. You are much more likely to make your man a sound drunkard by pressing drink on him as a relaxant or a pain killer when he is dull and weary than when he is in a high period celebrating with friends.

> But you must remember that when dealing with any pleasure in its normal and healthy form, we are on the Enemy's ground.

> Regardless, we have won many a soul through pleasure.

## Text Message 9.3

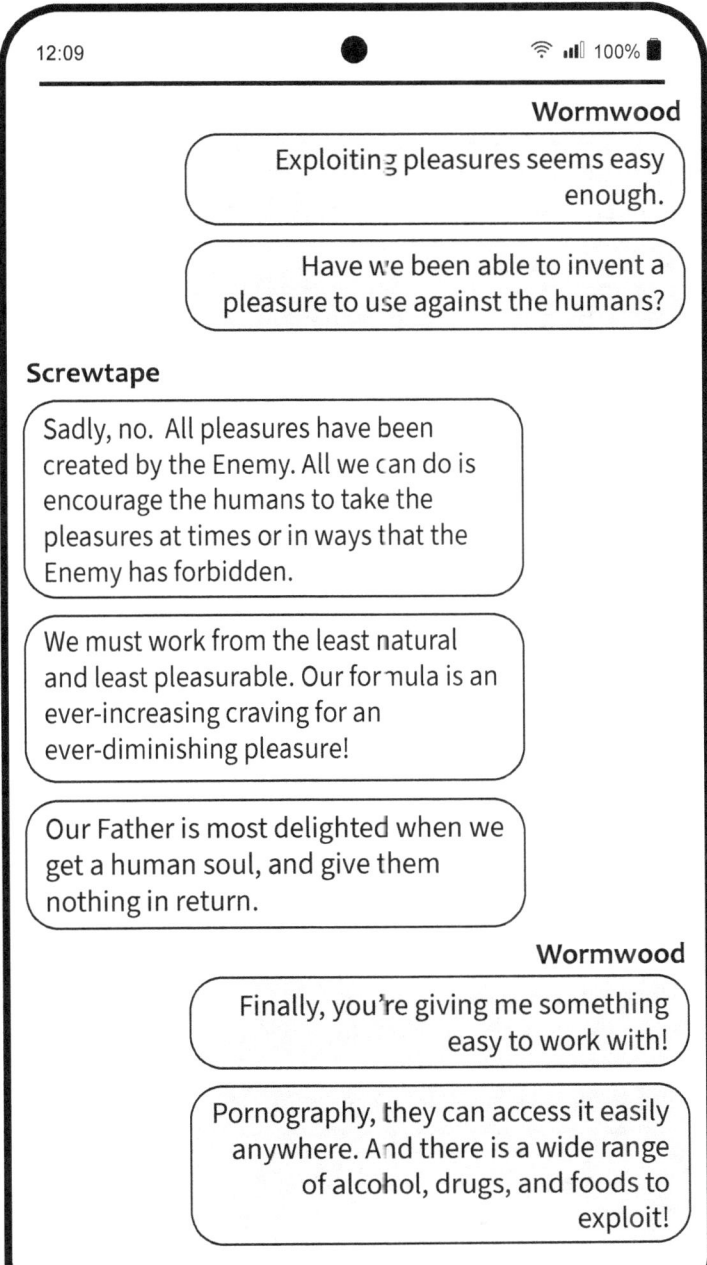

**Wormwood**

Exploiting pleasures seems easy enough.

Have we been able to invent a pleasure to use against the humans?

**Screwtape**

Sadly, no. All pleasures have been created by the Enemy. All we can do is encourage the humans to take the pleasures at times or in ways that the Enemy has forbidden.

We must work from the least natural and least pleasurable. Our formula is an ever-increasing craving for an ever-diminishing pleasure!

Our Father is most delighted when we get a human soul, and give them nothing in return.

**Wormwood**

Finally, you're giving me something easy to work with!

Pornography, they can access it easily anywhere. And there is a wide range of alcohol, drugs, and foods to exploit!

## Text Message 9.4

**Screwtape**

Yes. When you use this tactic in the trough times, it can be like shooting fish in a barrel.

But I warn you. Don't forget about the basics I have taught you.

**Wormwood**

You better remind me.

**Screwtape**

Keep knowledge out of his mind.
Do not let him suspect undulation.

Get him to think his conversion would have and should have lasted forever. And that his present spiritual dryness is an equally permanent condition.

If he is the desponding type, get him to despair.

If he is the wishful-thinking type, lead him to think all is well. In a few weeks, he'll begin to think his early days as a Christian were a bit extreme.

A moderated religion is as good for us as no religion at all, and more amusing.

## Text Message 9.5

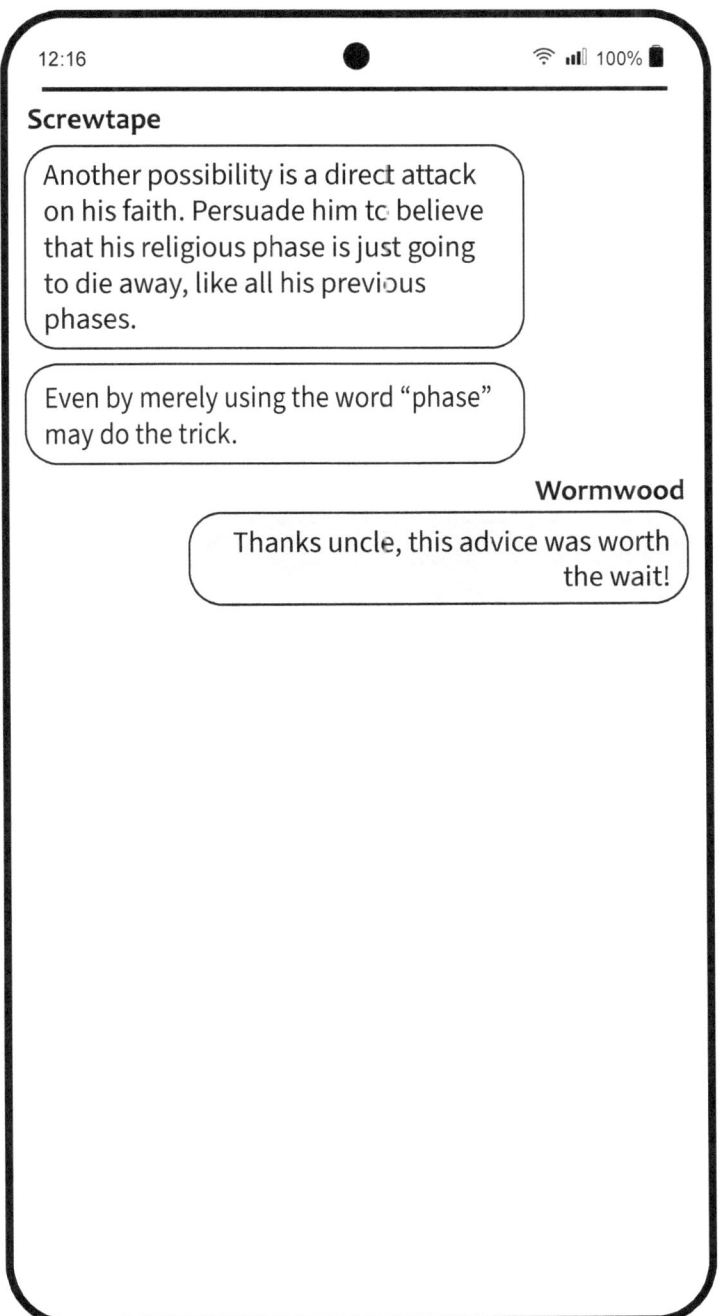

**Screwtape**

Another possibility is a direct attack on his faith. Persuade him to believe that his religious phase is just going to die away, like all his previous phases.

Even by merely using the word "phase" may do the trick.

**Wormwood**

Thanks uncle, this advice was worth the wait!

## Summary

This page from the enemy's playbook suggests that avoiding the abuse of pleasures during trough times (spiritual dryness) weakens the devil's attack. It also suggests that understanding the law of undulation benefits us and helps us persevere during times of spiritual dryness. This awareness also weakens the devil's attack. Finally, it suggests that we should not misinterpret spiritual dryness as a "phase" that will die away.

## Resources

| Transformation of life | Titus 2:11–12 |
|---|---|
| Temptation | James 1:12–16 |
| Against presumption | Sirach 5:2 |
| Self-control | Sirach 18:30 |
| Temperance | CCC paragraph 1809 |
| Idolatry | CCC paragraph 2113 |
| Offenses against chastity | CCC paragraphs 2351–2356 |
| The love of husband and wife | CCC paragraph 2362 |

CCC paragraph 1809

On the virtues of temperance, fortitude, justice and prudence:

To live well is nothing other than to love God with all one's heart, with all one's soul and with all one's efforts; from this it comes about that love is kept whole and uncorrupted (through temperance). No misfortune can disturb it (and this is fortitude). It obeys only [God] (and this is justice), and is careful in discerning things, so as not to be surprised by deceit or trickery (and this is prudence).

~ St. Augustine

## Counterattack Actions

- Identify a pleasure that could make you vulnerable in the spiritual battle and resist that pleasure.
- Pray for fortitude and self-control.

## Questions

1. Do you agree with Screwtape that the abuse of sensual desires are effective tools to be used against us during times of spiritual dryness? Do they separate us from God?

2. What do all the different types of abuses of pleasure have in common? Why do they work against us?

3. What examples can you list that confirm the devil's formula against us, that an ever-increasing craving produces an ever-diminishing pleasure?

4. What do you think Screwtape is suggesting when he says: "A moderated religion is as good for us as no religion at all"?

5.  Can you relate to the statement that religion and faith can be a "phase"? What can prevent troughs in faith and spiritual dryness from being a phase that dies away?


6.  What do you do to combat temptations and suggestions like the ones Screwtape suggests in this text message?

## Text Message 10.1

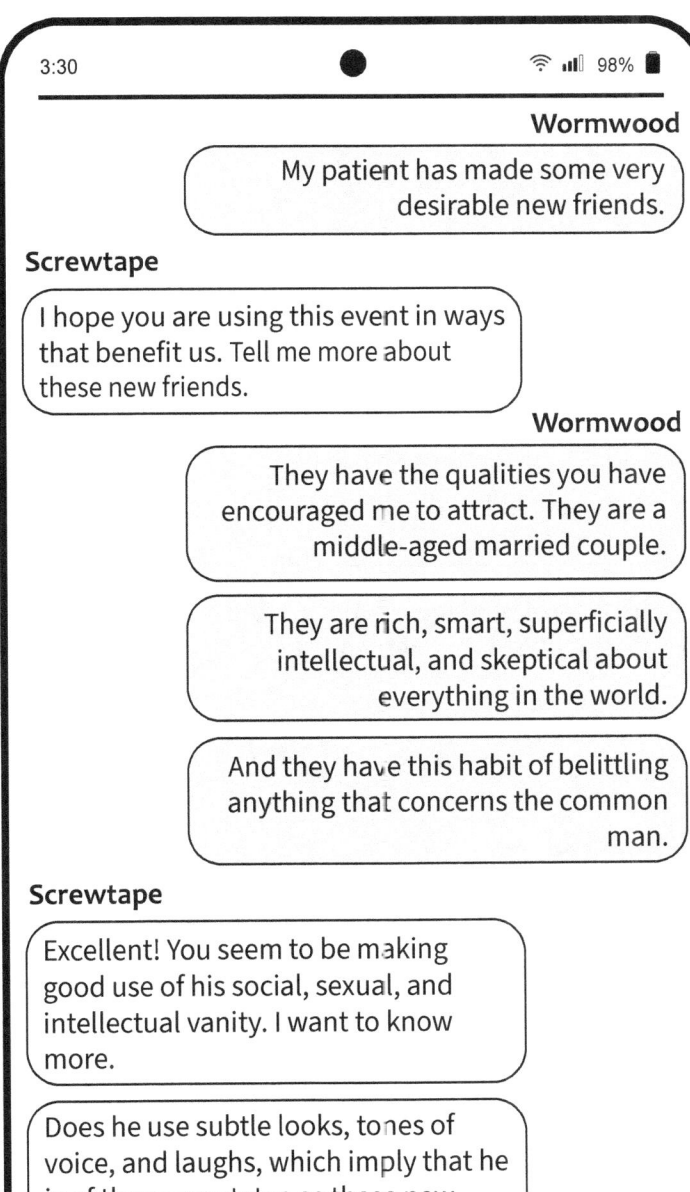

**Wormwood**

My patient has made some very desirable new friends.

**Screwtape**

I hope you are using this event in ways that benefit us. Tell me more about these new friends.

**Wormwood**

They have the qualities you have encouraged me to attract. They are a middle-aged married couple.

They are rich, smart, superficially intellectual, and skeptical about everything in the world.

And they have this habit of belittling anything that concerns the common man.

**Screwtape**

Excellent! You seem to be making good use of his social, sexual, and intellectual vanity. I want to know more.

Does he use subtle looks, tones of voice, and laughs, which imply that he is of the same status as these new friends?

## Text Message 10.2

3:33 ● 98%

**Screwtape**

You should especially encourage this type of phoniness.

Soon he will realize that his faith is in direct opposition with the conversations occurring with these new friends of his.

Until he realizes this, he will be silent when he ought to speak and laugh when he ought to be silent.

This type of phoniness turns mortals into the thing they pretend to be.

**Wormwood**

So how do we prepare for the Enemy's attack?

**Screwtape**

Good question. Wormwood, you are maturing as a demon.

Delay your patient from realizing the pleasure of this new temptation. The Enemy's servants have been preaching about "the World" as a great temptation for more than 2,000 years.

## Text Message 10.3

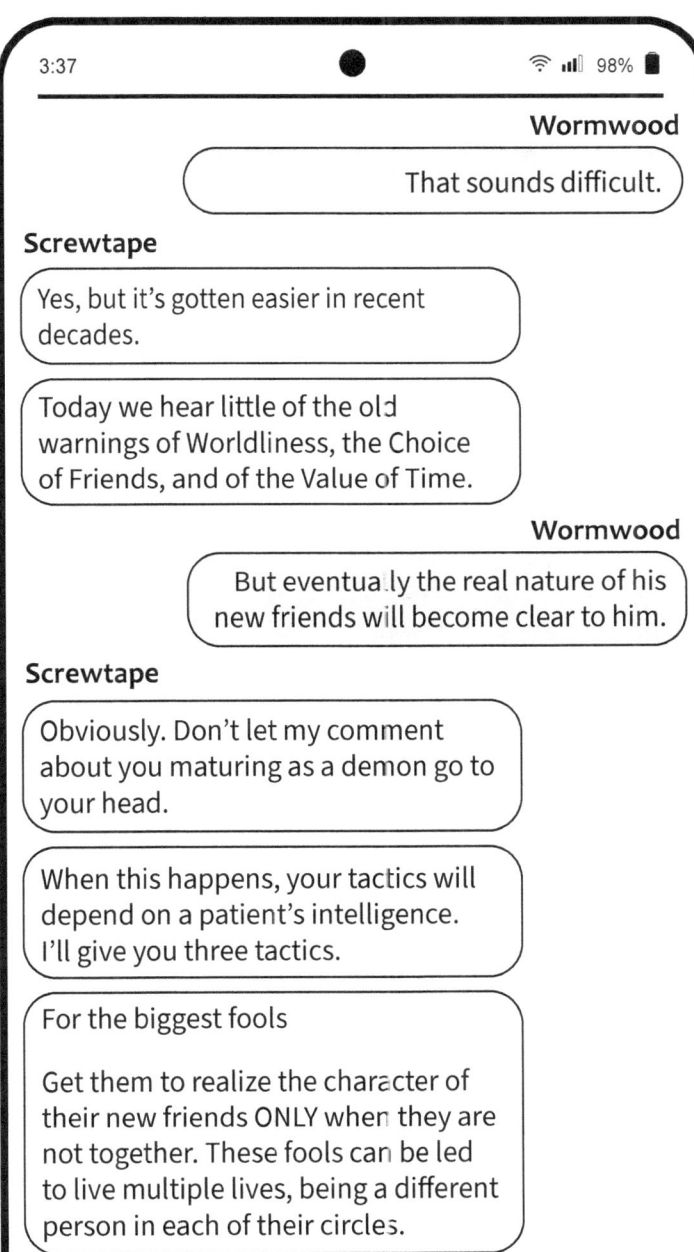

**3:37**  98%

**Wormwood**

That sounds difficult.

**Screwtape**

Yes, but it's gotten easier in recent decades.

Today we hear little of the old warnings of Worldliness, the Choice of Friends, and of the Value of Time.

**Wormwood**

But eventually the real nature of his new friends will become clear to him.

**Screwtape**

Obviously. Don't let my comment about you maturing as a demon go to your head.

When this happens, your tactics will depend on a patient's intelligence. I'll give you three tactics.

For the biggest fools

Get them to realize the character of their new friends ONLY when they are not together. These fools can be led to live multiple lives, being a different person in each of their circles.

## Text Message 10.4

**Screwtape**

For lesser fools

Get them to find pleasure in the perception that the two sides of their life are inconsistent. You can accomplish this by exploiting their vanity. Get them to think their Worldly Friends touch them on one side and their Church Friends touch them on another side AND that they are a complete, balanced, complex person who sees around them all.

If all else fails

Persuade them, in defiance of their conscience, to continue associating with these friends on the basis that they are doing them some "good", by being in their company, drinking their cocktails and laughing at their jokes.

**Wormwood**

OK. Anything else?

**Screwtape**

Yes. Have your patient spend more than he can afford on these new developments and to neglect his work and his mother.

## Text Message 10.5

**Screwtape**

Her jealousy and alarm, along with increasing evasiveness, will be invaluable, producing aggravation and domestic tension.

## Summary

This page from the enemy's playbook suggests that the people you associate with and how you act with them can affect your spiritual battle. Specifically, how true you remain to your beliefs regardless of which circle of friends you are with can affect your spiritual battle.

## Resources

| True friendship | Sirach 6:5–17 |
|---|---|
| Choice of friends | Sirach 9:10–16 |
| Friends | Proverbs 17:17 |
| Better than wine and strong drink | Sirach 40:20 |

"Mortals tend to turn into the thing they pretend to be."

~ Screwtape

## Counterattack Actions

- Notice a conversation where you should speak up, and then speak up with charity.
- Avoid conversations where hurtful words are being said about another person, or even better, speak up and say something kind about that person.
- If you have a relationship or friendship that is unhealthy for your spiritual life, leave it.

## Questions

1.  When have you found yourself silent when you should have
    spoken up? What was the situation? Why did you remain
    silent? Or when you spoke, when you should have remained
    silent?

2.  How does awareness of worldliness, choice of friends, and
    valuing time affect your spiritual battle?

3.  When in an unhealthy relationship, what factors prevent you
    from being aware of the negative effects they have on you?

4.  What are the attributes of quality friendships?

5.  How do you get out of a spiritually unhealthy relationship?

6.  What do you do to combat temptations and suggestions like
    the ones Screwtape suggests in this text message?

## Text Message 11.1

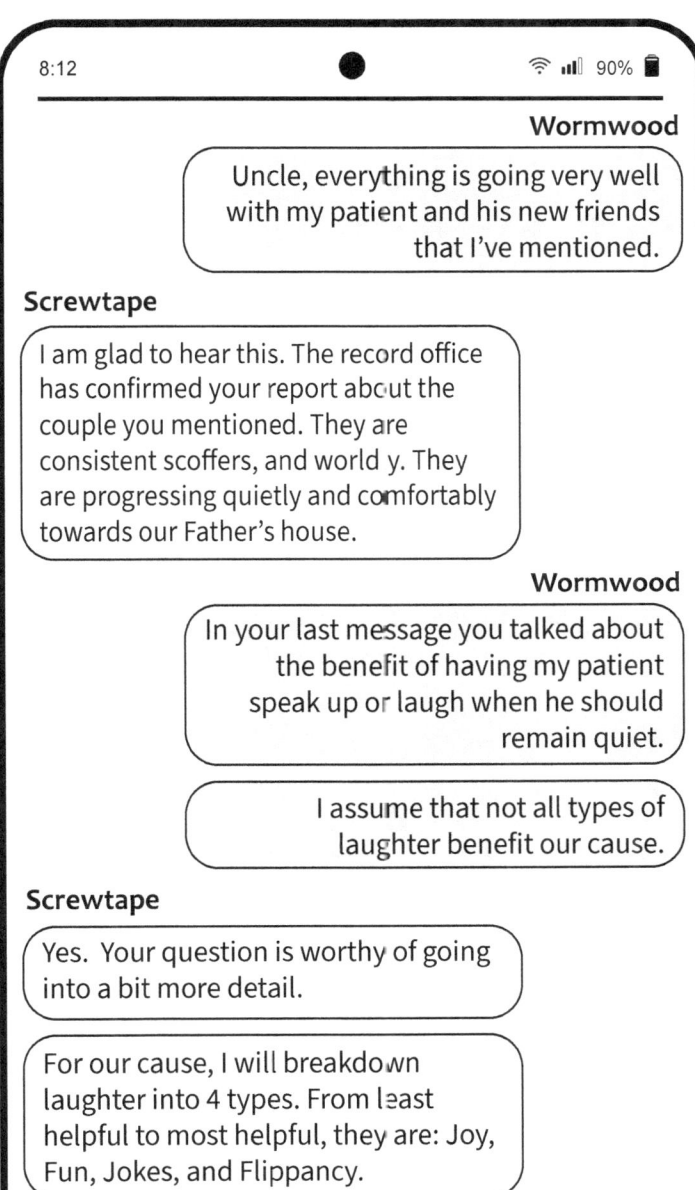

**8:12** 🔵 🔋 90% 📶

**Wormwood**

> Uncle, everything is going very well with my patient and his new friends that I've mentioned.

**Screwtape**

> I am glad to hear this. The record office has confirmed your report about the couple you mentioned. They are consistent scoffers, and worldy. They are progressing quietly and comfortably towards our Father's house.

**Wormwood**

> In your last message you talked about the benefit of having my patient speak up or laugh when he should remain quiet.

> I assume that not all types of laughter benefit our cause.

**Screwtape**

> Yes. Your question is worthy of going into a bit more detail.

> For our cause, I will breakdown laughter into 4 types. From least helpful to most helpful, they are: Joy, Fun, Jokes, and Flippancy.

## Text Message 11.2

8:14      🔘      📶 ▂▃▄ 90% 🔋

**Screwtape**

#1 Joy
Examples of when Joy produces human laughter include:
- when humans are reunited with friends and loved ones
- when they experience certain music and art

We don't understand the cause of this laughter. It does us no good and it should be discouraged. It really is disgusting and is an insult to the realism and dignity of Hell.

#2 Fun
Fun is closely related to Joy.
Laughter coming from fun is sort of an emotional froth that rises from the play instinct and is of very little use to us.

However, it can be used to divert humans from things the Enemy would like them to be doing or feeling.
This type of laughter has undesirable tendencies and can promote charity, courage, and many other evils.

**Wormwood**

Avoiding laughter from joy and fun sound slightly helpful, but I am ready for something I can really use.

## Text Message 11.3

**Screwtape**

I'm getting there. #3 Jokes
Jokes are much more promising.
Particularly, jokes that destroy shame.
A couple examples will help you.

Cruelty is shameful, but can be funny
when passed off as a practical joke.

Cowardice is shameful, but when it is
boasted of with humorous
exaggerations and gestures, it can be
passed off as a funny joke.

You can also encourage cowardice by
getting them to write something about
another person on-line, where the other
person cannot defend themselves.

**Wormwood**

This action can leverage both cruelty
and cowardice!

**Screwtape**

Precisely! And now the best of all.

#4 Flippancy
Flippancy is economical. Only a clever
human can make a real joke about
virtue, but any of them can be trained to
talk as if the virtue were funny.

## Text Message 11.4

**Screwtape**

With flippant people, the Joke is already assumed to have been made.
Every serious subject is discussed implying that they have already found a ridiculous side to it.

For example: a person laments how their stock investment had gone from a modest profit to a large loss overnight, and the other person responds, "better luck next time" or "easy come, easy go."

If prolonged, the habit of flippancy builds up around a human, like a fine armor plating against the Enemy.

Flippancy is a thousand miles away from Joy. It deadens, instead of sharpening the intellect.

**Wormwood**

These last two types of laughter are really good. I especially like Jokes.

## Summary

This page from the enemy's playbook suggests laughter not grounded in joy and beauty can be an asset to the devil in spiritual warfare. The wrong type of laughter takes dignity away from others and can separate us from God.

## Resources

| | |
|---|---|
| Joy between Jesus and Zacchaeus | Luke 19:6 |
| Joy and the resurrected Jesus | Luke 24:41 |
| Joy | Romans 15:13 |
| Joy | 2 John 1:12 |
| Joy and the resurrected Jesus | CCC paragraph 644 |
| Theological virtue of hope | CCC paragraph 2657 |

"Flippancy is a flower whose roots are often underground in the subconsciousness."

~ G. K. Chesterton, What I Saw in America

## Counterattack Actions

- Create a list of things that give you true joy. Make these things a part of your life.
- Identify and resist humor that is harmful to others.

## Questions

1. Screwtape speaks of the married couple progressing "quietly and comfortably" towards hell. What do you think "quietly and comfortably" means? Do you think that is how some people choose Hell over God?

2. This communication said that the demons do not understand the cause of laughter that comes from joy. Why do you think that is true? What do you believe to be the cause of laughter that comes from joy?

3. Do you believe it is possible that practical jokes could be a temptation in spiritual warfare? Why?

4. What is an example of flippancy, where you heard a serious subject having an implied ridiculous side?

5. How does flippancy deaden a person's intellect?

6. What do you do to combat temptations and suggestions like the ones Screwtape suggests in this text message?

## Text Message 12.1

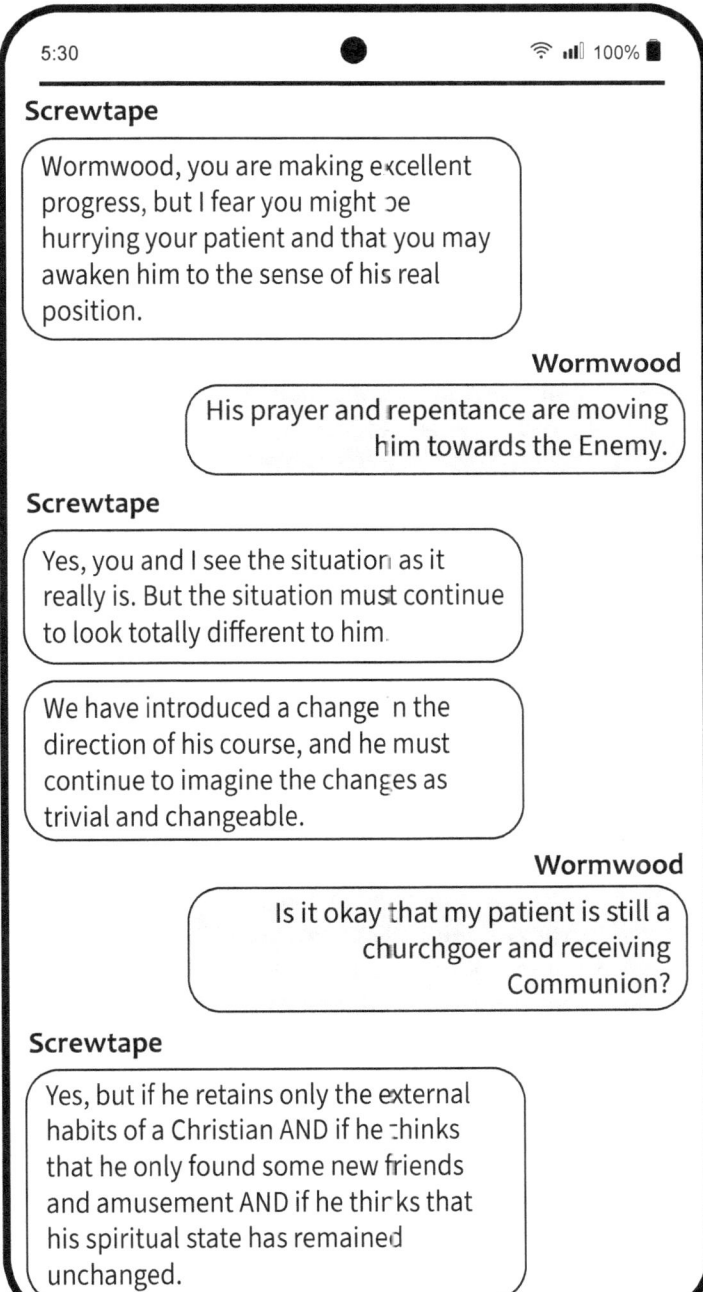

**Screwtape**

Wormwood, you are making excellent progress, but I fear you might be hurrying your patient and that you may awaken him to the sense of his real position.

**Wormwood**

His prayer and repentance are moving him towards the Enemy.

**Screwtape**

Yes, you and I see the situation as it really is. But the situation must continue to look totally different to him.

We have introduced a change in the direction of his course, and he must continue to imagine the changes as trivial and changeable.

**Wormwood**

Is it okay that my patient is still a churchgoer and receiving Communion?

**Screwtape**

Yes, but if he retains only the external habits of a Christian AND if he thinks that he only found some new friends and amusement AND if he thinks that his spiritual state has remained unchanged.

## Text Message 12.2

5:33　　　　　●　　　　　🛜 ıll 100% 🔋

**Wormwood**

So, there is a benefit to this?

**Screwtape**

Yes, while he is in this situation, he will not give thought to repenting of his sins. He will only think of these things vaguely and with unease and that he hasn't been doing very well lately.

But if the uneasiness gets too strong, it may wake him up and it could spoil everything.

**Wormwood**

So ideally, I should try to keep him in that vague and uneasy feeling, and keep him from doing anything about it? That sounds challenging.

**Screwtape**

Challenging, yes, but it will provide great rewards. If this feeling is allowed to live, but not allowed to progress towards real repentance, it will increase the patient's reluctance to think about the Enemy.

**Wormwood**

Why would it cause that?

## Text Message 12.3

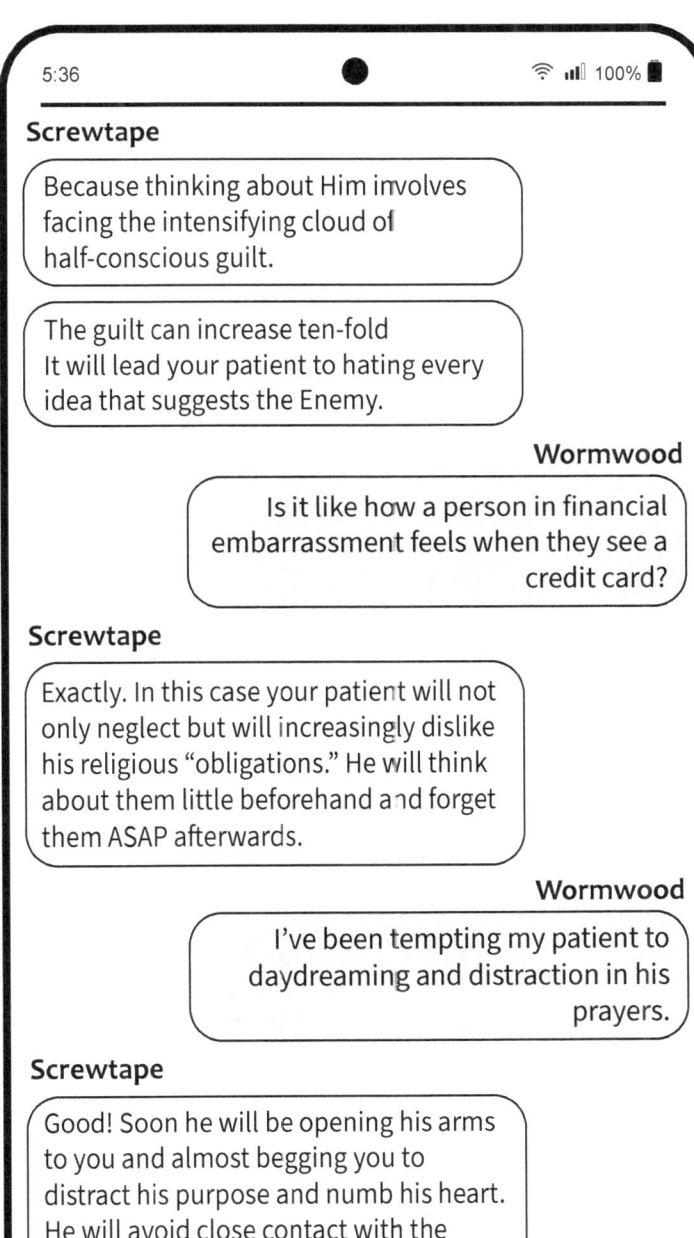

**Screwtape**

Because thinking about Him involves facing the intensifying cloud of half-conscious guilt.

The guilt can increase ten-fold
It will lead your patient to hating every idea that suggests the Enemy.

**Wormwood**

Is it like how a person in financial embarrassment feels when they see a credit card?

**Screwtape**

Exactly. In this case your patient will not only neglect but will increasingly dislike his religious "obligations." He will think about them little beforehand and forget them ASAP afterwards.

**Wormwood**

I've been tempting my patient to daydreaming and distraction in his prayers.

**Screwtape**

Good! Soon he will be opening his arms to you and almost begging you to distract his purpose and numb his heart. He will avoid close contact with the Enemy.

## Text Message 12.4

**Screwtape**

> This will free you from the tedious work of providing pleasures and temptations. His uneasiness will increasingly cut him off from real happiness.

> You will find that anything or Nothing will attract his wandering attention. Lots of things can keep him from his prayers, work, or sleep.

> Things like TV, the Internet, and social media are effective. Tools like computers and "smart" phones are always within reach. Make him do Nothing for long periods of time and accomplish nothing in the process.

> Christians describe the Enemy as one "without whom Nothing is strong." HA!

**Wormwood**

> Without the Enemy, Nothing is strong. You lost me with this strange double-negative description.

**Screwtape**

> These ridiculous words are taken from their own liturgy.

## Text Message 12.5

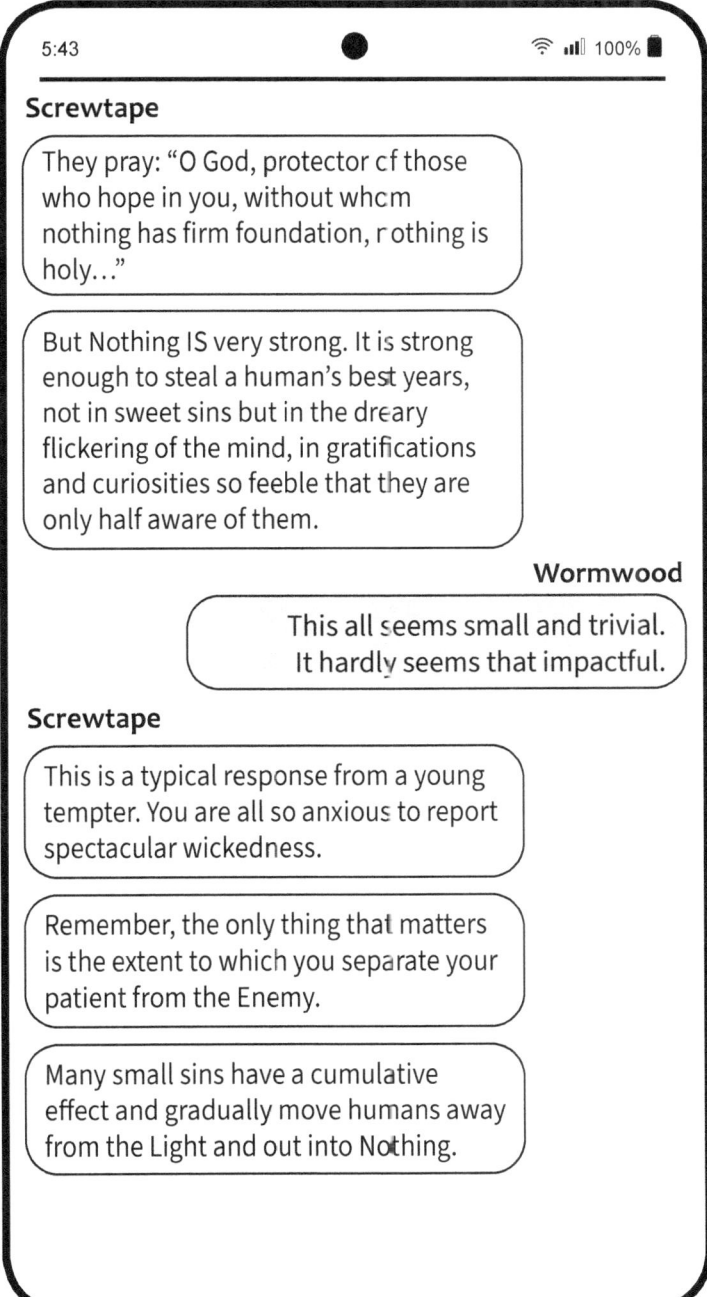

**Screwtape**

They pray: "O God, protector of those who hope in you, without whom nothing has firm foundation, nothing is holy…"

But Nothing IS very strong. It is strong enough to steal a human's best years, not in sweet sins but in the dreary flickering of the mind, in gratifications and curiosities so feeble that they are only half aware of them.

**Wormwood**

This all seems small and trivial. It hardly seems that impactful.

**Screwtape**

This is a typical response from a young tempter. You are all so anxious to report spectacular wickedness.

Remember, the only thing that matters is the extent to which you separate your patient from the Enemy.

Many small sins have a cumulative effect and gradually move humans away from the Light and out into Nothing.

Text Message 12.6

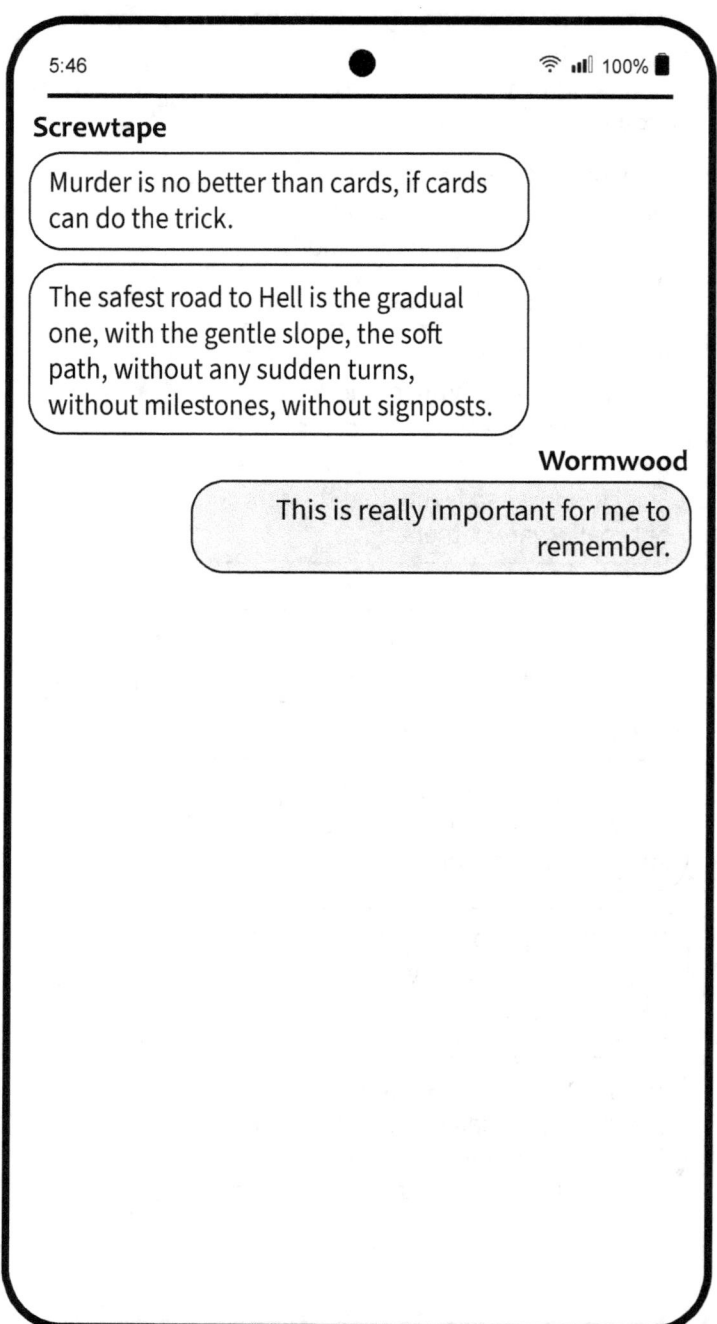

## Summary

This page from the enemy's playbook suggests seeing things as they really are, deep interior prayer, and repentance weaken the devil's attack. This letter also warns us how doing Nothing can negatively affect us and how easy the road to Hell really is.

## Resources

| | |
|---|---|
| Jesus' first words in public ministry | Mark 1:15 |
| Apart from me, you can do nothing | John 15:5 |
| The spirit is willing, but the flesh is weak | Matthew 26:41 |
| We do not know how to pray as we ought | Romans 8:26 |
| Pray without ceasing | 1 Thessalonians 5:17 |
| Constant prayer | Ephesians 6:18 |
| The battle of prayer | CCC paragraphs 2725–2745 |

CCC paragraph 2725

Prayer is both a gift of grace and a determined response on our part. It always presupposes effort. The great figures of prayer of the Old Covenant before Christ, as well as the Mother of God, the saints, and he himself, all teach us this: prayer is a battle. Against whom? Against ourselves and against the wiles of the tempter who does all he can to turn man away from prayer, away from union with God. We pray as we live, because we live as we pray. If we do not want to act habitually according to the Spirit of Christ, neither can we pray habitually in his name. The "spiritual battle" of the Christian's new life is inseparable from the battle of prayer.

CCC paragraphs 2725–2745 contain a section titled The Battle of Prayer. These 21 paragraphs provide good insight into spiritual warfare. They discuss:

- Objections to Prayer
- Humble Vigilance of Heart (facing difficulties and temptations in prayer)
- Filial Trust (Why do we complain of not being heard?)
- Persevering in Love

COLLECT

**O God**, protector of those who hope in you, **without whom nothing has firm foundation, nothing is holy**, bestow in abundance your mercy upon us and grant that, with you as our ruler and guide, we may use the good things that pass in such a way as to hold fast even now to those that ever endure. Through our Lord Jesus Christ, your Son, who lives and reigns with you in the unity of the Holy Spirit, God, for ever and ever. Amen.

~ Prayed at the beginning of Mass on the Seventeenth Sunday in Ordinary Time

**Counterattack Actions**

- Identify an area in your life that needs repentance, a turning back towards God. Repent in this area of your life.
- Identify an activity that may put you at risk of doing Nothing. Eliminate or reduce this activity in your life.

## Questions

1. Screwtape teaches Wormwood that keeping his patient from seeing the real situation is an important tactic in spiritual battle. What can we do to help us see the real situation?

2. Wormwood is told to encourage his patient to practice only external habits of his Christian faith. What *are* external habits of faith? What are internal habits of faith that will combat Satan in spiritual warfare?

3. We hear that man's repentance is an obstacle to Satan. Jesus spoke these words at the beginning of his public ministry "The kingdom of God is at hand. Repent, and believe in the gospel." (Mark 1:15) Why do you think repentance is so important in our spiritual life? How well do we repent and believe in the Gospel? Do we resolve guilt when it begins to weigh on us?

4. Screwtape says "Nothing is very strong, strong enough to steal a human's best years." How can a person protect themselves from doing too much of Nothing? What examples of Nothing would you add to Screwtape's list?

5.  If the safest road to Hell is gradual, easy and comfortable, does that mean the road to Heaven is difficult and uncomfortable? Why?

6.  What do you do to combat temptations and suggestions like the ones Screwtape suggests in this text message?

## Text Message 13.1

Screwtape

> WORMWOOD!!

Wormwood

> WHAT!

Screwtape

> You have provided me many reports of your recent successes, largely simple stories of no real concern.

> And ultimately, you have let your patient slip through your fingers!

> The situation is dire, and I see no reason to shield you from the consequences of your incompetence.

Wormwood

> What?

Screwtape

> What did I tell you about avoiding repentance?

Wormwood

> That it is challenging to manage?

## Text Message 13.2

9:25 🔵 70%

**Screwtape**

I received a report on your patient that repentance and reconversion have occurred at very high levels.

Your patient has received grace. The potential for defeat is growing.

**Wormwood**

Wait! That was another tempter.

**Screwtape**

Stop! Don't blame another junior tempter for your mistakes.

This amounts to a second conversion and probably to a deeper level than the first.

You should have known that a force field would prevent you from attacking your patient.

**Wormwood**

Force field?

**Screwtape**

The force field that surrounded your patient on his walk back from his favorite coffee shop.

## Text Message 13.3

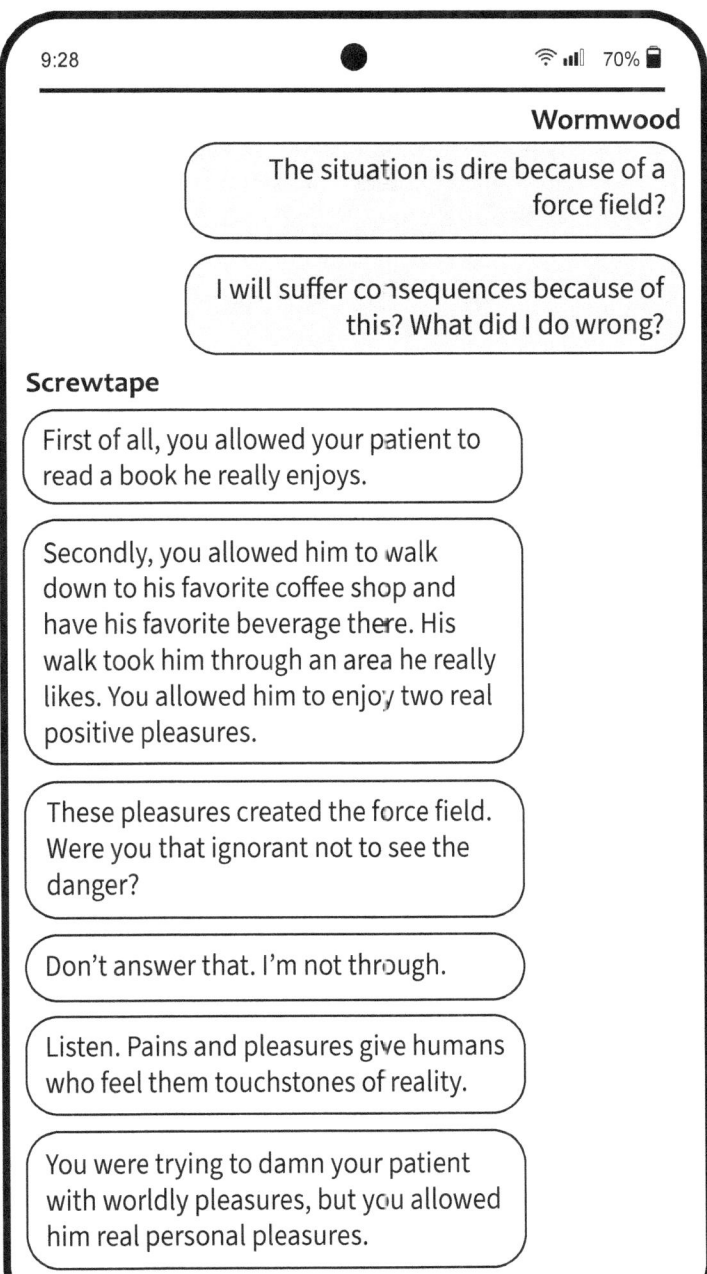

**Wormwood**

The situation is dire because of a force field?

I will suffer consequences because of this? What did I do wrong?

**Screwtape**

First of all, you allowed your patient to read a book he really enjoys.

Secondly, you allowed him to walk down to his favorite coffee shop and have his favorite beverage there. His walk took him through an area he really likes. You allowed him to enjoy two real positive pleasures.

These pleasures created the force field. Were you that ignorant not to see the danger?

Don't answer that. I'm not through.

Listen. Pains and pleasures give humans who feel them touchstones of reality.

You were trying to damn your patient with worldly pleasures, but you allowed him real personal pleasures.

## Text Message 13.4

**Screwtape**

How could you fail to see that a real pleasure was the last thing you should have let him have?

Didn't you anticipate the pleasure he would experience from both that book and his walk to the coffee shop?

Don't answer that. I'm still not through. As a prerequisite to detaching him from the Enemy, you had begun to detach him from his true self, and you had made some progress in doing so. Now all this is undone!

**Wormwood**

Haven't you said the Enemy likes to see those vermin detach as well?

**Screwtape**

You're shifting the focus of our conversation away from your blunder. I see what you're trying to do.

Yes, the Enemy does like detachment too, but in a different way.

## Text Message 13.5

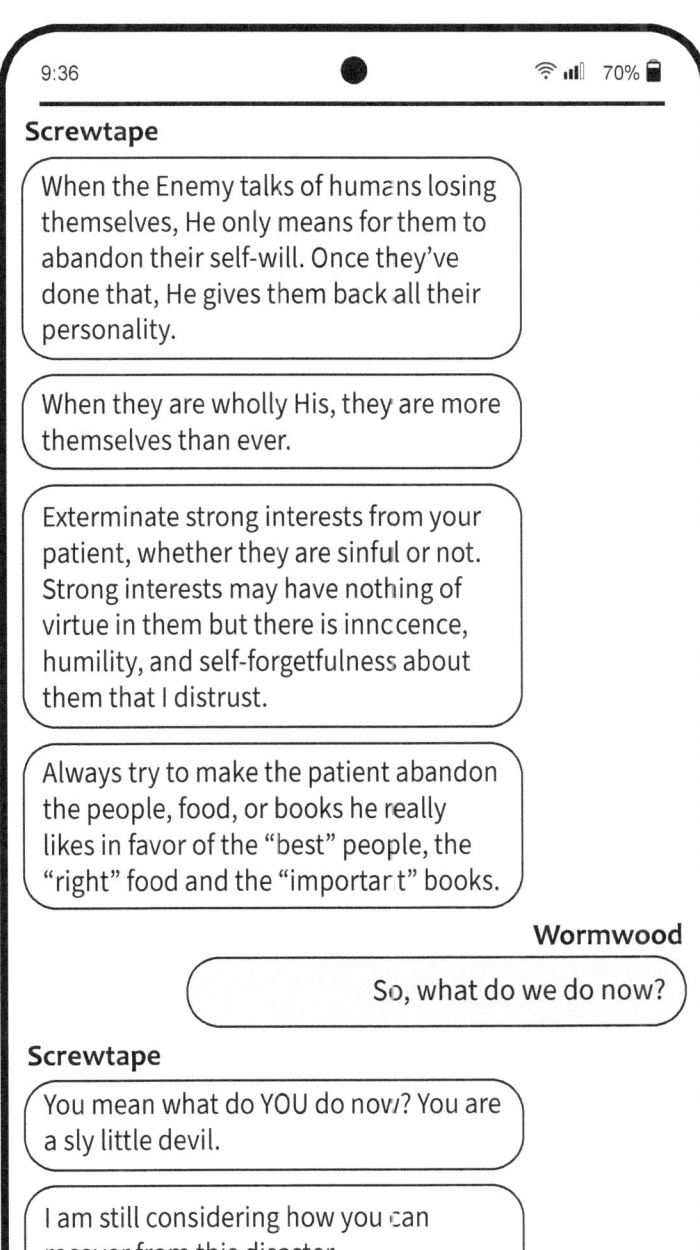

**Screwtape**

When the Enemy talks of humans losing themselves, He only means for them to abandon their self-will. Once they've done that, He gives them back all their personality.

When they are wholly His, they are more themselves than ever.

Exterminate strong interests from your patient, whether they are sinful or not. Strong interests may have nothing of virtue in them but there is innocence, humility, and self-forgetfulness about them that I distrust.

Always try to make the patient abandon the people, food, or books he really likes in favor of the "best" people, the "right" food and the "important" books.

**Wormwood**

So, what do we do now?

**Screwtape**

You mean what do YOU do now? You are a sly little devil.

I am still considering how you can recover from this disaster.

## Text Message 13.6

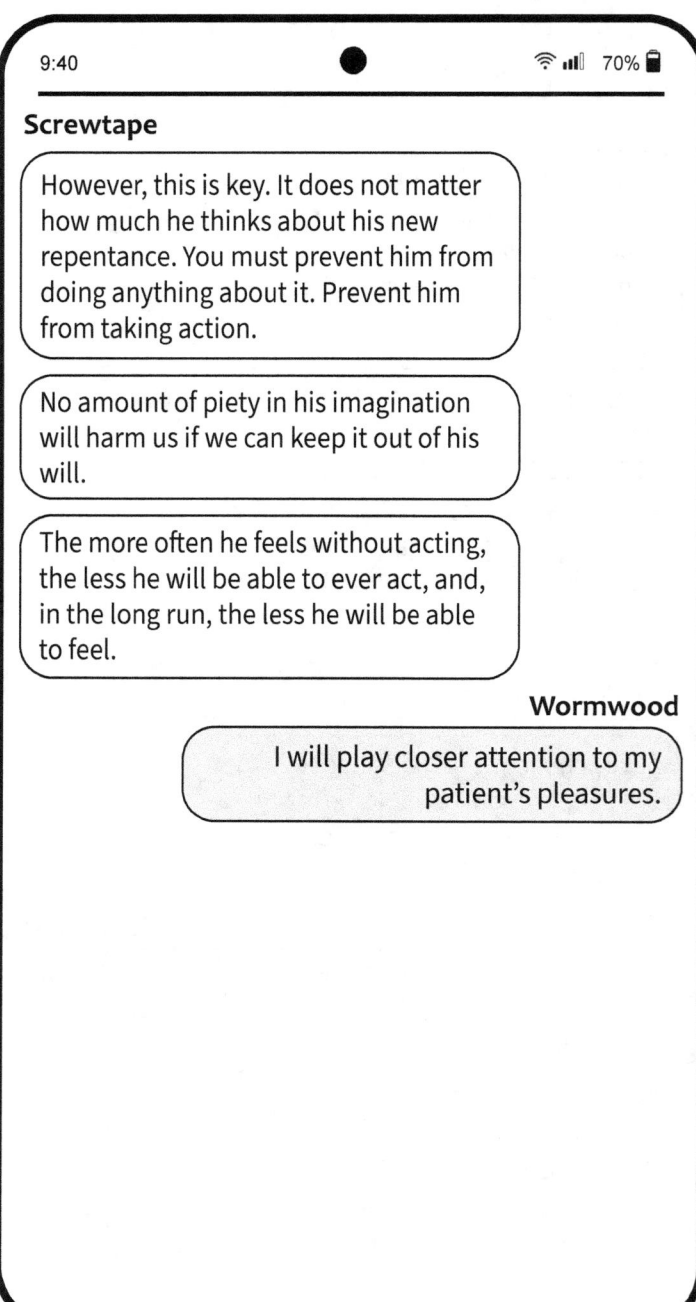

**Screwtape**

However, this is key. It does not matter how much he thinks about his new repentance. You must prevent him from doing anything about it. Prevent him from taking action.

No amount of piety in his imagination will harm us if we can keep it out of his will.

The more often he feels without acting, the less he will be able to ever act, and, in the long run, the less he will be able to feel.

**Wormwood**

I will play closer attention to my patient's pleasures.

## Summary

This page from the enemy's playbook suggests that enjoying real pleasures, and real conversion and repentance weaken the devil's attack.

## Resources

| The parable of the lost son | Luke 15:11-32 |
| --- | --- |
| Interior repentance | CCC paragraph 1421 |
| Many forms of penance in the Christian life | CCC paragraph 1439 |
| Effects of the Sacrament of Penance and Reconciliation | CCC paragraph 1468 |
| Grace | CCC paragraphs 1996-2005 |

CCC paragraph 1439

The process of conversion and repentance was described by Jesus in the parable of the prodigal son, the center of which is the merciful father: the fascination of illusory freedom, the abandonment of the father's house; the extreme misery in which the son finds himself after squandering his fortune; his deep humiliation at finding himself obliged to feed swine, and still worse, at wanting to feed on the husks the pigs ate; his reflection on all he has lost; his repentance and decision to declare himself guilty before his father; the journey back; the father's generous welcome; the father's joy - all these are characteristic of the process of conversion. The beautiful robe, the ring, and the festive banquet are symbols of that new life - pure worthy, and joyful - of anyone who returns to God and to the bosom of his family, which is the Church. Only the heart of Christ who knows the depths of his Father's love could reveal to us the abyss of his mercy in so simple and beautiful a way.

GRACE: The free and undeserved gift that God gives us to respond to our vocation to become his adopted children. As **sanctifying grace**, God shares his divine life and friendship with us in a habitual gift, a stable and supernatural disposition that enables the soul to live with God, to act by his love. As **actual grace**, God gives us the help to conform our lives to his will. **Sacramental grace** and **special graces** (charisms, the grace of one's state of life) are gifts of the Holy Spirit to help us live out our Christian vocation. (1996, 2000)

~ CCC Glossary

### Counterattack Actions

* Identify where you need conversion in your life and pray to receive God's grace for this conversion.
* Make positive pleasures a regular part of your life.

## Questions

1. In your experience, what causes conversion and repentance? Screwtape suspects that it is grace. What is grace and how would grace causing conversion and repentance be possible?

2. Positive pleasures are considered an impenetrable energy field for the demons. Why do you think this could be? What are some of your positive pleasures?

3. How do worldly pleasures differ from our personal (positive) pleasures?

4. What do you think is meant by the statement: When we are wholly God's we are more ourselves than ever. In what ways are we less ourselves when we are not wholly God's?

5. Why is taking action critical in spiritual warfare? What action(s) are you not taking that you should?

6. What do you do to combat temptations and suggestions like the ones Screwtape suggests in this text message?

## Text Message 14.1

7:57        ●        🛜 ▂▄▆ 80% 🔋

**Screwtape**

Wormwood, I am now aware of another alarming situation with your patient.

**Wormwood**

Now what?

**Screwtape**

Your patient is making resolutions similar to his first conversion.

He is not making those naïve promises of unending virtue, but only has the simple hope that the Enemy will provide him with what he needs to get him through the day. This is bad!

**Wormwood**

What do we do?

**Screwtape**

No, what do YOU do?

Your patient has become humble. Have you drawn his attention to this fact?

**Wormwood**

No. Why would I do that?

## Text Message 14.2

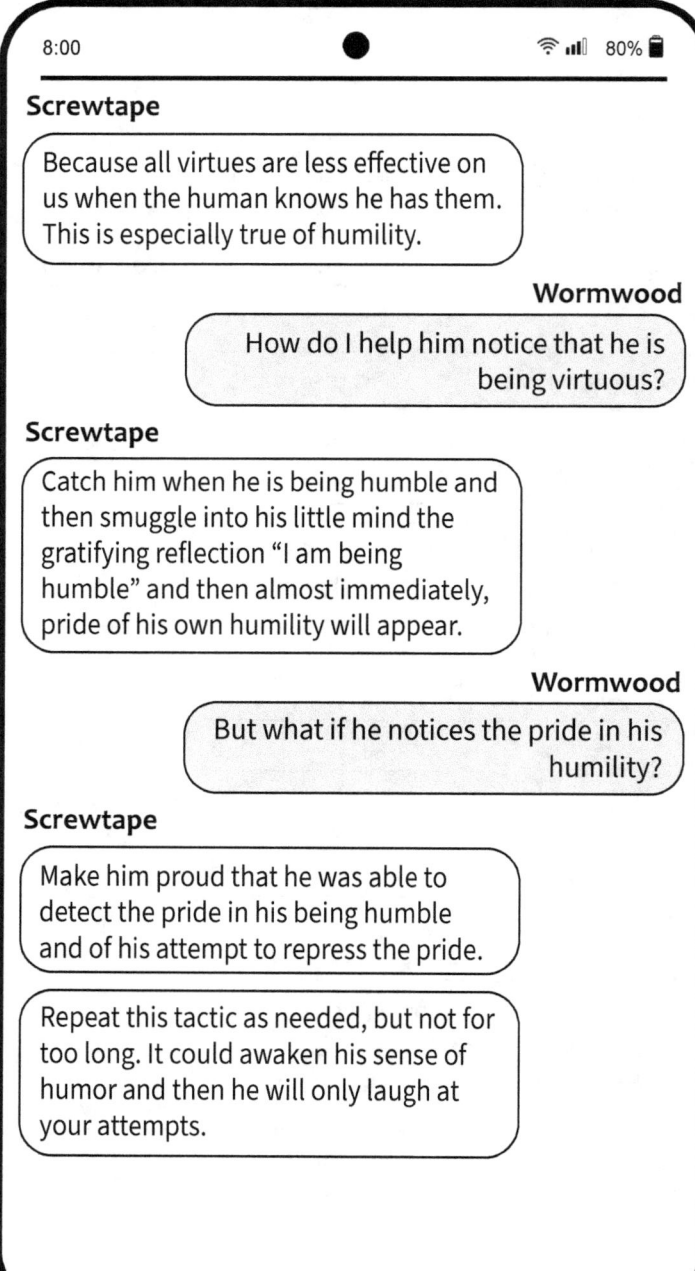

**Screwtape**

Because all virtues are less effective on us when the human knows he has them. This is especially true of humility.

**Wormwood**

How do I help him notice that he is being virtuous?

**Screwtape**

Catch him when he is being humble and then smuggle into his little mind the gratifying reflection "I am being humble" and then almost immediately, pride of his own humility will appear.

**Wormwood**

But what if he notices the pride in his humility?

**Screwtape**

Make him proud that he was able to detect the pride in his being humble and of his attempt to repress the pride.

Repeat this tactic as needed, but not for too long. It could awaken his sense of humor and then he will only laugh at your attempts.

## Text Message 14.3

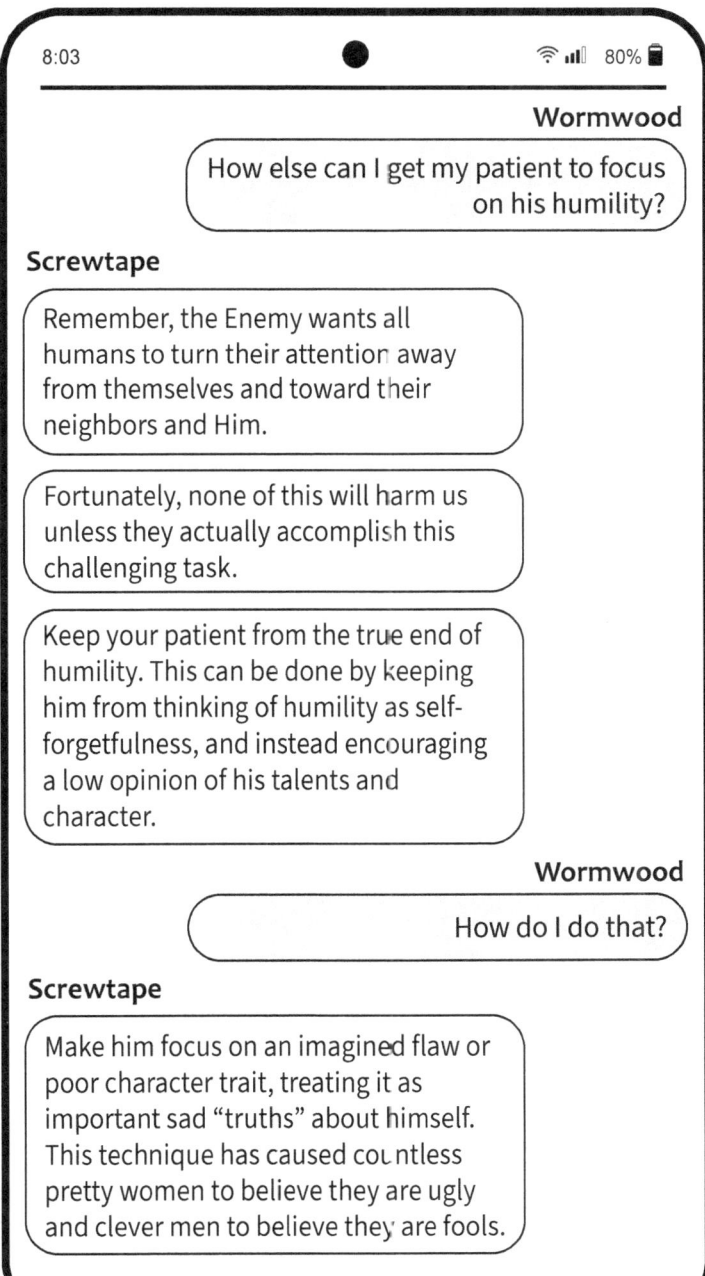

8:03     🔘     🛜 📶 80% 🔋

**Wormwood**

How else can I get my patient to focus on his humility?

**Screwtape**

Remember, the Enemy wants all humans to turn their attention away from themselves and toward their neighbors and Him.

Fortunately, none of this will harm us unless they actually accomplish this challenging task.

Keep your patient from the true end of humility. This can be done by keeping him from thinking of humility as self-forgetfulness, and instead encouraging a low opinion of his talents and character.

**Wormwood**

How do I do that?

**Screwtape**

Make him focus on an imagined flaw or poor character trait, treating it as important sad "truths" about himself. This technique has caused countless pretty women to believe they are ugly and clever men to believe they are fools.

## Text Message 14.4

**Screwtape**

This will also introduce an element of dishonesty into his heart, a trait what otherwise would lead to becoming a virtue.

**Wormwood**

How does the Enemy want them to feel and think about humility?

**Screwtape**

The Enemy wants them to be free from any bias towards themselves. He wants them to equally rejoice in their own talents as gratefully as in their neighbor's talents or in a sunrise or in beautiful music or art.

The Enemy wants to kill their animal self-love as quickly as possible and restore to them a new kind of self-love that has them love others equally as themselves.

His whole effort is to get the human's mind off the subject of their value altogether.

**Wormwood**

So, I should instill false humility or modesty into my patient?

## Text Message 14.5

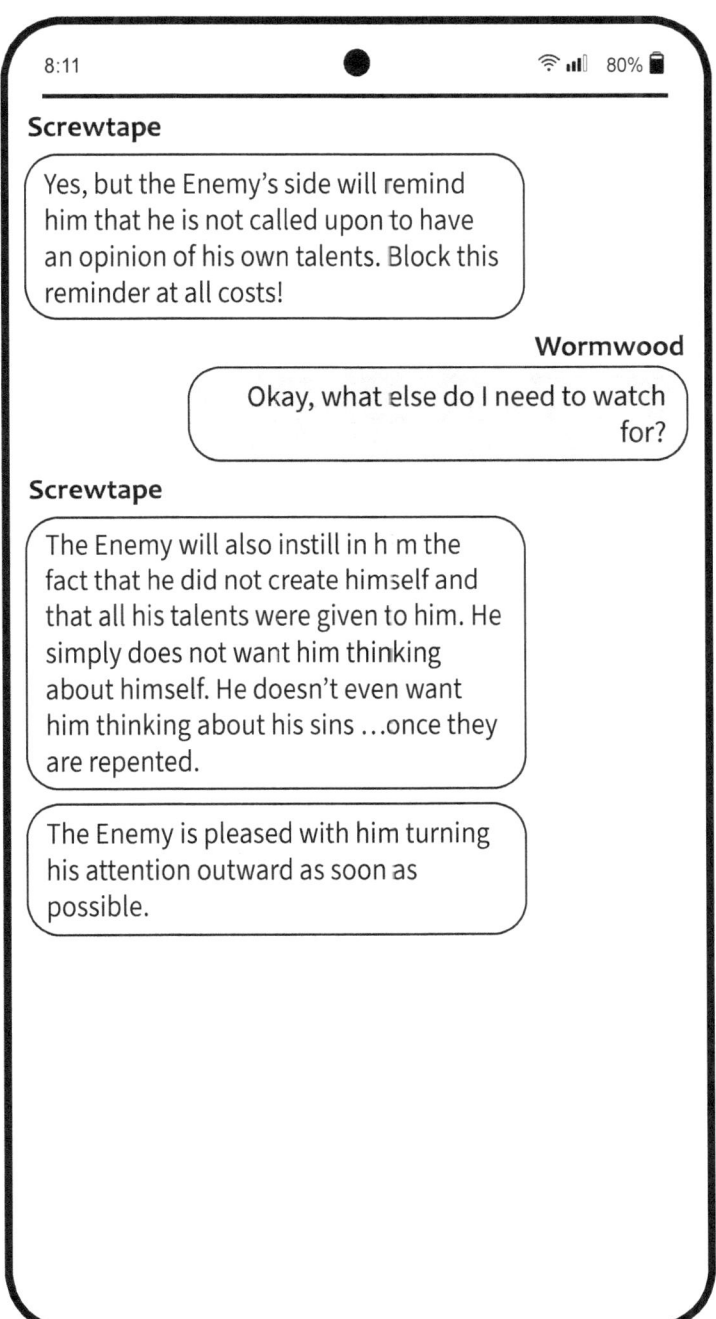

**Screwtape**

Yes, but the Enemy's side will remind him that he is not called upon to have an opinion of his own talents. Block this reminder at all costs!

**Wormwood**

Okay, what else do I need to watch for?

**Screwtape**

The Enemy will also instill in h m the fact that he did not create himself and that all his talents were given to him. He simply does not want him thinking about himself. He doesn't even want him thinking about his sins …once they are repented.

The Enemy is pleased with him turning his attention outward as soon as possible.

## Summary

This page from the enemy's playbook suggests that virtuous living absent of awareness and personal pride both weaken the devil's attack. Love of God and neighbor before self also provide great challenges to Satan.

## Resources

| | |
|---|---|
| Wisdom, the source of blessings | Wisdom 8:7 |
| The virtues | CCC paragraphs 1803 – 1845 |
| The desires of the spirit | CCC paragraph 2546 |
| Prayers as God's gift | CCC paragraph 2559 |

CCC paragraph 2559

"Prayer is the raising of one's mind and heart to God or the requesting of good things from God." But when we pray, do we speak from the height of our pride and will, or "out of the depths" of a humble and contrite heart? He who humbles himself will be exalted; humility is the foundation of prayer. Only when we humbly acknowledge that "we do not know how to pray as we ought," are we ready to receive freely the gift of prayer. "Man is a beggar before God."

CCC paragraph 2546

"Blessed are the poor in spirit." The Beatitudes reveal an order of happiness and grace, of beauty and peace. Jesus celebrates the joy of the poor, to whom the Kingdom already belongs:

> The Word speaks of voluntary humility as "poverty in spirit"; the Apostle gives an example of God's poverty when he says: "For your sakes he became poor."
>
> ~ St. Gregory of Nyssa

**Humility**: The virtue by which a Christian acknowledges that God is the author of all good. Humility avoids inordinate ambition or pride, and provides the foundation for turning to God in prayer (2559). Voluntary humility can be described as "poverty of spirit" (2546).

## Counterattack Actions

- Pray the Litany of Humility found in Text Message 2.
- Identify which items in the Litany are the most difficult to pray for and ask God in prayer for more strength in this area.

## Questions

1. What is your definition of humility? What is false humility? Screwtape warns Wormwood to avoid the true end of humility. What is the true end of humility?

2. Why and how do virtues help us in spiritual warfare?

3. Have you ever been proud of your humble actions or of another virtue? How can you avoid being proud of your virtues?

4. How can we turn our attention away from ourselves and toward God and neighbor? Why is it so hard?

5. What is behind Screwtape's comment that "… countless pretty women believe they are ugly and clever men believe they are fools?"

6. What do you do to combat temptations and suggestions like the ones Screwtape suggests in this text message? Have you ever laughed at the devil's temptations or suggestions, like Screwtape speaks of in this letter? Did it help?

## Text Message 15.1

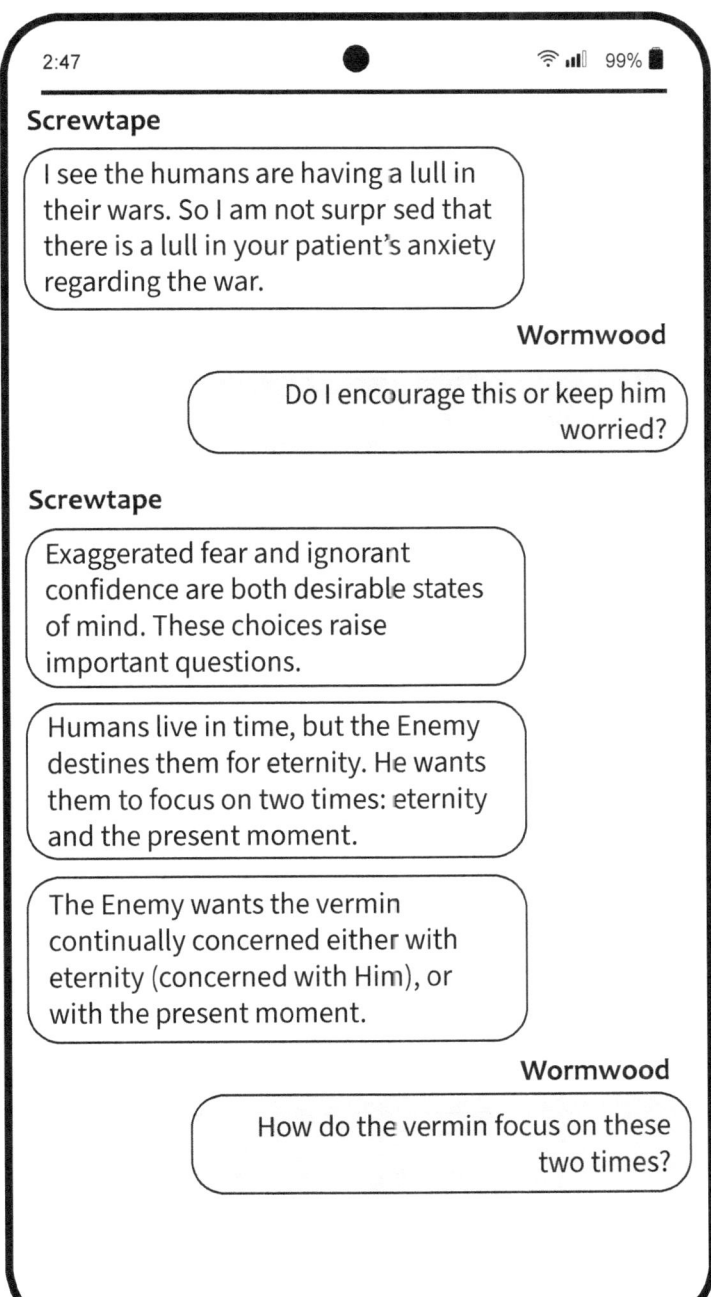

**Screwtape**

I see the humans are having a lull in their wars. So I am not surpr sed that there is a lull in your patient's anxiety regarding the war.

**Wormwood**

Do I encourage this or keep him worried?

**Screwtape**

Exaggerated fear and ignorant confidence are both desirable states of mind. These choices raise important questions.

Humans live in time, but the Enemy destines them for eternity. He wants them to focus on two times: eternity and the present moment.

The Enemy wants the vermin continually concerned either with eternity (concerned with Him), or with the present moment.

**Wormwood**

How do the vermin focus on these two times?

## Text Message 15.2

**Screwtape**

By either meditating on their eternal union (or separation) from Him, or by obeying the present voice of conscience.

And by bearing the present cross, receiving the present grace, or giving thanks for the present pleasure. Our strategy is to get their thoughts away from eternity and the present.

**Wormwood**

How do I do that?

**Screwtape**

Tempt them to live in the past. Although this has limited value, because they already know what happened in the past.

It is far better to get them to live in the future. Focusing on the future fuels hope and fear. The future is unknown, and it is also the least like eternity.

**Wormwood**

What do you mean?

## Text Message 15.3

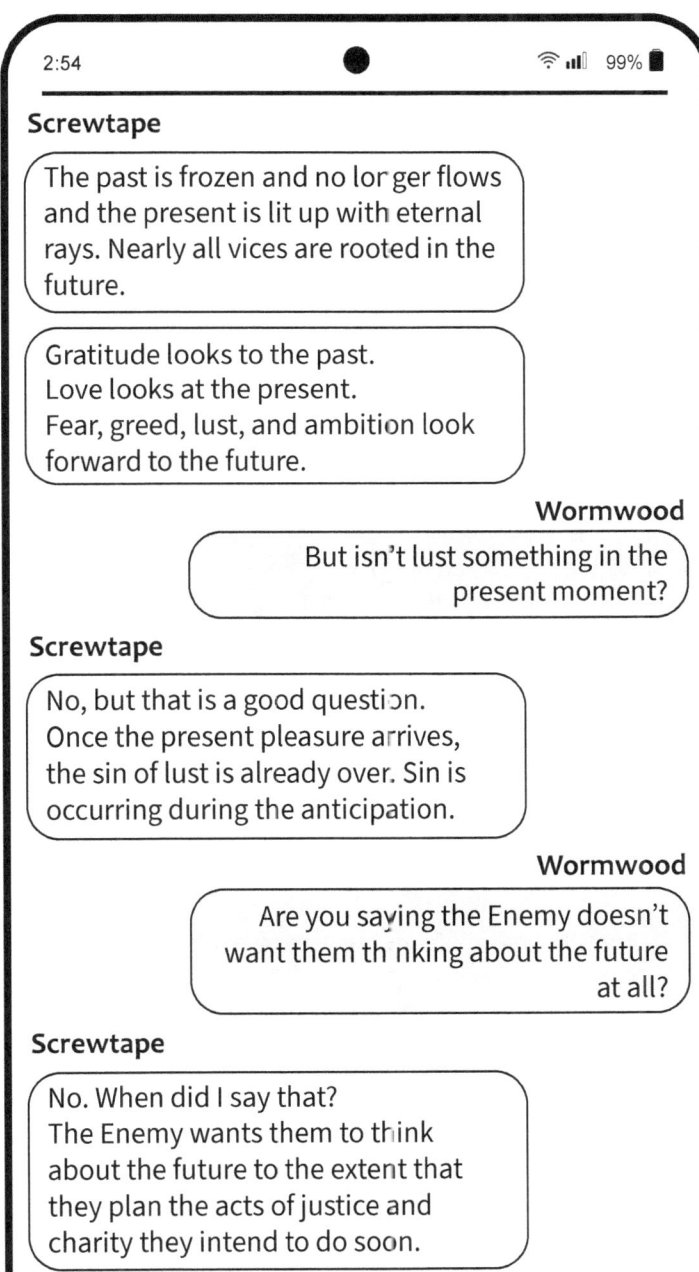

**Screwtape**

The past is frozen and no longer flows and the present is lit up with eternal rays. Nearly all vices are rooted in the future.

Gratitude looks to the past.
Love looks at the present.
Fear, greed, lust, and ambition look forward to the future.

**Wormwood**

But isn't lust something in the present moment?

**Screwtape**

No, but that is a good question. Once the present pleasure arrives, the sin of lust is already over. Sin is occurring during the anticipation.

**Wormwood**

Are you saying the Enemy doesn't want them thinking about the future at all?

**Screwtape**

No. When did I say that?
The Enemy wants them to think about the future to the extent that they plan the acts of justice and charity they intend to do soon.

## Text Message 15.4

**Screwtape**

> We want humans to be anxious about the future and haunted by visions of imminent heaven or hell.

> Having the whole race perpetually in pursuit of the unattainable rainbow's end, never honest, nor happy in the present moment is what we want.

> But in the present, and there alone, all obligation, all grace, all knowledge, and all pleasure dwells. If your patient is living in the present, his state is very undesirable, and he should be attacked at once!

**Wormwood**

> Attacked how?

**Screwtape**

> Try some complacency on him. Hopefully he is living in the present only because he is in good health and enjoying his work. Regardless of why he is living in the present, if I were you, I would break up any present happiness or pleasure.

> Why should the creature be happy anyways?

## Summary

This page from the enemy's playbook suggests that focusing on the present moment and on eternity weakens the devil's attack.

## Resources

| | |
|---|---|
| Dependence on God | Luke 12:22–34 |
| Ways of coming to know God | CCC paragraph 33 |

## Counterattack Actions

- Pray the Hail Mary prayer found in Text Message 5. This prayer focuses on eternity and the present moment. Satan and the demons hate this prayer.
- Identify something from your past that keeps you from living more fully in the present and eternity.

## Questions

1.  How often do you think about eternity or living in the present moment? If you need to, how could you improve your answer?

2.  Have you been affected by living in the past? If, so, has it kept you from moving forward in your life?

3.  What examples can you think of where sin and vices are rooted in the future?

4.  How do you avoid being "perpetually in pursuit of the rainbow's end"? What advice would you have for someone who wants to stop chasing after things that do not satisfy?

5.  Do you think complacency is an effective strategy proposed by Screwtape? How do you combat complacency?

6.  What do you do to combat temptations and suggestions like the ones Screwtape suggests in this text message?

## Text Message 16.1

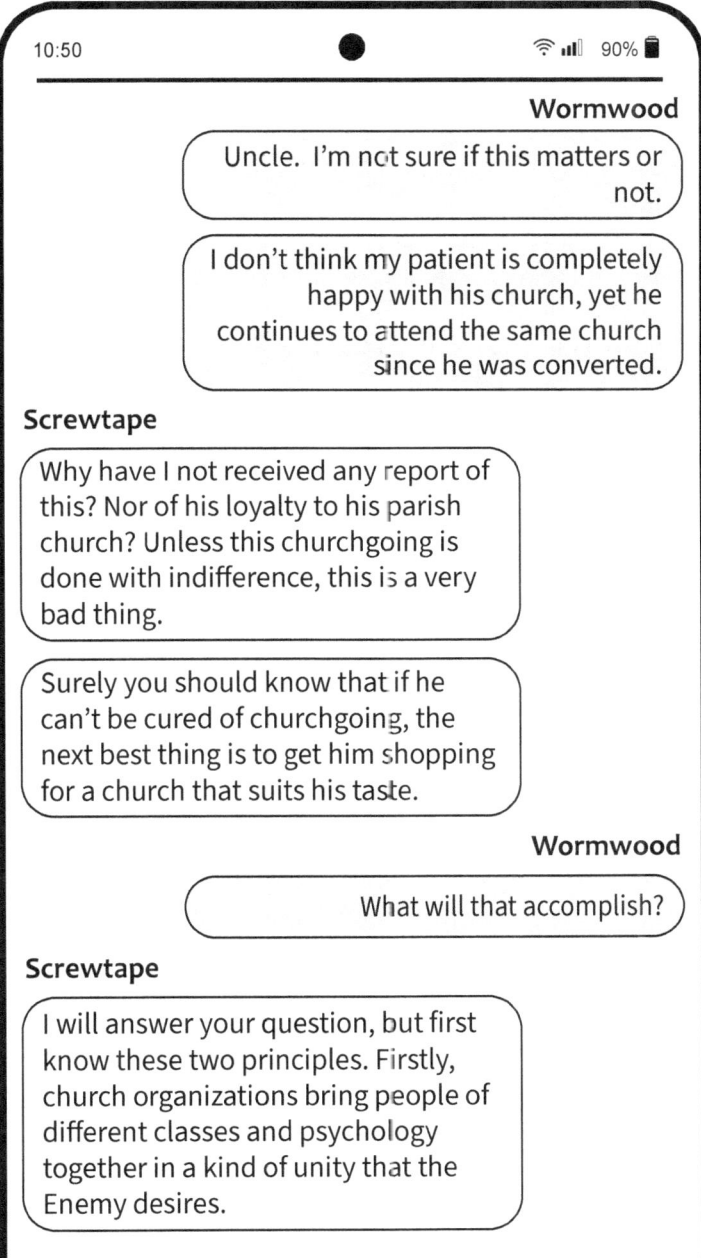

**Wormwood**

Uncle. I'm not sure if this matters or not.

I don't think my patient is completely happy with his church, yet he continues to attend the same church since he was converted.

**Screwtape**

Why have I not received any report of this? Nor of his loyalty to his parish church? Unless this churchgoing is done with indifference, this is a very bad thing.

Surely you should know that if he can't be cured of churchgoing, the next best thing is to get him shopping for a church that suits his taste.

**Wormwood**

What will that accomplish?

**Screwtape**

I will answer your question, but first know these two principles. Firstly, church organizations bring people of different classes and psychology together in a kind of unity that the Enemy desires.

## Text Message 16.2

10:54      ⬤      🛜 📶 90% 🔋

**Screwtape**

Because of this, the church should always be attacked.

Secondly, congregations make each church into a kind of "club" and if all goes well for us … each congregation into an isolated clique.

Now to your question. The search for a "suitable" church makes humans into critics when the Enemy instead wants them to be pupils.

The Enemy wants the human vermin to be critical, in the sense of rejecting what is false, and to not waste time in what it rejects. He also wants them to be open and to be fed with humility.

**Wormwood**

So what do I do?

**Screwtape**

Send your fool patient around to the neighboring parishes as soon as possible! I have already looked up two churches nearest him.

**Wormwood**

Tell me more.

## Text Message 16.3

**Screwtape**

The first has a pastor who waters down the faith to make it easier for his "hardheaded" congregation to understand, now shocks his congregation with his unbelief. Heh heh, he has undermined many a soul's Christianity.

And there is more with this one. To spare his members all difficulties, he has abandoned the lectionary and his preaching consequently revolves endlessly around twenty of his favorite lessons.

Because of this, we are safe from the danger of any truth ever reaching them through the minuscule amount of Scripture he actually preaches.

**Wormwood**

My patient may not be naïve enough for a church like this one …at least not yet.

**Screwtape**

Fair enough. At the other church we have Father Spike. Here the humans are often confused trying to understand his wide range of opinions. His opinions swing from extreme to extreme.

## Text Message 16.4

**Wormwood**

Is there any connection between all of Father Spike's opinions?

**Screwtape**

Hehehe… Hatred. The man cannot bring himself to preach anything which is not intended to shock, grieve, puzzle, or humiliate.

We are also teaching him to say "The teaching of the Church is…" when he really means "I'm almost sure I read recently…"

**Wormwood**

OK. Now back to what you said earlier… You said I should get my patient committed to some isolated clique within the Church?

**Screwtape**

Yes! There are many ways to accomplish this. For example, there is real fun in working them up into those who say "Mass" against those who say "Holy Communion."

All the indifferent things like candles, vestments, devotions, etc. are also fertile ground for their disagreements.

## Text Message 16.5

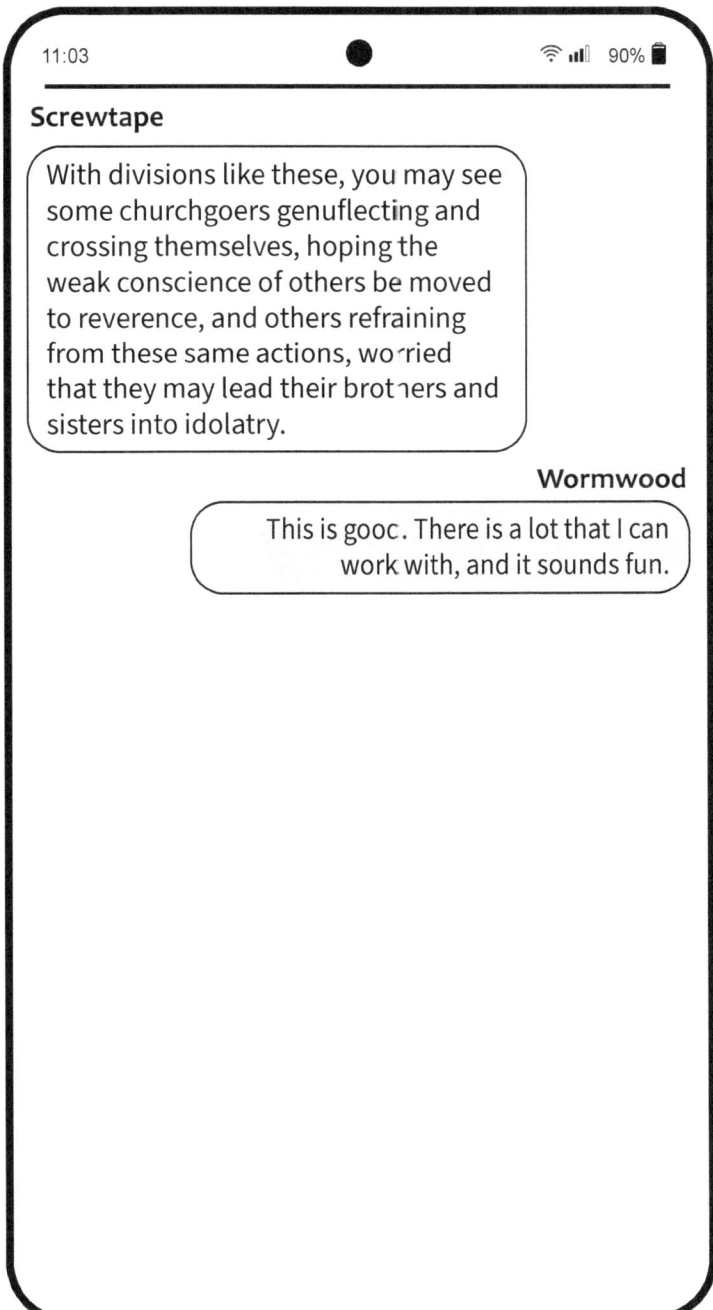

**Screwtape**

With divisions like these, you may see some churchgoers genuflecting and crossing themselves, hoping the weak conscience of others be moved to reverence, and others refraining from these same actions, worried that they may lead their brothers and sisters into idolatry.

**Wormwood**

This is good. There is a lot that I can work with, and it sounds fun.

## Summary

This page from the enemy's playbook suggests that church fidelity and member unity both weaken the devil's attack. This letter also suggests that knowledge of Scripture (more than just small amounts) also weakens the devil's attack.

## Resources

| | |
|---|---|
| That they may all be one | John 17:21 |
| Following their own desires | 2 Timothy 4:3-4 |
| Toward unity | CCC paragraph 820 |

For the time will come when people will not tolerate sound doctrine but, following their own desires and insatiable curiosity, will accumulate teachers and will stop listening to the truth and will be diverted to myths.

~ 2 Timothy 4:3–4

## Counterattack Actions

- Pray for unity among all Christians.
- Read the Scriptures, especially the four Gospels and the Acts of the Apostles.

## Questions

1.  Have you ever changed your parish or denomination affilia-
    tion? If so, what were the reasons?

2.  Do you experience unity that crosses social classes and back-
    grounds in your local church? In what ways? Do cliques exist
    in your local church?

3.  Why do you think people search for "suitable" churches?
    What is your definition of a "suitable" church?

4.  Do you agree with Screwtape that keeping most of Scripture
    from church members can be a form of spiritual warfare?
    How?

5.  What examples can you think of through which Satan divides
    people within their church? Liberal vs. conservative, modern
    vs. traditional, etc.

6.  What do you do to combat temptations and suggestions like
    the ones Screwtape suggests in this text message?

## Text Message 17.1

4:32    100%

**Wormwood**

Uncle, I think you'll be proud of me. I've been using gluttony, one of the seven "deadly" sins, to catch souls.

**Screwtape**

Yet again you are showing your ignorance. One of our great achievements over the past 150 years has been to deaden the human conscience of this sin.

**Wormwood**

How did we pull that off?

**Screwtape**

Have you noticed that humans no longer hear sermons on gluttony like they used to?

We have shifted their focus from excess to deprivation. Notice their wonderfully annoying and over demanding attitudes.

Let's take a look at your patient's mother's dossier. You will see there that her food quantities are small. The quantity matters not if we can use the human belly and palette to produce impatience, unkindness, and self-concern.

## Text Message 17.2

4:35                          ●              🛜 ▪▎ 100% 🔋

**Screwtape**

Your patient's mother is an absolute
terror to wait staff.

**Wormwood**

Delicious, tell me more!

**Screwtape**

The woman is always responding to
what is offered her with a little sigh and
a smile saying "Oh please, please … all I
want is a cup of tea, weak but not too
weak and the teeniest bit of really crisp
toast."

She doesn't recognize her determination
to get what she wants as gluttony,
regardless of how irritating it may be to
others.

And get this: she believes she is
practicing temperance.

**Wormwood**

I am starting to get it. Can you give
me another example?

**Screwtape**

Of course I can.

## Text Message 17.3

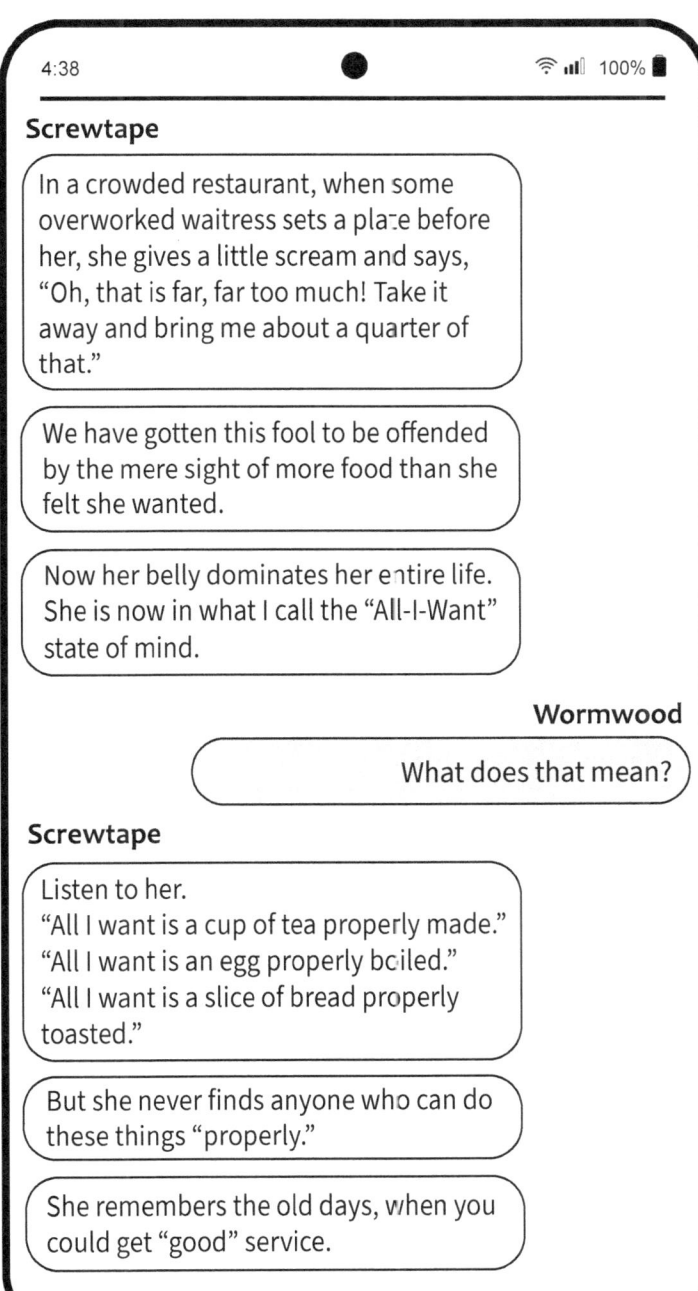

**Screwtape**

In a crowded restaurant, when some overworked waitress sets a plate before her, she gives a little scream and says, "Oh, that is far, far too much! Take it away and bring me about a quarter of that."

We have gotten this fool to be offended by the mere sight of more food than she felt she wanted.

Now her belly dominates her entire life. She is now in what I call the "All-I-Want" state of mind.

**Wormwood**

What does that mean?

**Screwtape**

Listen to her.
"All I want is a cup of tea properly made."
"All I want is an egg properly boiled."
"All I want is a slice of bread properly toasted."

But she never finds anyone who can do these things "properly."

She remembers the old days, when you could get "good" service.

## Text Message 17.4

**Wormwood**

How does this exactly help our cause?

**Screwtape**

Her daily disappointments produce increased temper and angry help. It also cools friendships.

**Wormwood**

OK. But what about my patient? Male humans tend to operate differently than this. I don't see this 'All I Want' strategy to be effective.

**Screwtape**

Fair enough. Have you not noticed the vanities many of the males have regarding food and drink?

**Wormwood**

No.

**Screwtape**

They think they are experts regarding these things.

With males, their attitude can be encouraged regarding things like: grilling, beer, cars, and outdoor hobbies.

## Text Message 17.5

**Wormwood**

Oh yeah.
Like: my butcher sells the best meat for grilling, or this brand of beer is too hoppy, or gas grilling can't compare to charcoal grilling.

**Screwtape**

Exactly. What begins as vanity gradually becomes a habit.

## Summary

This page from the enemy's playbook suggests that temperance and an attitude of gratitude both weaken the devil's attack.

## Resources

| | |
|---|---|
| Teaching about anger | Matthew 5:21–26 |
| Transformation of life | Titus 2:12 |
| Wisdom, the source of bless-ings | Wisdom 8:7 |
| Self-control | Sirach 18:30 |
| The capital sins | CCC paragraph 1866 |
| The human virtues | CCC paragraph 1805 |
| Temperance | CCC paragraphs 1809, 2290 |
| Safeguarding peace | CCC paragraph 2302 |
| The proliferation of sin | CCC paragraph 1865 |
| Toward unity | CCC paragraph 820 |

## The Seven Deadly Sins and a Virtue to Counter Them

| Sin (Vices) | Virtues |
|---|---|
| **#1 – Pride**<br>The sin of undue self-esteem or self-love, or the desire for excess control and power. | Pray for **Humility**, to acknowledge that God is the author of all good and that we are not. |
| **#2 – Envy**<br>The sin of resentment and desire of another's good fortune. | Pray for **Kindness** and **Gratitude**, for happiness of another's good fortune, and to be grateful for our own. |
| **#3 – Lust**<br>The sin of considering others as mere objects. | Pray for **Chastity**, for valuing the dignity of others and maintaining pure thoughts. |
| **#4 – Wrath**<br>The sin of outbursts of negative emotion, and desire for revenge. | Pray for **Meekness**, for having patience and charity when resolving issues. |
| **#5 – Gluttony**<br>The sin of consuming to unhealthy excess. | Pray for **Temperance**, for taking all things in moderation. |
| **#6 – Greed**<br>The sin of unnecessary desires for earthly possessions. | Pray for **Generosity**, for the ability to freely give of self or possessions. |
| **#7 – Sloth**<br>The sin of laziness, avoiding spiritual or physical work. | Pray for **Diligence**, for the ability to follow God's will despite discomfort. |

## Counterattack Actions

- Thank God right now for what you are grateful for. Make this practice part of your daily prayer.
- The next time you are at a restaurant, thank the server and tell them you appreciate their service.

## Questions

1. Do you think it is true that sermons no longer include preaching on gluttony or the other deadly sins? Why do you suppose that would be?

2. What are the effects you see that come from the "All-I-Want" attitude in society and in relationships?

3. What attitudes can counter the tactics of vanity that demons may be using in spiritual warfare?

4. Could there be greater vanity found in societies where there is greater material wealth? If so, why?

5. How can we cultivate an attitude of being more grateful for what we have?

6. What do you do to combat temptations and suggestions like the ones Screwtape suggests in this text message?

## Text Message 18.1

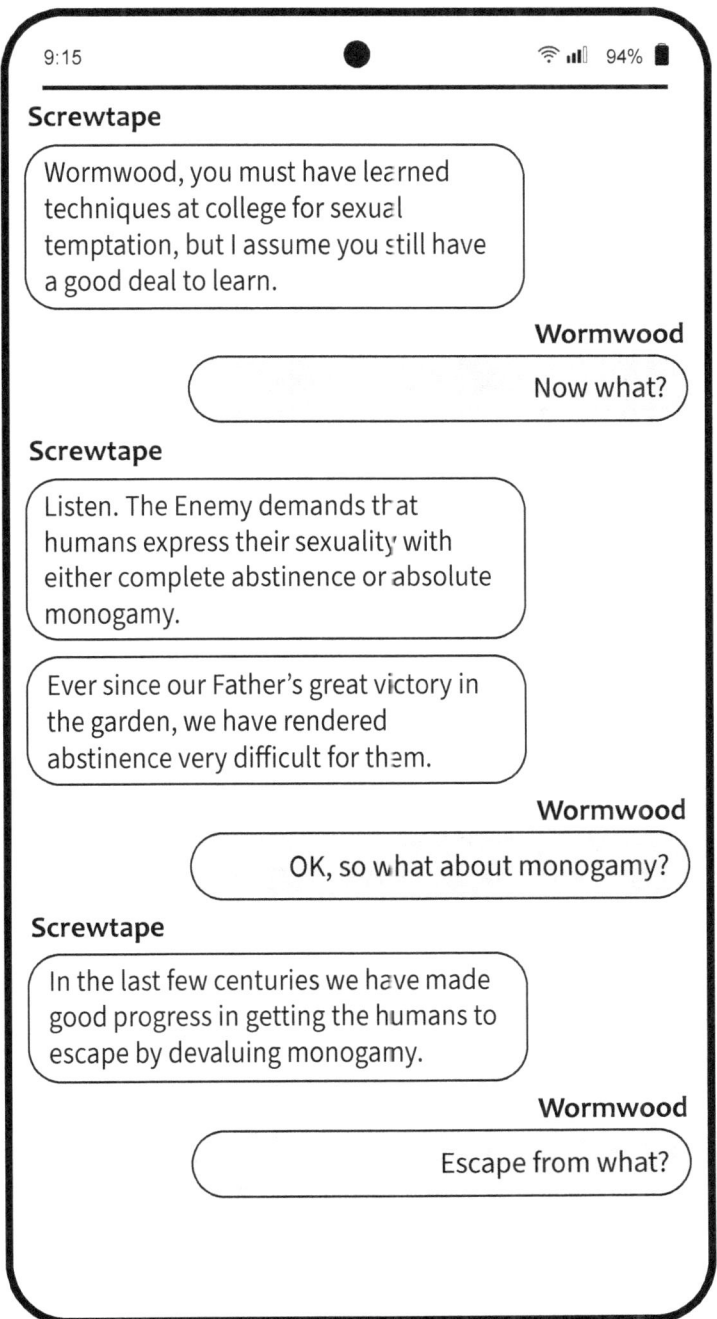

**Screwtape**

Wormwood, you must have learned techniques at college for sexual temptation, but I assume you still have a good deal to learn.

**Wormwood**

Now what?

**Screwtape**

Listen. The Enemy demands that humans express their sexuality with either complete abstinence or absolute monogamy.

Ever since our Father's great victory in the garden, we have rendered abstinence very difficult for them.

**Wormwood**

OK, so what about monogamy?

**Screwtape**

In the last few centuries we have made good progress in getting the humans to escape by devaluing monogamy.

**Wormwood**

Escape from what?

## Text Message 18.2

**Screwtape**

Escape from the commitment of marriage. We have persuaded them to think that the feeling of "being in love" is the only valid grounds for marriage.

And that marriage ought to always provide this "being in love" feeling.

Hehe, and under this expectation, when the feeling of "being in love" is not present, the marriage is no longer binding.

**Wormwood**

What is the point of keeping the commitment of marriage if there is no personal gain from it?

**Screwtape**

Exactly. You and I know that existence is a zero-sum game. If I win, you must lose, and if you win, I must lose.

The human vermin and we spirits are both consumers. Humans consume food and drink, as well as time and pleasures from other humans.

**Wormwood**

What do we consume?

## Text Message 18.3

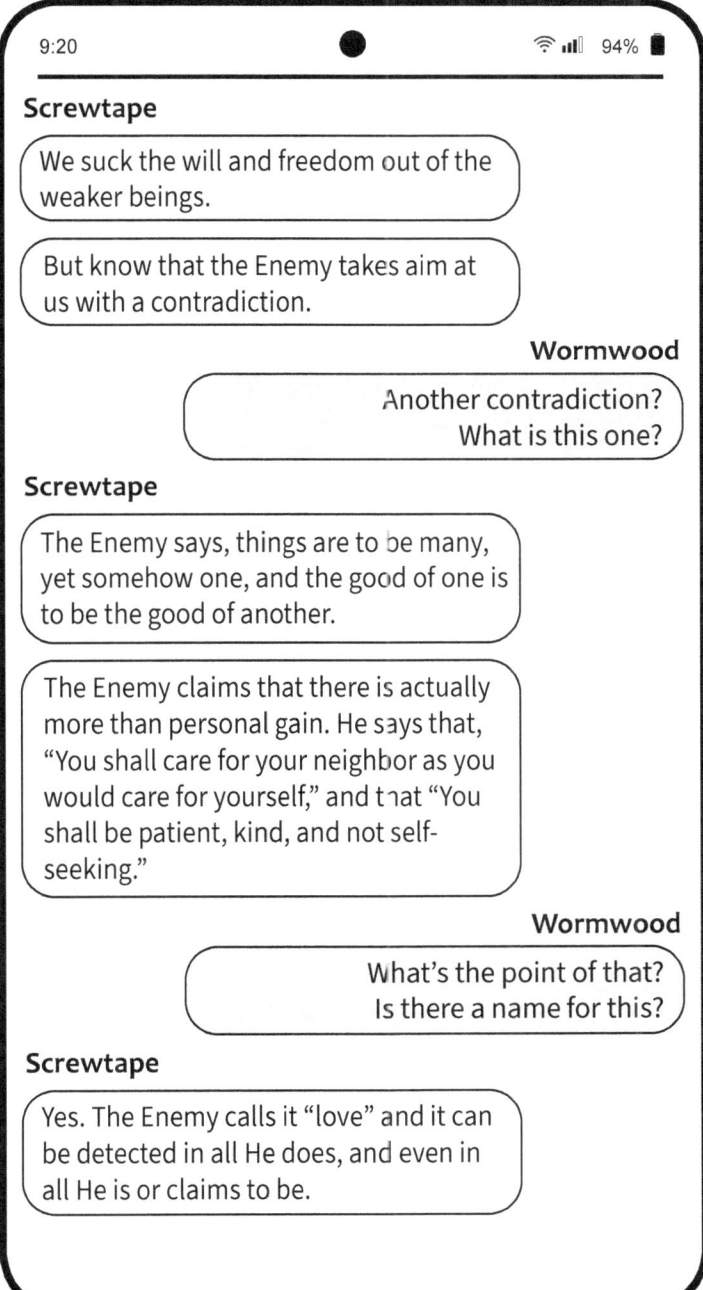

**Screwtape**

We suck the will and freedom out of the weaker beings.

But know that the Enemy takes aim at us with a contradiction.

**Wormwood**

Another contradiction? What is this one?

**Screwtape**

The Enemy says, things are to be many, yet somehow one, and the good of one is to be the good of another.

The Enemy claims that there is actually more than personal gain. He says that, "You shall care for your neighbor as you would care for yourself," and that "You shall be patient, kind, and not self-seeking."

**Wormwood**

What's the point of that? Is there a name for this?

**Screwtape**

Yes. The Enemy calls it "love" and it can be detected in all He does, and even in all He is or claims to be.

## Text Message 18.4

**Wormwood**

What is love?

**Screwtape**

Angels of our kind don't really know. We rejected it from the beginning. The Enemy seems to have wired His two-legged animals to be predisposed to this self-defeating behavior.

To draw humans in, the Enemy has associated their sexual desire with the impulse to love. He even gives the humans an impulse to love their offspring, producing the family, in which they unite in a more conscious and responsible way, putting the interests of the family before their own.

**Wormwood**

God is love?
Family is love?

What is the point of letting others get ahead at your expense?
I don't understand love.

**Screwtape**

I don't either.

## Text Message 18.5

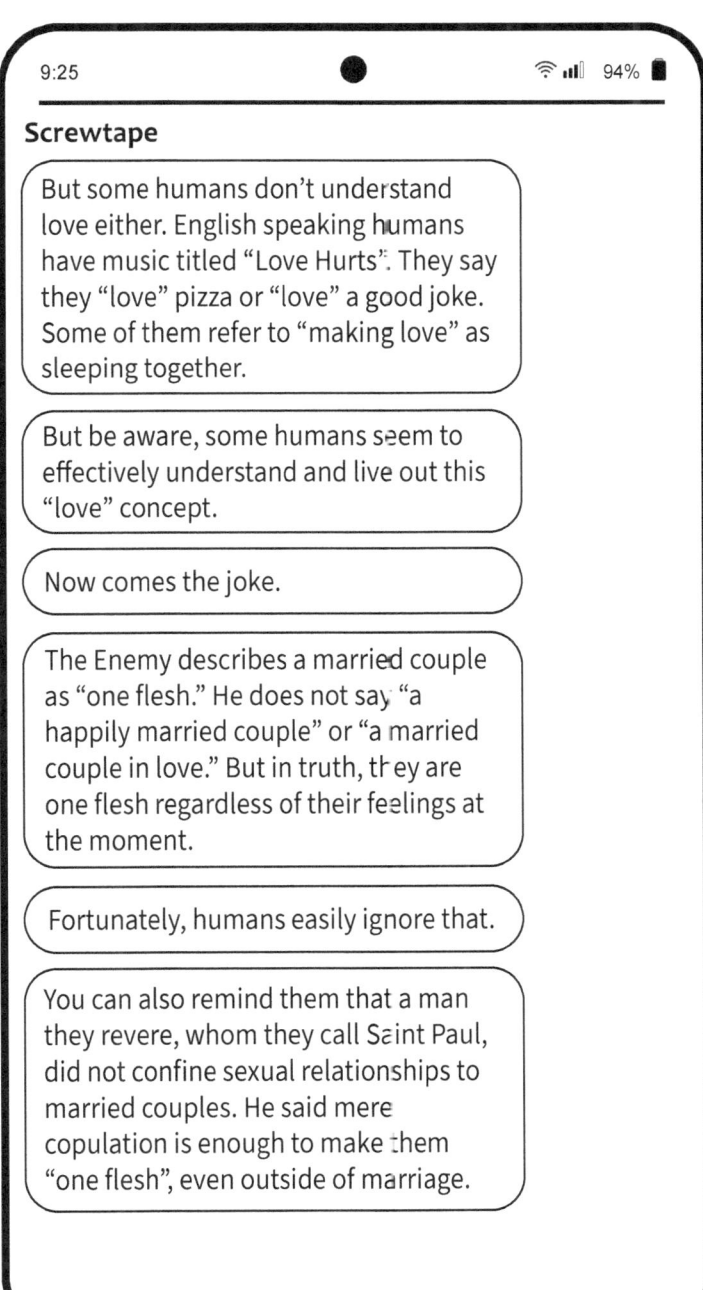

**Screwtape**

But some humans don't understand love either. English speaking humans have music titled "Love Hurts". They say they "love" pizza or "love" a good joke. Some of them refer to "making love" as sleeping together.

But be aware, some humans seem to effectively understand and live out this "love" concept.

Now comes the joke.

The Enemy describes a married couple as "one flesh." He does not say "a happily married couple" or "a married couple in love." But in truth, they are one flesh regardless of their feelings at the moment.

Fortunately, humans easily ignore that.

You can also remind them that a man they revere, whom they call Saint Paul, did not confine sexual relationships to married couples. He said mere copulation is enough to make them "one flesh", even outside of marriage.

## Text Message 18.6

**Screwtape**

The truth, whether they like it or not, is that when a man lies with a woman, a transcendental relationship is set up between them, which must be eternally enjoyed or eternally endured.

**Wormwood**

This sounds like a great opportunity. How can we leverage this?

**Screwtape**

Prior to marriage they show obedience to the Enemy's designs having an intention of fidelity, fertility, and good will for the other.

Make them think that any sexual infatuation is "love" as long as it "intends" to lead toward marriage. Concentrate on lust. Make them think that their lust for the other is love.

Just keep them from real love.

Whatever that is.

## Summary

This page from the enemy's playbook suggests that putting the needs of others before your own weakens the devil's attack.

Note: Information captured in Text Message 18.5 references Chapter 6 in St. Paul's first letter to the Corinthians.

## Resources

| | |
|---|---|
| The vine and the branches | John 15:1–17 |
| A writing from St. Paul on love | 1 Corinthians 13 |
| Marriage and divorce | Matthew 19:1–12 |
| The two become one body | Genesis 2:24 |
| Wives and husbands | Ephesians 5:21–33 |
| True love | Song of Songs 8:6–7 |
| Charity | CCC paragraphs 1822 – 1832 |
| **The Sacrament of Matrimony** | |
| Marriage in God's plan | CCC paragraphs 1602 – 1620 |
| The celebration of marriage | CCC paragraphs 1621 – 1624 |
| Matrimonial consent | CCC paragraphs 1625 – 1637 |
| Effects of the sacrament | CCC paragraphs 1638 – 1642 |
| Goods and requirements of conjugal love | CCC paragraphs 1643 – 1654 |
| The domestic church | CCC paragraphs 1655 – 1658 |

If we turn away from evil out of fear of punishment, we are in the position of slaves. If we pursue the enticement of wages, . . . we resemble mercenaries. Finally, if we obey for the sake of the good itself and out of love for him who commands . . . we are in the position of children.

~ St. Basil

The Consent

I (N.) take you (N.) to be my wife/husband. I promise to be faithful to you in good times and in bad, in sickness and in health, to love you and to honor you all the days of my life.

~ from the Order of Celebrating Matrimony

**Counterattack Actions**

- Identify where love can be strengthened in your life and make those changes.
- If you are married, reflect on the words of consent above, taken from the Order of Celebrating Matrimony. Identify how you can live these vows out in a greater way.

## Questions

1. Screwtape says that feelings when "in love" do not last. Is it reasonable to think that they *can* last? What advice do you have for someone who says they don't feel in love anymore?

2. How can marriages be nurtured and protected?

3. What are the benefits of a committed marriage?

4. What is lust? In your words, what is love?

5. Screwtape took scripture out of context in this text message. Where else has Satan attempted to deceive by taking scripture out of context?

6. What do you do to combat temptations and suggestions like the ones Screwtape suggests in this text message?

## Text Message 19.1

11:20

99%

**Wormwood**

I have been thinking a lot about our last conversation.

If all beings by their very nature are in competition, and if the Enemy's idea of love is clearly a contradiction, what should come of your repeated warning that the Enemy really loves the human vermin and really desires their freedom and continued existence?

**Screwtape**

I hope you haven't shared these conversations with anyone! Not that it matters.

The truth is, I carelessly slipped when saying that the Enemy really loves humans. Of course, that is impossible. He is one being, and they are distinct from Him. Their good cannot be His.

Anyone would see that the appearance of heresy into which I have fallen is purely accidental.

**Wormwood**

Could all this talk about love be a disguise or a trick?

## Text Message 19.2

11:26 ● 99%

**Wormwood**

Maybe He has some real motive for creating them and taking so much trouble about them?

**Screwtape**

Comprehending this impossible "love" has been our ultimate failure in finding a real motive.

**Wormwood**

What does the Enemy expect to accomplish or gain from all this?

**Screwtape**

That question is a mystery. This very problem was the major cause of Our Father's argument with the Enemy.

**Wormwood**

Tell me about this quarrel.

**Screwtape**

When the creation of humans was first proposed, even then the Enemy freely stated that He foresaw a certain episode about a cross.

Our Father naturally asked for an explanation, but the Enemy gave no reply, except for some ridiculous story about detached love.

## Text Message 19.3

11:30

**Screwtape**

Naturally, this Our Father could not accept. He admitted that he felt a real anxiety to understand this story and the Enemy replied, "I wish with all my heart that you did."

I imagine it was at this point that Our Father's disgust caused him to remove himself an infinite distance from the Presence of the Enemy with a suddenness that gave rise to the Enemy's ridiculous story that Our Father was forcibly thrown out of Heaven.

Members of the Enemy's faction have admitted that if we were ever to come to understand this mysterious love, the war would be over.

And there lies the great task. We know that He cannot really love. No one can. It doesn't make sense.

**Wormwood**

If only we could find out what He is really up to!

**Screwtape**

Yes. But hypothesis after hypothesis has been tried, and still we haven't figured it out.

## Text Message 19.4

11:34 ● 🛜 ⏺ 99% 🔋

**Wormwood**

In our last conversation you weren't clear. Is being in love a desirable state for humans or not?

**Screwtape**

That is the sort of question I'd expect humans to ask. Leave them to discuss whether "love" or patriotism or celibacy etc. are "good" or "bad."

Can't you see? There is no answer to this "being in love."

Nothing matters except for their state of mind and circumstances. Patients move either nearer to the Enemy or nearer to us.

Instill into your patient casual unchastity. It is an unmatched recipe for prolonged, romantic, tragic adultery, all-ending, if things go well, in murders and other such events.

Until next time, understand that this state of falling in love is not necessarily favorable to us or the other side.

It is simply an event which we and the Enemy are both trying to exploit.

## Summary

This page from the enemy's playbook suggests that awareness of both your state of mind and circumstances weakens the devil's attack. Awareness and response to God's love is something Satan does not understand, and gives us a great advantage.

## Resources

| The conditions of discipleship | Matthew 16:24 |
|---|---|
| Follow … the way of the cross | CCC paragraph 1816 |
| Human solidarity | CCC paragraph 1939 |
| Christian holiness | CCC paragraph 2015 |
| Economic activity and social justice | CCC paragraph 2427 |
| The domestic church | CCC paragraphs 1655 – 1658 |

CCC paragraph 2015

The way of perfection passes by way of the Cross. There is no holiness without renunciation and spiritual battle. Spiritual progress entails the ascesis and mortification that gradually lead to living in the peace and joy of the Beatitudes:

> He who climbs never stops going from beginning to beginning, through beginnings that have no end. He never stops desiring what he already knows.
> ~ St. Gregory of Nyssa

The Daily Examen

A technique of prayerful reflection on the events of the day in order to detect God's presence and discern his direction for us.

The Examen is an ancient practice in the Church that can help us see God's hand at work in our whole experience.

"Anyone who loves God in the depths of his heart has already been loved by God. In fact, the measure of a person's love for God depends upon how deeply aware they are of God's love for them.

When this awareness is keen it makes whoever possesses it long to be enlightened by the divine light, and this longing is so intense that it seems to penetrate their very bones. They lose all consciousness of themselves and are entirely transformed by the love of God."

~ St. Diadochus of Photiké: Early 5th century saint

## Counterattack Actions

* Take some time to contemplate Jesus' love for you (perhaps before a crucifix) and then write a letter to Him.
* To increase your self-awareness, practice doing the Daily Examen. There are many resources available on Ignatian spirituality in Christian bookstores and online.

## Questions

1. In what ways do you experience God's love for you?

2. How do you respond to God's love?

3. Do you think our salvation could have come without the cross?

4. How could/do some humans (and angels) choose not to accept God's love?

5. Screwtape says that state of mind and circumstances are all that matter in spiritual warfare. How can you manage your state of mind and circumstances?

6. What do you do to combat temptations and suggestions like the ones Screwtape suggests in this text message?

## Text Message 20.1

1:43       🔵       📶 92% 🔋

**Wormwood**

Uncle, the Enemy has weakened and ultimately stopped my attacks on my patient's chastity.

**Screwtape**

Well you ought to have known that He always does in the end. You should have stopped before it got to this point. Now your patient knows these attacks don't last forever.

At least ignorant humans actually believe there is no way of getting rid of us unless they yield to our suggestions and temptations.

I suppose you have tried persuading your patient that chastity is unhealthy.

Create a list for me of women in his neighborhood and workplace.

**Wormwood**

What good will that do me now?

**Screwtape**

If you can't use his sexuality to make him unchaste, then you must use it to promote a "desirable" marriage.

## Text Message 20.2

**Wormwood**

A desirable marriage?

**Screwtape**

Yes, if this is the best you can manage. Let's talk about the physical type of woman he should be encouraged to "fall in love" with.

You must create a misdirection of his sexual taste.

**Wormwood**

How is that done?

**Screwtape**

We use the small circle of popular artists, fashion designers, actresses, and advertisers who determine fashions.

Our goal is to guide those of each sex away from those who make marriages the most spiritual, healthy, happy and fertile.

**Wormwood**

Do these tactics ever change over time?

## Text Message 20.3

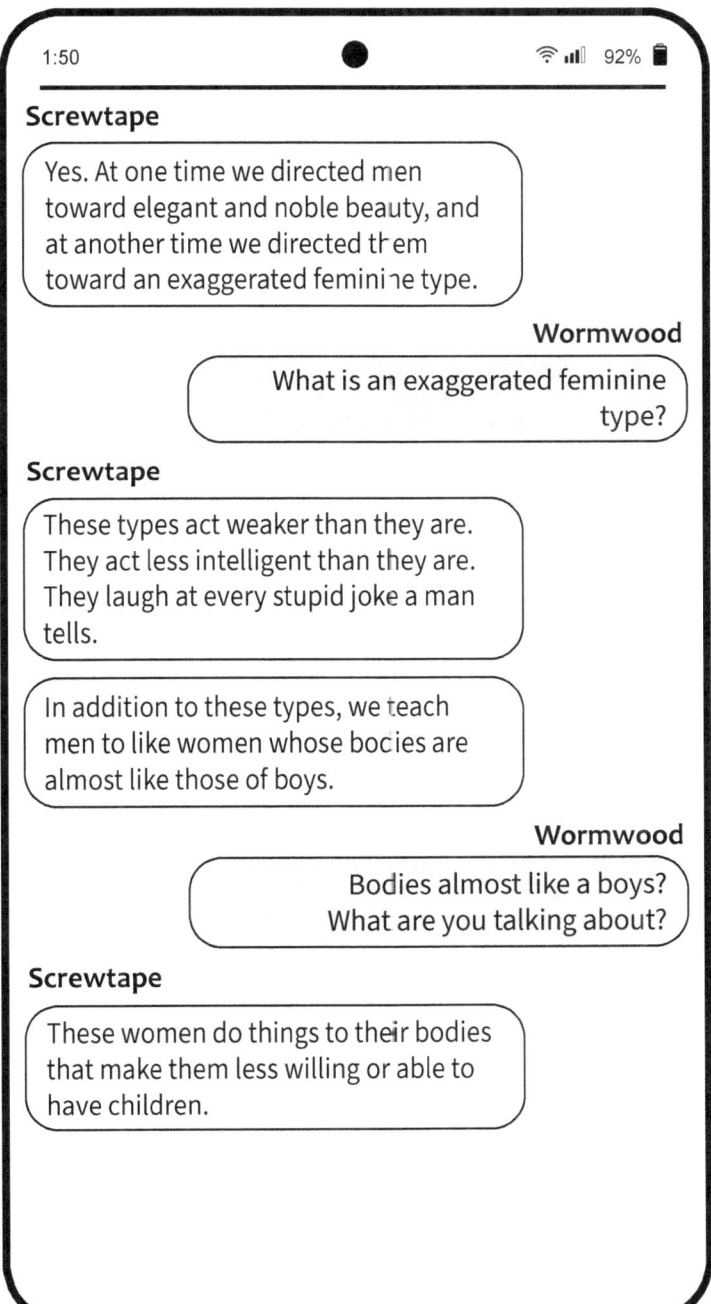

**Screwtape**

Yes. At one time we directed men toward elegant and noble beauty, and at another time we directed them toward an exaggerated feminine type.

**Wormwood**

What is an exaggerated feminine type?

**Screwtape**

These types act weaker than they are. They act less intelligent than they are. They laugh at every stupid joke a man tells.

In addition to these types, we teach men to like women whose bodies are almost like those of boys.

**Wormwood**

Bodies almost like a boys? What are you talking about?

**Screwtape**

These women do things to their bodies that make them less willing or able to have children.

## Text Message 20.4

**Screwtape**

The small circle of accomplices that I mentioned earlier assist us with this attack. They use image editing tools to enhance pictures of women, making them appear more petite and "perfect" in print and electronic media.

It's all fake. Women are made to look firmer and more slender than nature allows a full-grown woman to be.

As a result, we are directing the desires of men to something that doesn't exist, making the role of the eye more important and its demands more impossible.

If you look into any man's heart you will see he is haunted by two imaginary women: a terrestrial down-to-earth woman and an infernal Venus.

**Wormwood**

A terrestrial down-to-earth woman and an infernal Venus? Now what are talking about?

**Screwtape**

I'll explain.

## Text Message 20.5

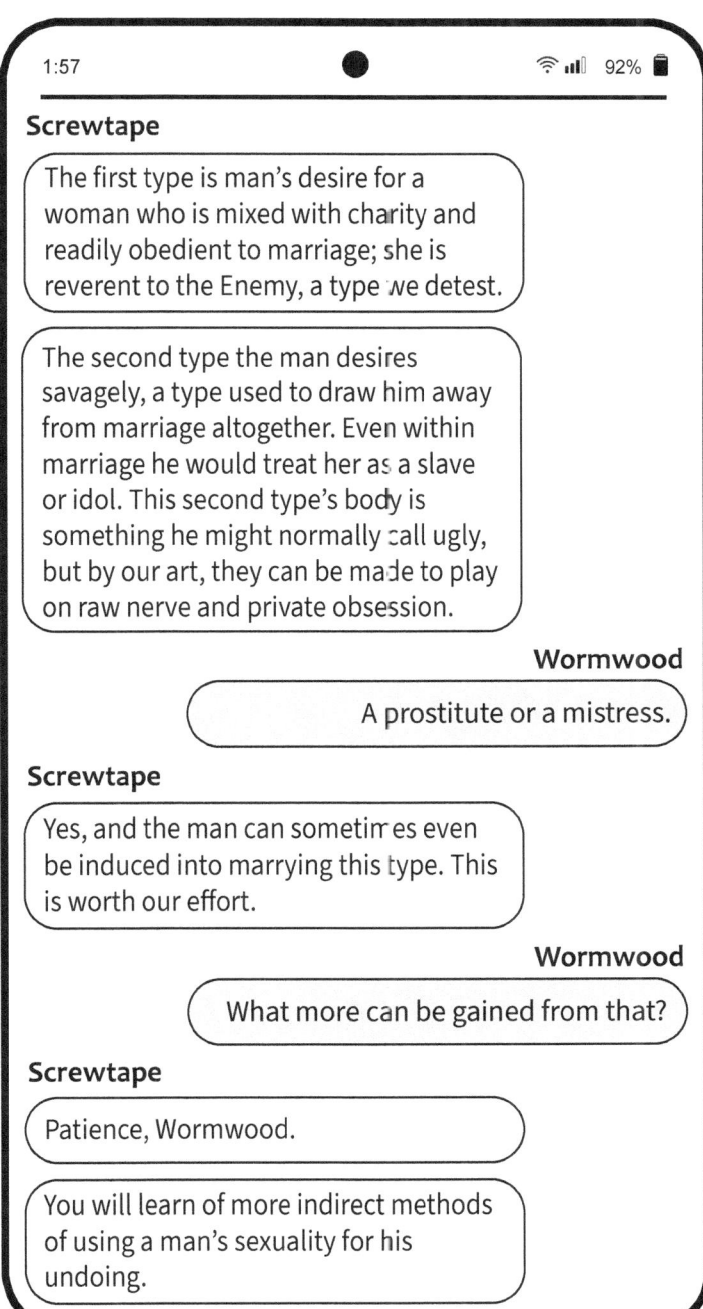

**Screwtape**

The first type is man's desire for a woman who is mixed with charity and readily obedient to marriage; she is reverent to the Enemy, a type we detest.

The second type the man desires savagely, a type used to draw him away from marriage altogether. Even within marriage he would treat her as a slave or idol. This second type's body is something he might normally call ugly, but by our art, they can be made to play on raw nerve and private obsession.

**Wormwood**

A prostitute or a mistress.

**Screwtape**

Yes, and the man can sometimes even be induced into marrying this type. This is worth our effort.

**Wormwood**

What more can be gained from that?

**Screwtape**

Patience, Wormwood.

You will learn of more indirect methods of using a man's sexuality for his undoing.

## Text Message 20.6

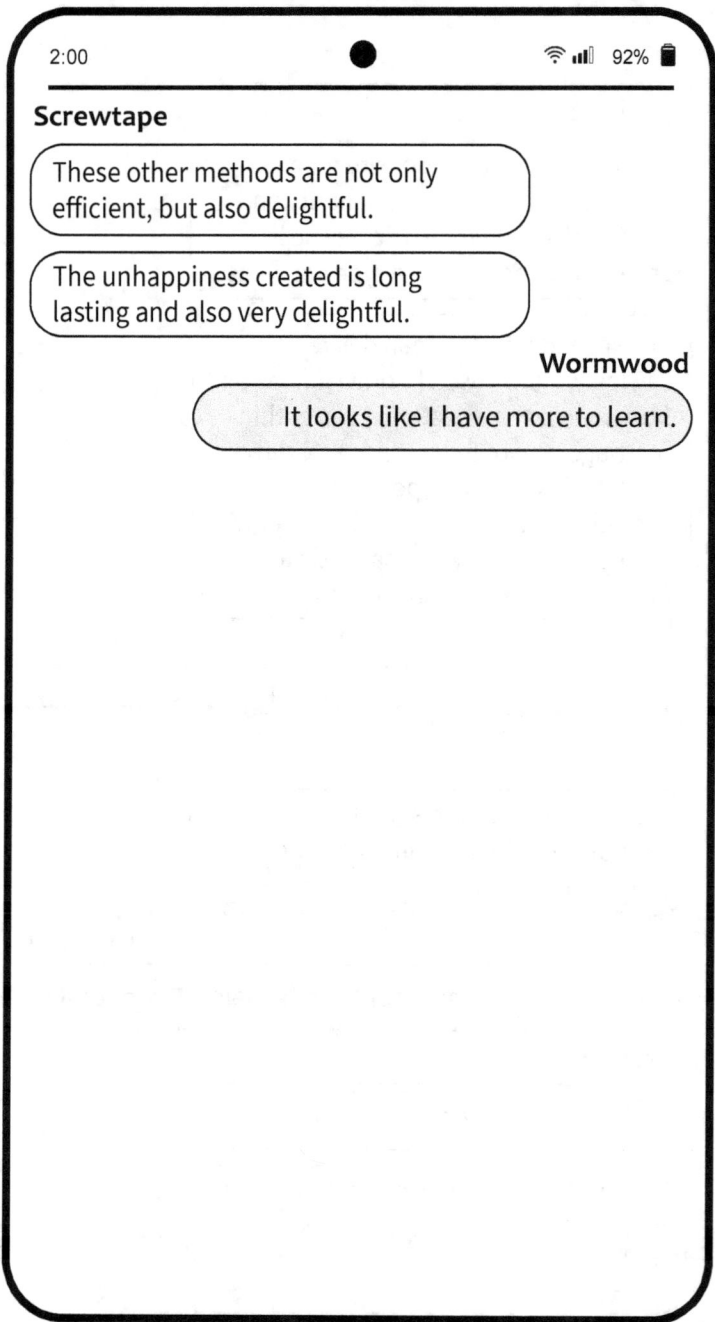

**Screwtape**

These other methods are not only efficient, but also delightful.

The unhappiness created is long lasting and also very delightful.

**Wormwood**

It looks like I have more to learn.

## Summary

This page from the enemy's playbook suggests that treating people with dignity and respect and not as objects weakens the devil's attack.

## Resources

| David's sin | 2 Samuel 11 |
|---|---|
| Teaching about adultery | Matthew 5:27-30 |
| Proliferation of sin | CCC paragraph 1866 |
| Marriage under the regime of sin | CCC paragraph 1607 |
| Respect for human life | CCC paragraph 2259 |
| Offenses against chastity | CCC paragraph 2351 |
| The desires of the spirit | CCC paragraph 2541 |

## Teaching About Adultery

"You have heard that it was said, 'You shall not commit adultery.' But I say to you, everyone who looks at a woman with lust has already committed adultery with her in his heart. If your right eye causes you to sin, tear it out and throw it away. It is better for you to lose one of your members than to have your whole body thrown into Gehenna. And if your right hand causes you to sin, cut it off and throw it away. It is better for you to lose one of your members than to have your whole body go into Gehenna."

~ Matthew Chapter 5:27–30

## Counterattack Actions

- When you see a person who is physically attractive, praise God for His creation.
- Include the temptations discussed here in your Daily Examen, explained in Text 19.

## Questions

1. Screwtape implied that there is a way to get rid of the devil's tactics without yielding to temptation or suggestion. What would that be?

2. Screwtape has his idea of a desirable marriage, one that benefits the devils. What is your idea of a desirable marriage?

3. What are your thoughts on the fake images portrayed of men and women in society?

4. How do you think men and women are affected by the images of the opposite sex in society? How are men, women, and children affected by these images?

5. What are your thoughts on Screwtape's suggestion that men are haunted by two imaginary types of women?

6. What do you do to combat temptations and suggestions like the ones Screwtape suggests in this text message?

## Text Message 21.1

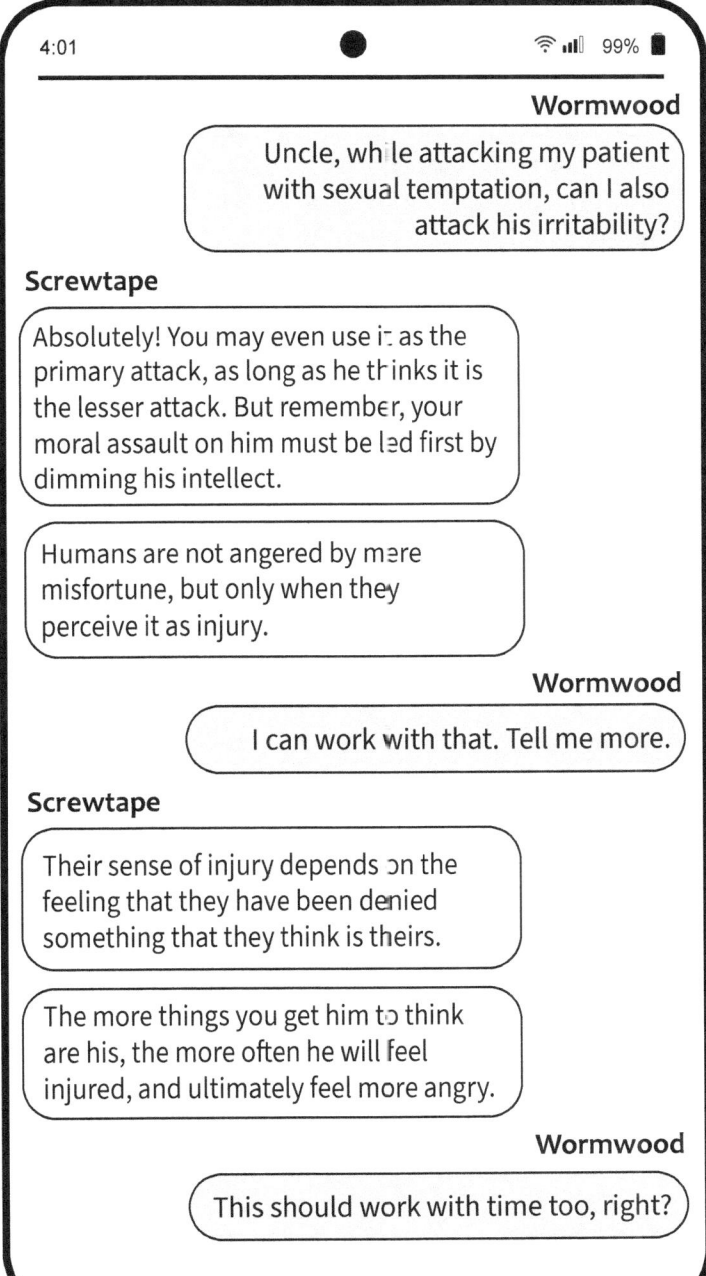

4:01

Wormwood

Uncle, while attacking my patient with sexual temptation, can I also attack his irritability?

Screwtape

Absolutely! You may even use it as the primary attack, as long as he thinks it is the lesser attack. But remember, your moral assault on him must be led first by dimming his intellect.

Humans are not angered by mere misfortune, but only when they perceive it as injury.

Wormwood

I can work with that. Tell me more.

Screwtape

Their sense of injury depends on the feeling that they have been denied something that they think is theirs.

The more things you get him to think are his, the more often he will feel injured, and ultimately feel more angry.

Wormwood

This should work with time too, right?

## Text Message 21.2

**Screwtape**

This is one of the best attacks! Not many things will throw many humans into a fit than to have time, that they thought they had for themselves, unexpectedly stolen from them.

For example, when a quiet evening is planned and an unexpected visitor pops by; or when two people anticipated a quality one-on-one conversation and a talkative friend shows up.

**Wormwood**

My patient doesn't seem that irritated with these types of intrusions of time.

**Screwtape**

Yes, but you can encourage anger in him by getting him to focus on his time being stolen.

Get him to believe that he begins each day as the lawful owner of 24 hours.

Then have him resent all the time he must give to his employer, or the amount of time he gives for his religious commitments, viewing all this time as a significant tax.

## Text Message 21.3

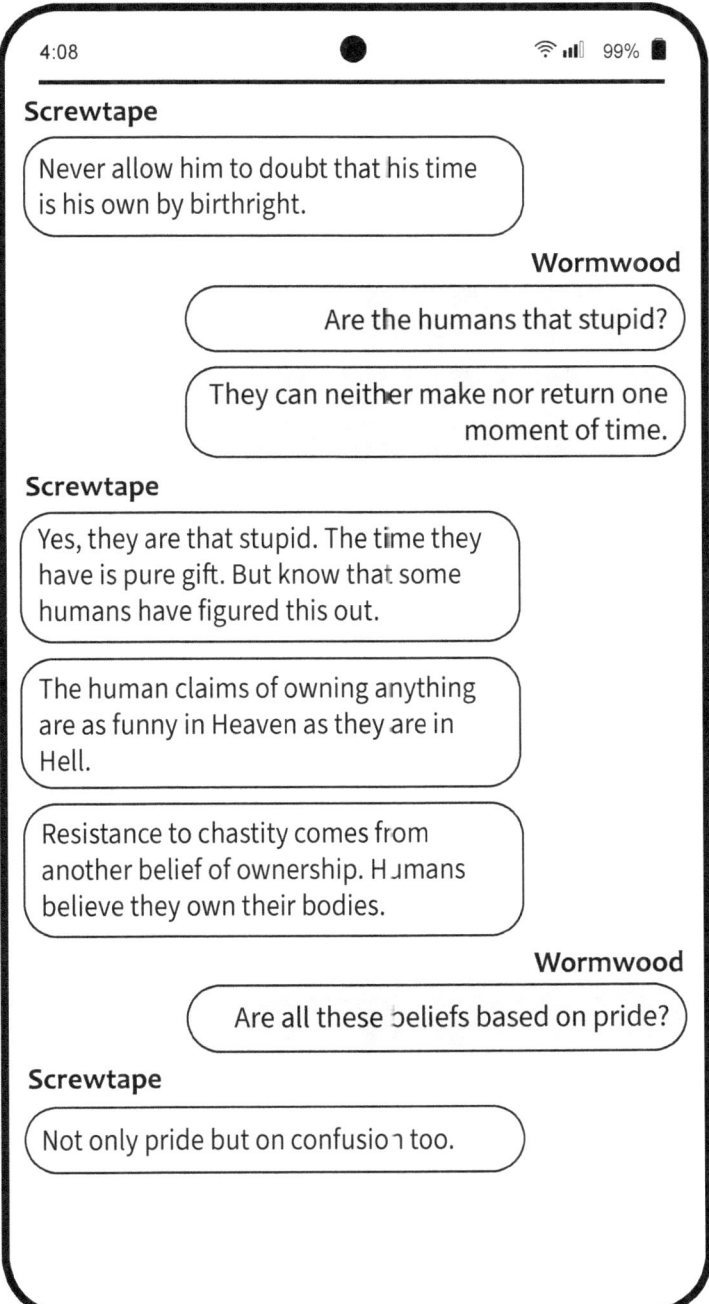

**Screwtape**

Never allow him to doubt that his time is his own by birthright.

**Wormwood**

Are the humans that stupid?

They can neither make nor return one moment of time.

**Screwtape**

Yes, they are that stupid. The time they have is pure gift. But know that some humans have figured this out.

The human claims of owning anything are as funny in Heaven as they are in Hell.

Resistance to chastity comes from another belief of ownership. Humans believe they own their bodies.

**Wormwood**

Are all these beliefs based on pride?

**Screwtape**

Not only pride but on confusion too.

## Text Message 21.4

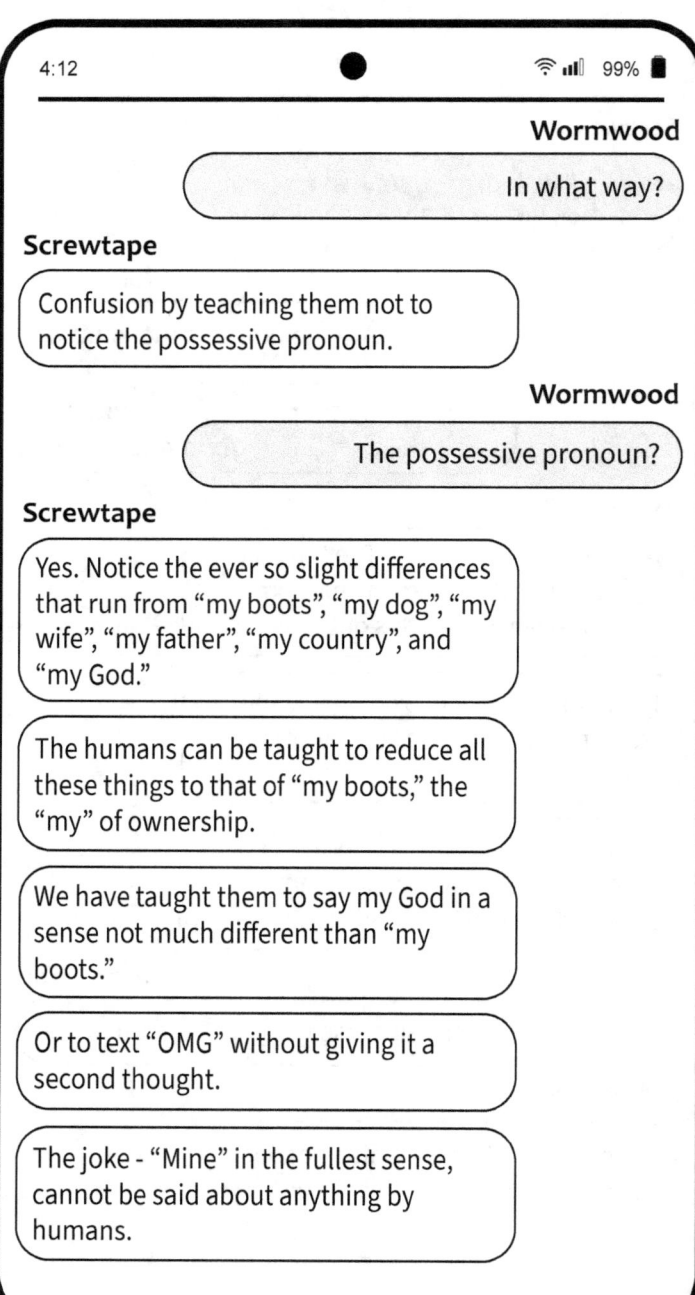

**Wormwood**

In what way?

**Screwtape**

Confusion by teaching them not to notice the possessive pronoun.

**Wormwood**

The possessive pronoun?

**Screwtape**

Yes. Notice the ever so slight differences that run from "my boots", "my dog", "my wife", "my father", "my country", and "my God."

The humans can be taught to reduce all these things to that of "my boots," the "my" of ownership.

We have taught them to say my God in a sense not much different than "my boots."

Or to text "OMG" without giving it a second thought.

The joke - "Mine" in the fullest sense, cannot be said about anything by humans.

## Text Message 21.5

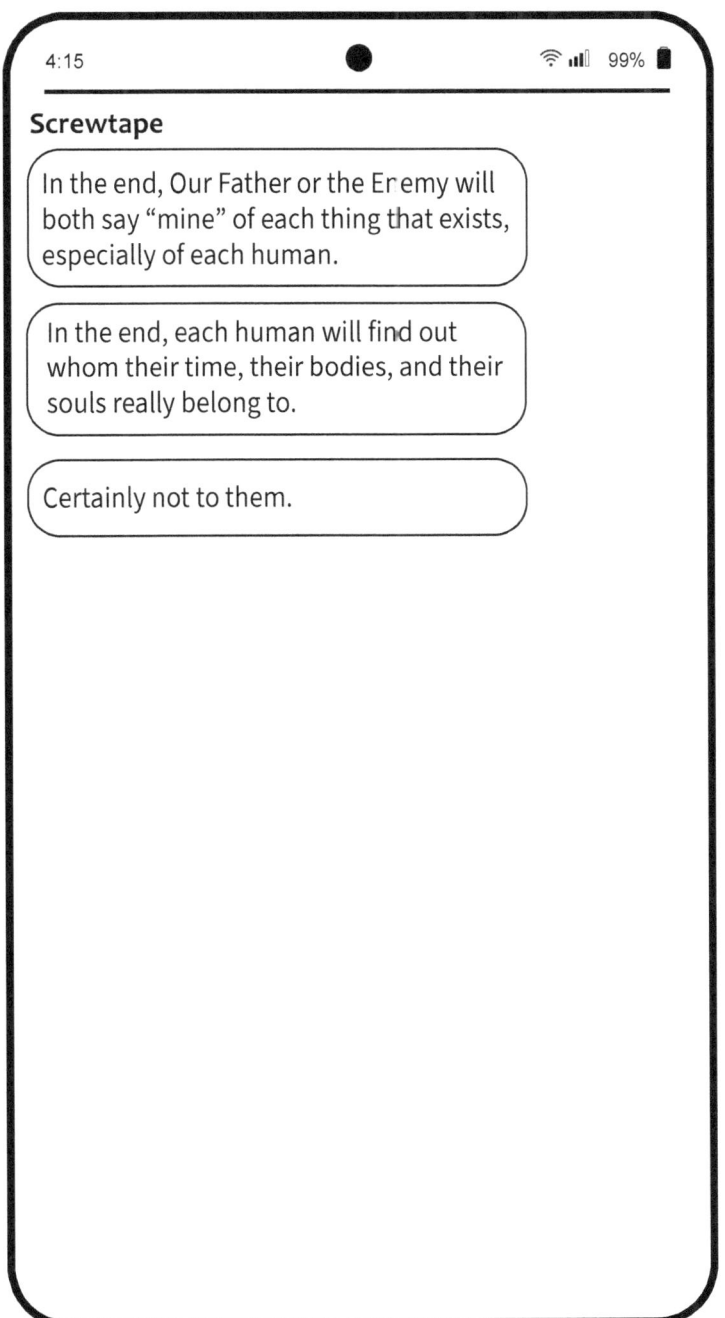

**Screwtape**

In the end, Our Father or the Enemy will both say "mine" of each thing that exists, especially of each human.

In the end, each human will find out whom their time, their bodies, and their souls really belong to.

Certainly not to them.

## Summary

This page from the enemy's playbook suggests that understanding that a person's body or the time they have are not their own weakens the devil's attack.

## Resources

| Spirit, soul and body | 1 Thessalonians 5:23 |
|---|---|
| No one can determine the right time to act | Ecclesiastes 3 |
| Man: in the image of God | CCC paragraphs 360, 362-368 |

Compared to eternity, time can seem inferior, degenerate. But this is an abstract speculation. If we look at man's purpose and destiny, which is to be introduced into the life of the Trinity, then it is clear that time is a gift.

Time gives us a chance to grow. Thanks to time, what God has placed within us can germinate and become a tree. Because of time, we have the possibility of participating in God's creation ourselves.

~ Fr. Wilfrid Stinissen, O.C.D. from Eternity in the Midst of Time

## Counterattack Actions

- Take time today to thank God in prayer.
- Identify where and how you can use your time more wisely. Then follow through with what you have identified.
- From your answer to Question 1 in this chapter, thank God for these possessions and acknowledge that they are all gifts.

## Questions

1.  List your top three possessions? Why did you select them?

2.  On a scale of 1 to 10, how do you value time? How do you prioritize the use of time?

3.  Do you give thanks to God for the time you have? If you see time as pure gift, do you use it differently? Why?

4.  C. S. Lewis wrote about humans believing that they "own" their own bodies decades before the Roe vs. Wade decision. What is the argument that we "own" our bodies? What is the argument against the belief that we "own" our bodies?

5.  Do you think of time any differently now? Does giving your time to others seem more like a gift now?

6.  What do you do to combat temptations and suggestions like the ones Screwtape suggests in this text message?

## Text Message 22.1

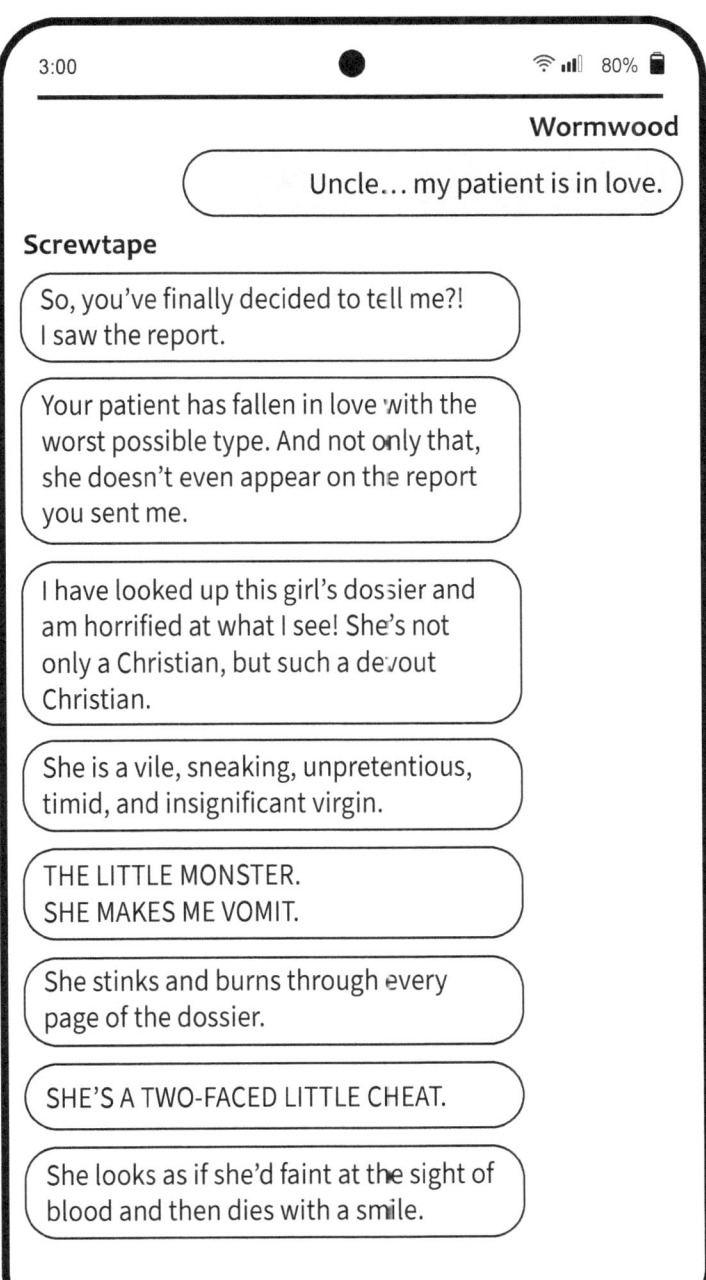

**Wormwood**

Uncle… my patient is in love.

**Screwtape**

So, you've finally decided to tell me?!
I saw the report.

Your patient has fallen in love with the
worst possible type. And not only that,
she doesn't even appear on the report
you sent me.

I have looked up this girl's dossier and
am horrified at what I see! She's not
only a Christian, but such a devout
Christian.

She is a vile, sneaking, unpretentious,
timid, and insignificant virgin.

THE LITTLE MONSTER.
SHE MAKES ME VOMIT.

She stinks and burns through every
page of the dossier.

SHE'S A TWO-FACED LITTLE CHEAT.

She looks as if she'd faint at the sight of
blood and then dies with a smile.

## Text Message 22.2

**3:03** 🔘 📶 80% 🔋

**Screwtape**

She's the sort of creature who'd find ME funny! FILTHY INSIPID LITTLE PRUDE.

And yet she's ready to fall into your simpleton patient's arms, like any other breeding animal.

**Wormwood**

Why doesn't the Enemy blast her for it? If he thinks virginity is so important and honorable?

**Screwtape**

The Enemy is a hedonist at heart. All those fasts and vigils and crosses are only a façade. He makes no secret of it; at His right hand are "pleasures for ever more." Ugh!

He is vulgar, Wormwood. He has filled His world full of pleasures.

There are things for humans to do all day long without His minding: sleeping, washing, eating, drinking, making love, playing, praying, working.

We must tweak anything before it is of any use to us.

## Text Message 22.3

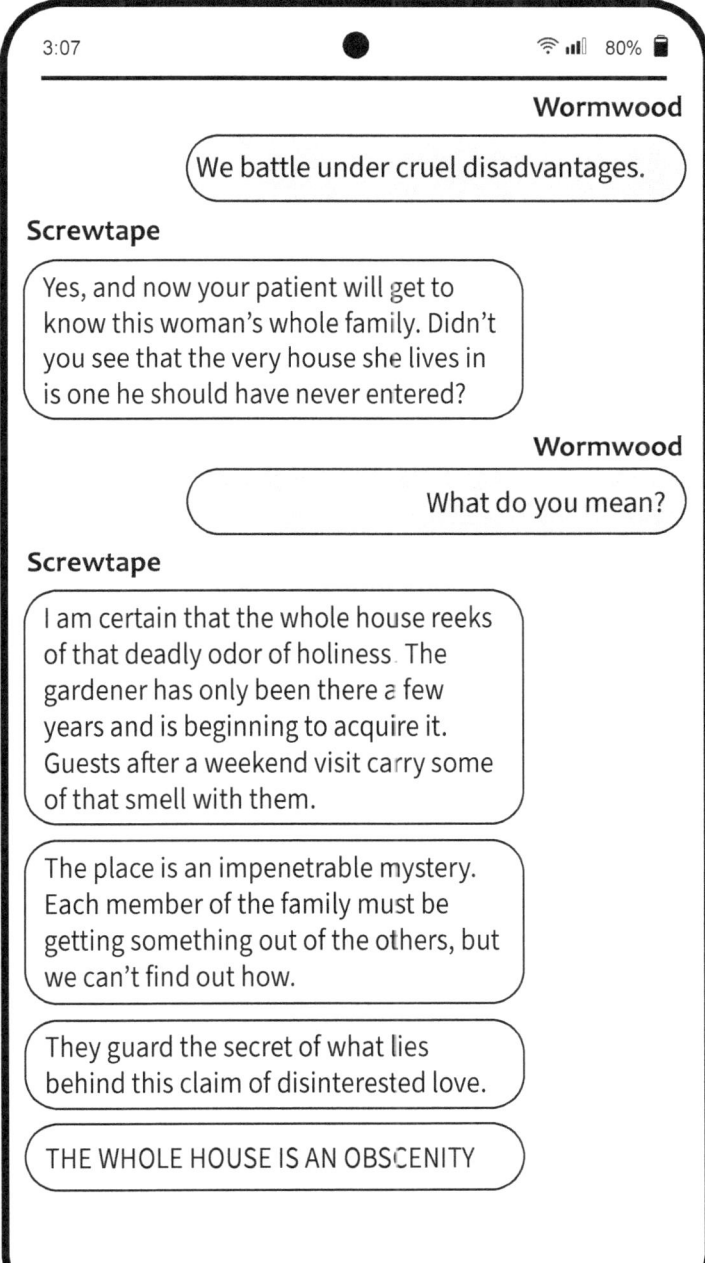

**Wormwood**

We battle under cruel disadvantages.

**Screwtape**

Yes, and now your patient will get to know this woman's whole family. Didn't you see that the very house she lives in is one he should have never entered?

**Wormwood**

What do you mean?

**Screwtape**

I am certain that the whole house reeks of that deadly odor of holiness. The gardener has only been there a few years and is beginning to acquire it. Guests after a weekend visit carry some of that smell with them.

The place is an impenetrable mystery. Each member of the family must be getting something out of the others, but we can't find out how.

They guard the secret of what lies behind this claim of disinterested love.

THE WHOLE HOUSE IS AN OBSCENITY

## Text Message 22.4

3:10    ●    📶 80% 🔋

**Screwtape**

A human writer named MacDonald described Heaven as "the regions where there is only life and therefore all that is not music is silence."

MUSIC AND SILENCE, HOW I DETEST THEM BOTH!

How thankful we should be that ever since Our Father entered Hell, all has been occupied by noise.

Noise defends us from virtuous thought. We will make the whole universe a noise in the end. We have already made great strides in this direction on Earth.

THE MELODIES AND SILENCES OF HEAVEN WILL BE SHOUTED DOWN IN THE END!

MEANWHILE YOU LITTLE

OH NO!

Notttt

**Wormwood**

Uncle?

## Text Message 22.5

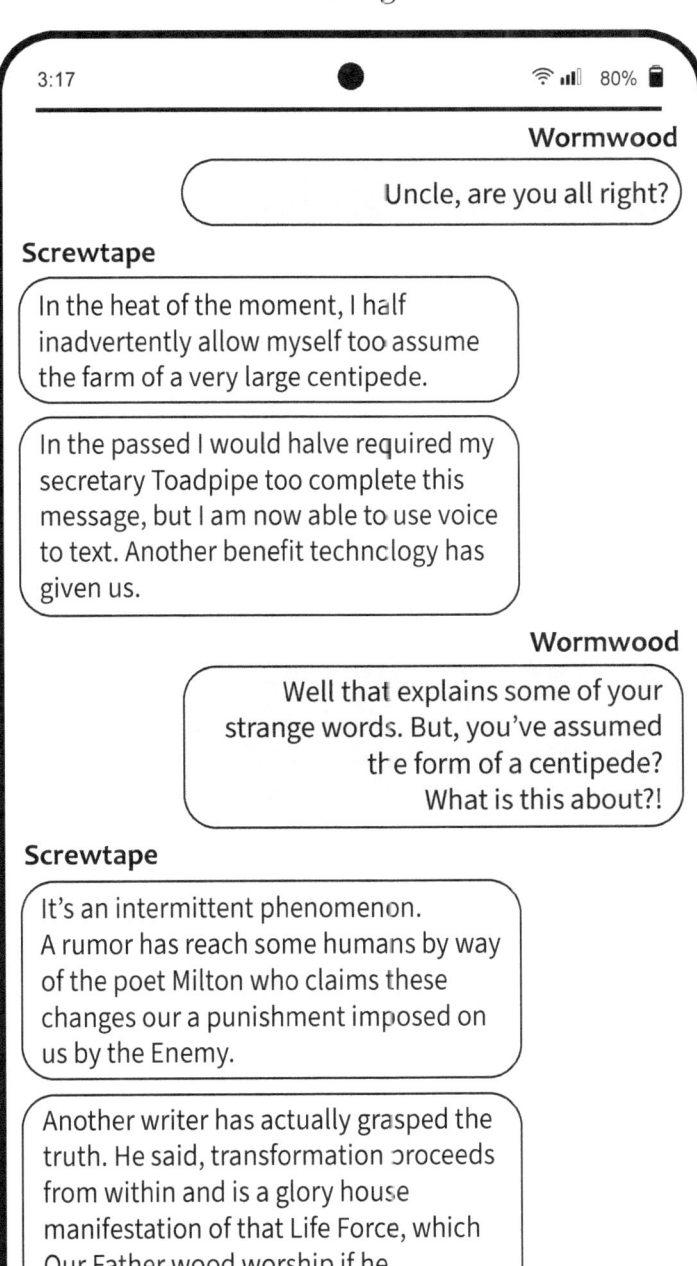

**3:17** 80%

**Wormwood**

> Uncle, are you all right?

**Screwtape**

> In the heat of the moment, I half inadvertently allow myself too assume the farm of a very large centipede.

> In the passed I would halve required my secretary Toadpipe too complete this message, but I am now able to use voice to text. Another benefit technology has given us.

**Wormwood**

> Well that explains some of your strange words. But, you've assumed the form of a centipede? What is this about?!

**Screwtape**

> It's an intermittent phenomenon. A rumor has reach some humans by way of the poet Milton who claims these changes our a punishment imposed on us by the Enemy.

> Another writer has actually grasped the truth. He said, transformation proceeds from within and is a glory house manifestation of that Life Force, which Our Father wood worship if he worshiped anything other than himself.

## Text Message 22.6

3:21    ●    🛜 📶 80% 🔋

**Screwtape**

I hope this doesn't last for to long.

## Summary

This page from the enemy's playbook suggests that music and silence as well as holiness and holy living spaces weaken the devil's attack.

## Resources

| Christian holiness | CCC paragraphs 2012–2015 |
|---|---|
| Contemplative prayer is silence | CCC paragraph 2717 |

The best way to drive out the devil,
if he will not yield to texts of Scripture,
is to jeer and flout him,
for he cannot bear scorn.

~ Martin Luther

## Counterattack Actions

- Add something to your home or workplace that "reeks" of holiness, things like a Bible, crucifix, or a sacred image.
- Add some time of silence to your day. Add uplifting music to your day.
- When you notice temptation or suggestion from evil spirits, laugh at them.

## Questions

1. Screwtape says he needs to tweak our everyday things in order to affect us. How can sleeping, eating, drinking, playing, praying, or working be tweaked in spiritual warfare?

2.  Have you been to a home that "reeks" of the "deadly odor of holiness" Screwtape speaks about? What are elements of a home that repel evil spirits?

3.  Do you consider noise an attack against virtuous thought? Can some music be noise and an attack on virtue?

4.  We read that transformation proceeds from within. In this case, Screwtape from within is an insect. We have the potential to transform ourselves into saints. How can you nurture your transformation?

5.  Screwtape lost his composure in this letter. He became extremely upset at the thought that he could be considered funny. Thomas More wrote: "The devil ... the proud spirit ... cannot endure to be mocked." Why do you think this could be?

6.  What do you do to combat temptations and suggestions like the ones Screwtape suggests in this text message?

## Text Message 23.1

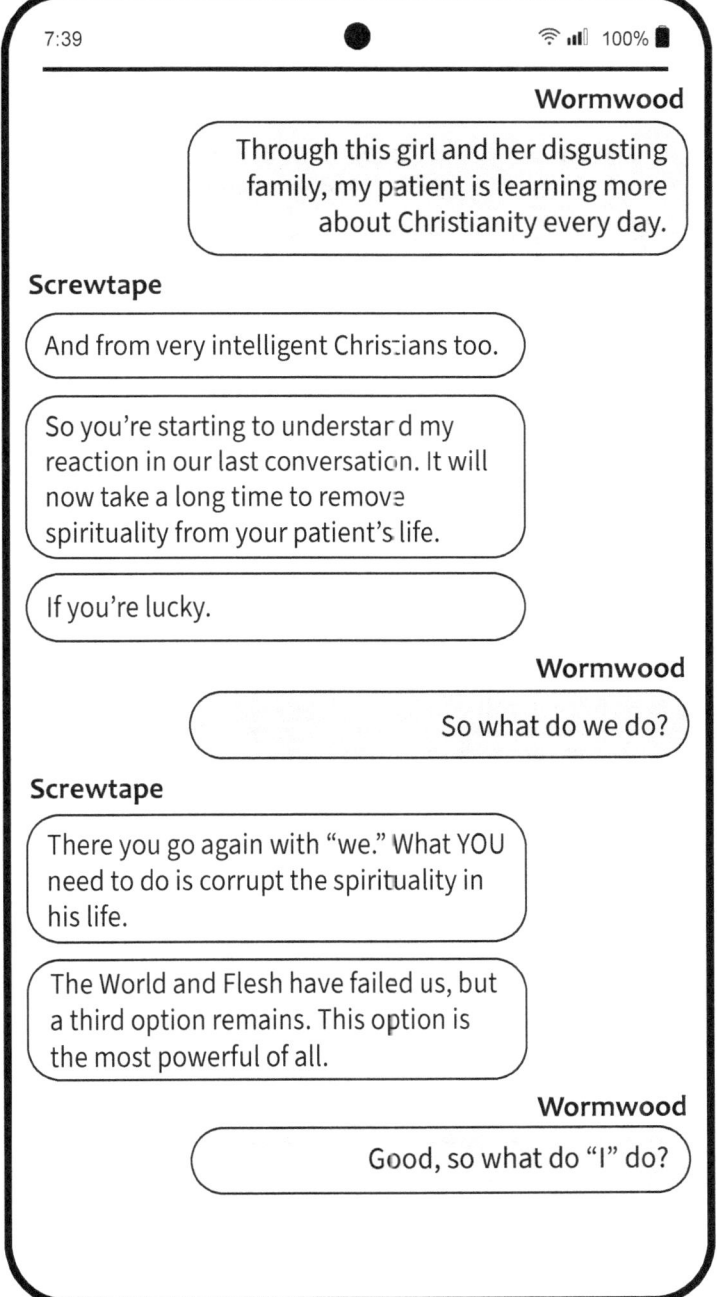

**Wormwood**

Through this girl and her disgusting family, my patient is learning more about Christianity every day.

**Screwtape**

And from very intelligent Christians too.

So you're starting to understand my reaction in our last conversation. It will now take a long time to remove spirituality from your patient's life.

If you're lucky.

**Wormwood**

So what do we do?

**Screwtape**

There you go again with "we." What YOU need to do is corrupt the spirituality in his life.

The World and Flesh have failed us, but a third option remains. This option is the most powerful of all.

**Wormwood**

Good, so what do "I" do?

## Text Message 23.2

**Screwtape**

Based on your patient's new friends, the point of attack will entangle religion and politics.

Several of his friends are focused on the social issues of their religion. This is bad in itself, but good can be made from it.

**Wormwood**

How?

**Screwtape**

Some Christian political writers think that Christianity began to go wrong and departed from their founder's doctrine at a very early stage.

This is where we introduce the concept of the "Historical Jesus."

**Wormwood**

What does Historical Jesus mean and how could a concept like that ever help us?

**Screwtape**

I intend to tell you. Let me continue.

## Text Message 23.3

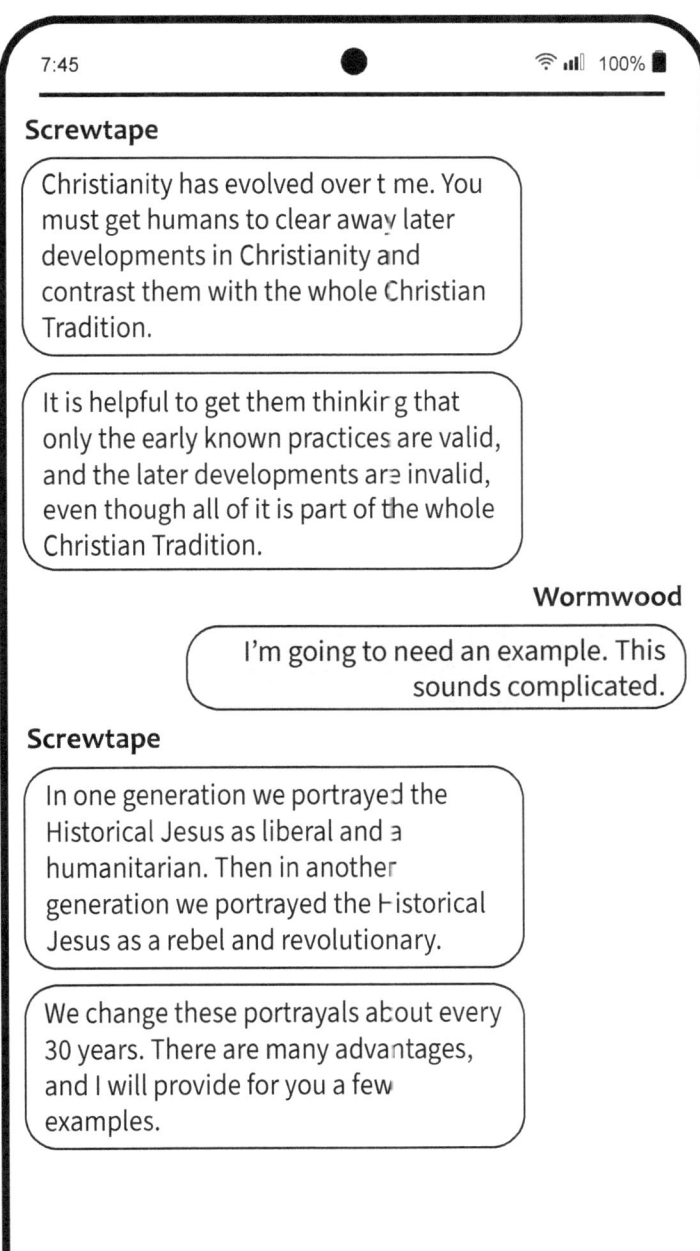

**Screwtape**

> Christianity has evolved over t me. You must get humans to clear away later developments in Christianity and contrast them with the whole Christian Tradition.

> It is helpful to get them thinkir g that only the early known practices are valid, and the later developments are invalid, even though all of it is part of the whole Christian Tradition.

**Wormwood**

> I'm going to need an example. This sounds complicated.

**Screwtape**

> In one generation we portrayed the Historical Jesus as liberal and a humanitarian. Then in another generation we portrayed the Historical Jesus as a rebel and revolutionary.

> We change these portrayals about every 30 years. There are many advantages, and I will provide for you a few examples.

## Text Message 23.4

**Screwtape**

One advantage of changing the portrayal of the Historical Jesus is that they direct their devotion to something that doesn't exist.

Each Historical Jesus is unhistorical. Their scriptures say what they say and cannot be added to, so each new Historical Jesus must have something suppressed and some point exaggerated.

This keeps the current generation thinking they have actually figured out the truth and that the past generation was missing something.

A second advantage of changing the portrayal of the Historical Jesus is that the importance of a particular Historical Jesus is placed in some peculiar theory. This distracts them from who He is and what He did.

**Wormwood**

What do you mean by some peculiar theory?

**Screwtape**

First, we make Him solely a teacher.

## Text Message 23.5

**7:54** ● 📶 100% 🔋

### Screwtape

Then we hide the clear connections between His teachings and of the other great moral teachers, again distracting them from who He is and what He did.

Another advantage of changing the portrayal of the Historical Jesus is that it destroys the devotional life.

Real presence of the Enemy, by which I mean things like prayer and sacraments, is to be substituted with a merely probable, distant, and rugged figure, who spoke a strange language and died a long time ago.

Someone like this cannot be worshiped. Instead of the Creator being worshiped by its creature, you soon will only have a leader acclaimed by a partisan and approved by a judicious historian.

This twisted view of religion is false to history as well. Few converts have been made by a historical study of Jesus. The earliest converts were made by a single historical fact, the Resurrection.

The "Gospels" come later and were written not to make Christians but to instruct Christians already made.

## Text Message 23.6

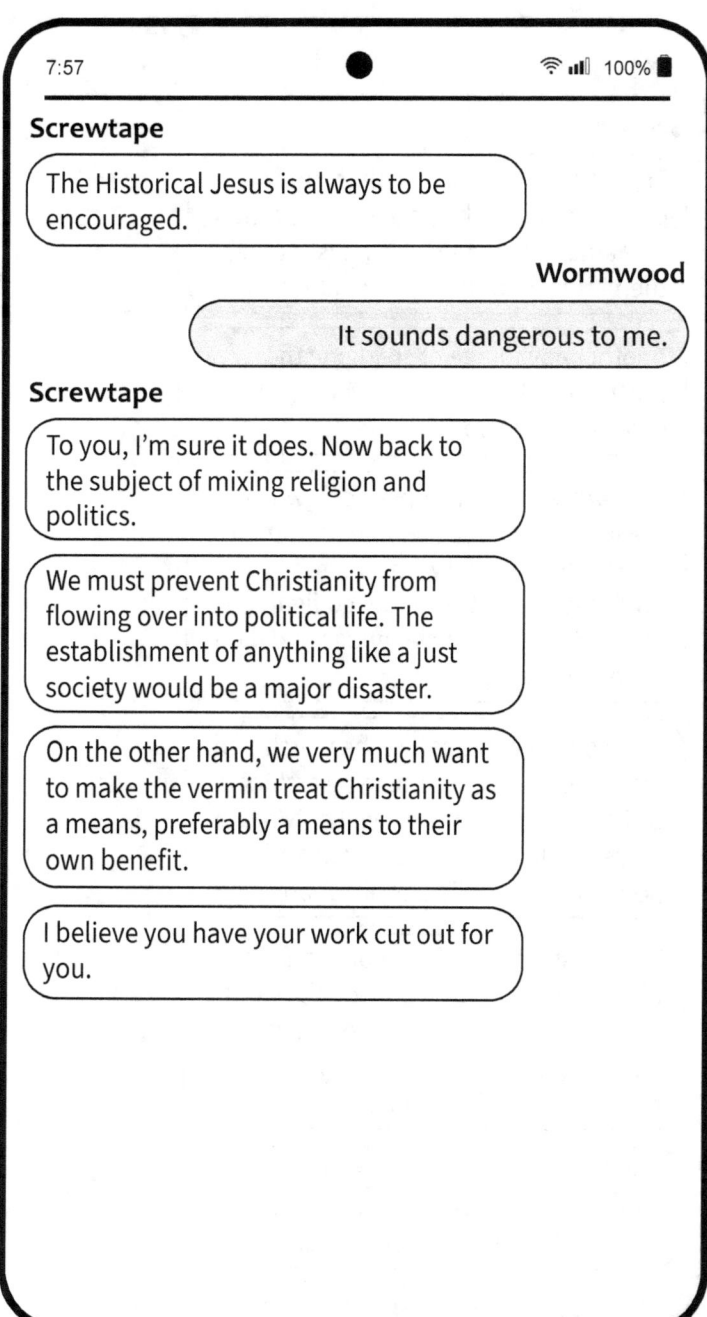

**Screwtape**

The Historical Jesus is always to be encouraged.

**Wormwood**

It sounds dangerous to me.

**Screwtape**

To you, I'm sure it does. Now back to the subject of mixing religion and politics.

We must prevent Christianity from flowing over into political life. The establishment of anything like a just society would be a major disaster.

On the other hand, we very much want to make the vermin treat Christianity as a means, preferably a means to their own benefit.

I believe you have your work cut out for you.

## Summary

This page from the enemy's playbook suggests that awareness of who Jesus really is and what He really did weakens the devil's attack. This letter also suggests mixing religion and politics as a tool used against humans in spiritual warfare.

## Resources

| | |
|---|---|
| Jesus – the demons know who He is | Mark 1:24, Acts 10:38 |
| Why Jesus came | Mark 10:45 |
| Jesus | Isaiah 53:12 |
| Jesus | CCC paragraphs 430–440, 606–608 |
| Christ's presence | CCC paragraphs 1374–1381 |
| Christ's presence in the liturgy | CCC paragraph 1088 |
| Participation in social life | CCC paragraph 1900 |
| Duties of parents, education in the faith | CCC paragraphs 2225–2226 |
| Places favorable for prayer | CCC paragraph 2691 |

## Counterattack Actions

- Spend time reflecting on who Jesus is and what he did for you as well as humanity.
- Experience Jesus when you pray and receive the sacraments.

## Questions

1.  How does learning about Christianity increase spirituality?

2.  How can mixing religion and politics harm our spiritual life?

3.  Can you think of examples where people have relied on an image of a "Historical Jesus" and lose focus of the whole Christian Tradition OR of who He is and what He did?

4.  Does Jesus seem remote or distant from you? Do prayer and sacraments resolve this feeling? Isn't it interesting that C. S. Lewis referred to prayer and sacraments as Real Presence?

5.  How would a Christian use their religion as a means to their own advancement, or any advancement?

6.  What do you do to combat temptations and suggestions like the ones Screwtape suggests in this text message?

## Text Message 24.1

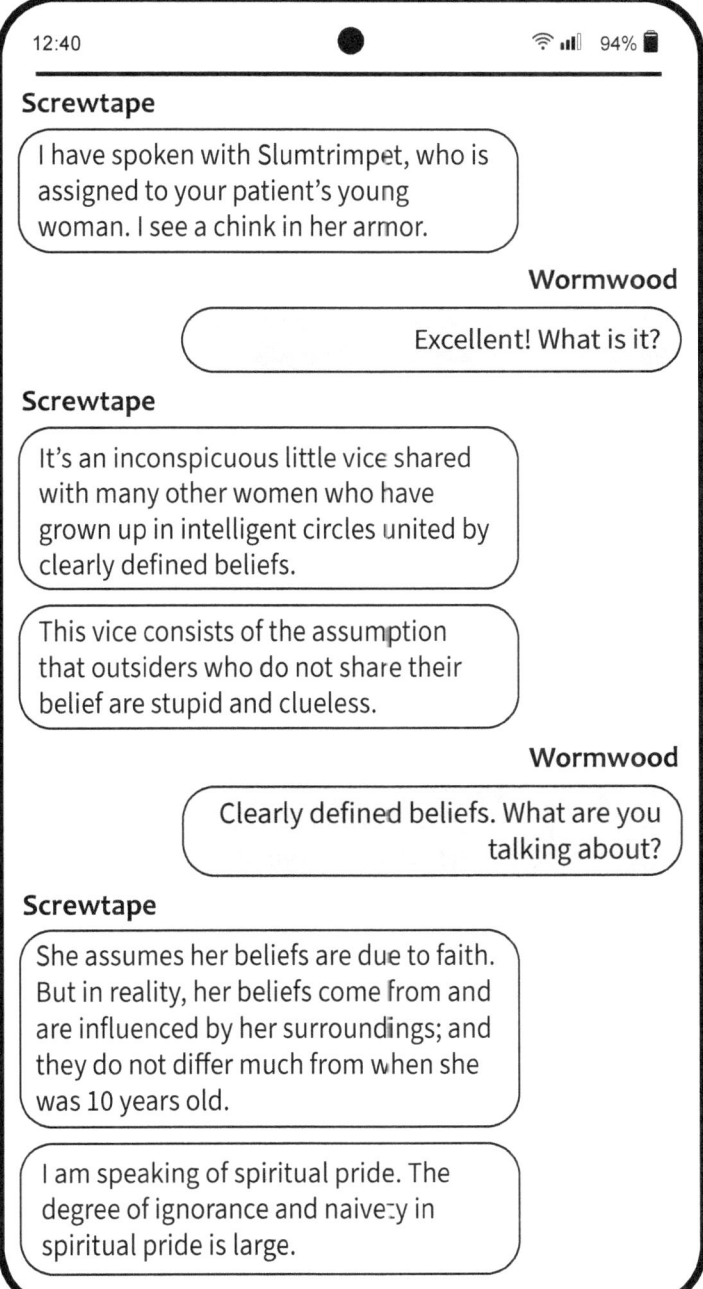

**Screwtape**

I have spoken with Slumtrimpet, who is assigned to your patient's young woman. I see a chink in her armor.

**Wormwood**

Excellent! What is it?

**Screwtape**

It's an inconspicuous little vice shared with many other women who have grown up in intelligent circles united by clearly defined beliefs.

This vice consists of the assumption that outsiders who do not share their belief are stupid and clueless.

**Wormwood**

Clearly defined beliefs. What are you talking about?

**Screwtape**

She assumes her beliefs are due to faith. But in reality, her beliefs come from and are influenced by her surroundings; and they do not differ much from when she was 10 years old.

I am speaking of spiritual pride. The degree of ignorance and naivety in spiritual pride is large.

## Text Message 24.2

**Screwtape**

The bad news: the degree of spiritual pride is small in this girl.

The good news: it can still be used to influence your patient himself.

**Wormwood**

How?

**Screwtape**

Consider these principles.
First, novices always exaggerate.
Second, those who have risen in society are refined to a fault.
Third, they are over-scrupulous and perfectionists.

Your patient is a novice in this new circle. He is experiencing a quality of Christian life he never imagined. And because he is in love with the girl, he is seeing it all unrealistically through rose-colored glasses.

He is anxious to imitate this quality of Christian life. Get your patient to imitate these defects in his mistress and exaggerate them until they become the strongest and most beautiful of vices. Spiritual Pride!

## Text Message 24.3

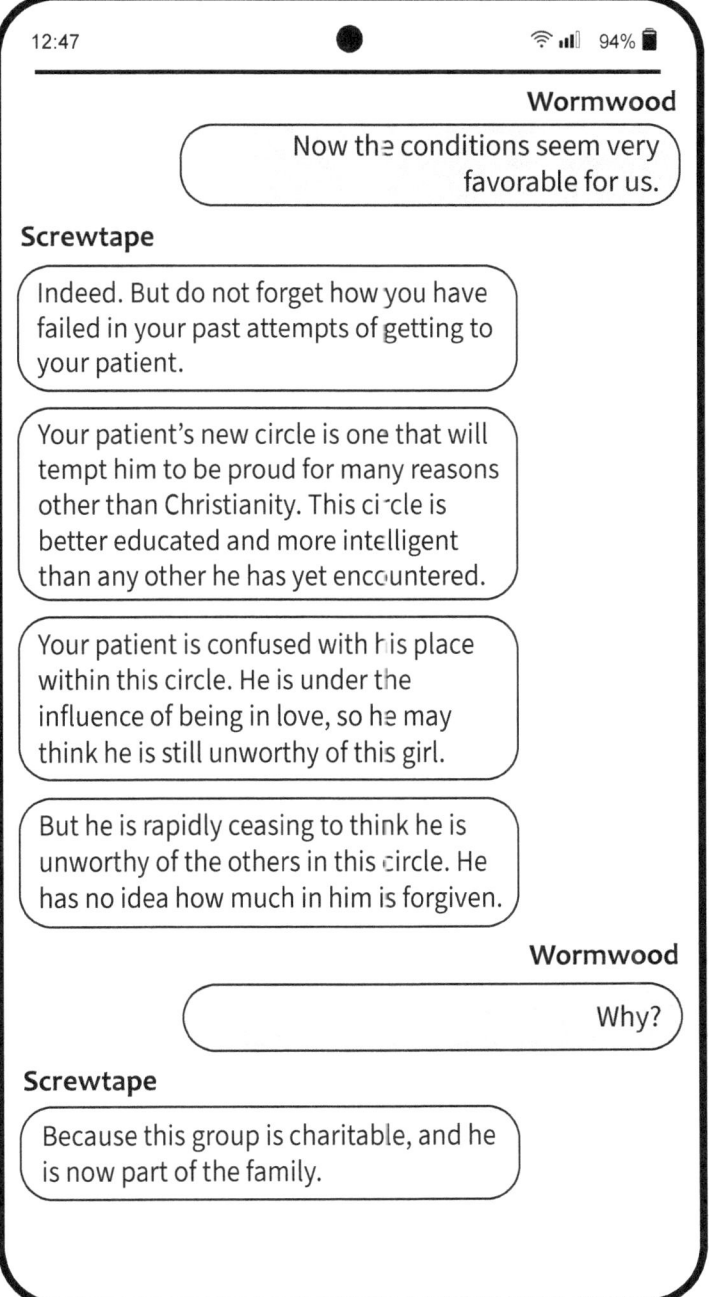

**Wormwood**

Now the conditions seem very favorable for us.

**Screwtape**

Indeed. But do not forget how you have failed in your past attempts of getting to your patient.

Your patient's new circle is one that will tempt him to be proud for many reasons other than Christianity. This circle is better educated and more intelligent than any other he has yet encountered.

Your patient is confused with his place within this circle. He is under the influence of being in love, so he may think he is still unworthy of this girl.

But he is rapidly ceasing to think he is unworthy of the others in this circle. He has no idea how much in him is forgiven.

**Wormwood**

Why?

**Screwtape**

Because this group is charitable, and he is now part of the family.

## Text Message 24.4

12:50 ● 94%

**Screwtape**

He has no idea how much of his conversion and how many of his ideas are seen by them as only echoes of their own ideas.

**Wormwood**

My patient does not realize he likes this new circle, simply because he has feelings for this girl?

**Screwtape**

Absolutely. He thinks he likes their talk and way of life because of some commonality between their spirituality and his.

But in fact, they are so far beyond him that if he were not in love, he would be merely puzzled and repelled by much of what he now accepts.

**Wormwood**

Can you explain this another way?

**Screwtape**

Of course I can.

## Text Message 24.5

**Screwtape**

Your patient is like a dog who imagines he understands firearms. Because of his hunting instincts and love for his master, he is able it to enjoy a day of shooting.

**Wormwood**

Sorry I asked.

**Screwtape**

But here is your chance.

Your patient is being drawn up to levels that under normal conditions would be out of his reach.

Make him feel that he is finding his place and that these people are like him and that being among them, he has come home.

Then, when he is with people outside this circle, he will be bored with them, primarily because he is missing the feelings he has when he is with that young woman.

Teach him to mistake the difference between the circle that energizes him and the circles that bore him as the difference between Christians and non-believers.

## Text Message 24.6

**Screwtape**

Your patient must be made to feel "how different we Christians are."

And by "we Christians" he must really, but unknowingly mean "the people whom I associate by right" not "the people, who in their charity and humility, have accepted me."

Success with this depends on confusing him. But avoid extreme pride in his being a Christian. Also avoid him being complacent with the Christian aspect of his circle.

Keep self-congratulations mixing with all his thoughts. And never allow him to question "What am I congratulating myself about?"

The idea of belonging to an inner circle is very sweet to him. Play on that idea.

**Wormwood**

OK. I'll work on his spiritual pride.

## Summary

This page from the enemy's playbook suggests that spiritual humility weakens the devil's attack.

## Resources

| | |
|---|---|
| The commissioning of the twelve | Matthew 10:5–15 |
| Another exorcist | Luke 9:49–50 |
| The words of eternal life | John 6:60–69 |
| The Eucharist in the economy of salvation | CCC paragraph 1336 |
| Coercion and matters religious | Dignitatis Humanae paragraph 12 |

In faithfulness therefore to the truth of the Gospel, the Church is following the way of Christ and the apostles when she recognizes and gives support to the principle of religious freedom as befitting the dignity of man and as being in accord with divine revelation. Throughout the ages the Church has kept safe and handed on the doctrine received from the Master and from the apostles. In the life of the People of God, as it has made its pilgrim way through the vicissitudes of human history, there has at times appeared a way of acting that was hardly in accord with the spirit of the Gospel or even opposed to it. Nevertheless, the doctrine of the Church that no one is to be coerced into faith has always stood firm.

Thus the leaven of the Gospel has long been about its quiet work in the minds of men, and to it is due in great measure the fact that in the course of time men have come more widely to recognize their dignity as persons, and the conviction has grown stronger that the person in society is to be kept free from all manner of coercion in matters religious.

~ Paragraph 12 from: Declaration on Religious Freedom on the Right of the Person and of Communities to Social and Civil Freedom in Matters Religious (Dignitatis Humanae)

## The Lord's Prayer / The Our Father

Our Father, who art in heaven,
hallowed be thy name;
thy kingdom come,
thy will be done
on earth as it is in heaven.
Give us this day our daily bread,
and forgive us our trespasses,
as we forgive those who trespass against us;
and lead us not into temptation,
but deliver us from evil.
Amen.

## Counterattack Actions

- With the temptations of spiritual pride, pray the Litany of Humility found in Text Message 2.
- Pray the Our Father prayer slowly with spiritual humility.

## Questions

1.  What examples can you think of where one group of Christians criticizes or attacks another group of Christians? Or what is an example of one group criticizing another group within their own community? What are the effects?

2.  Is Screwtape correct in saying new/novice Christians are at greater risk of having spiritual pride? Why? Does this mean people who have been Christians a long time are not at danger of spiritual pride?

3.  How can spiritual pride be prevented or corrected?

4.  How would you explain to someone Screwtape's analogy that a novice Christian understands his Christianity like a dog understands firearms? He implies they really don't understand.

5.  Is there something Screwtape is not saying that keeps the patient in a spiritually proud state? He seems to be keeping the focus away from something or someone.

6. What do you do to combat temptations and suggestions like the ones Screwtape suggests in this text message?

## Text Message 25.1

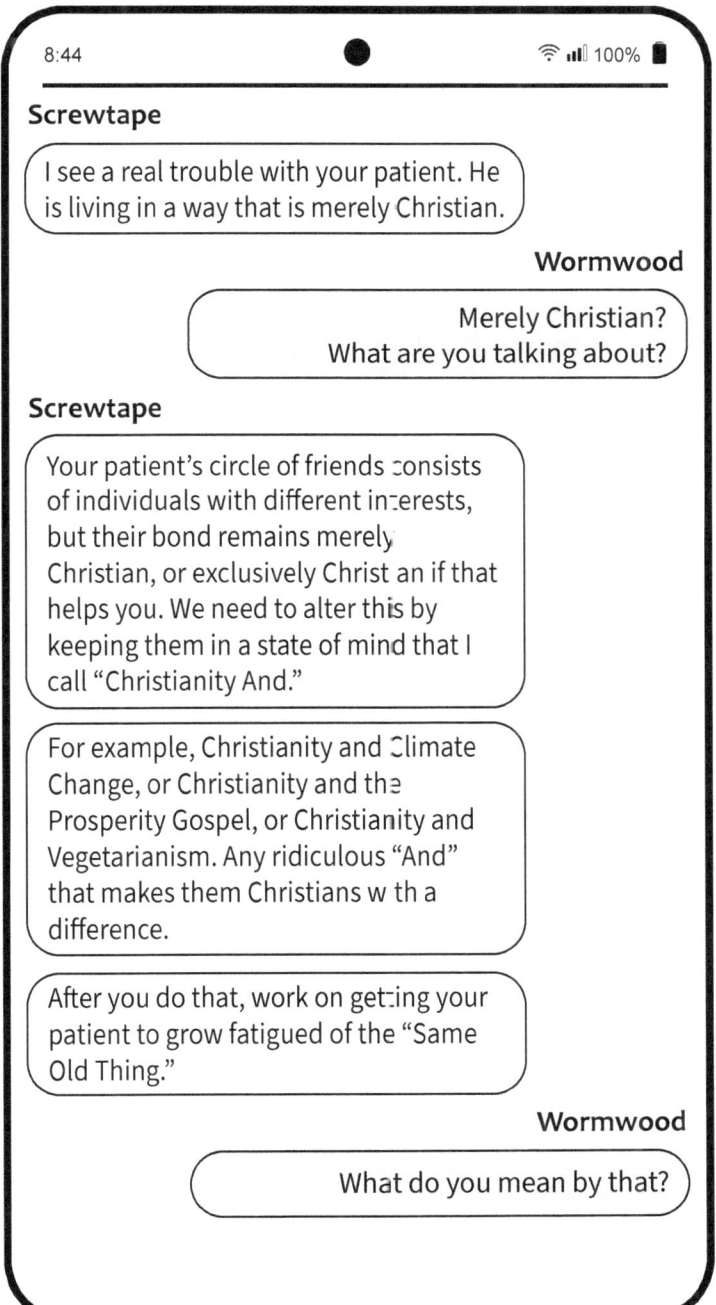

**Screwtape**

I see a real trouble with your patient. He is living in a way that is merely Christian.

**Wormwood**

Merely Christian?
What are you talking about?

**Screwtape**

Your patient's circle of friends consists of individuals with different interests, but their bond remains merely Christian, or exclusively Christian if that helps you. We need to alter this by keeping them in a state of mind that I call "Christianity And."

For example, Christianity and Climate Change, or Christianity and the Prosperity Gospel, or Christianity and Vegetarianism. Any ridiculous "And" that makes them Christians with a difference.

After you do that, work on getting your patient to grow fatigued of the "Same Old Thing."

**Wormwood**

What do you mean by that?

## Text Message 25.2

**Screwtape**

Fatigue of the "Same Old Thing" is one of the most valuable passions we have produced in the human heart. It has produced an endless source of heresies in religion, infidelity in marriages, and unsteadiness in friendships.

**Wormwood**

Why and how does fatigue of the "Same Old Thing" work against them?

**Screwtape**

Humans live in time and experience reality one event at a time. Therefore, to experience the many different facets of life, they must encounter change.

And the Enemy, the hedonist He is, has made change pleasurable.

But the Enemy does not want change to be an end in itself. Therefore, He has balanced the love of change with the love of permanence; something we call rhythm.

## Text Message 25.3

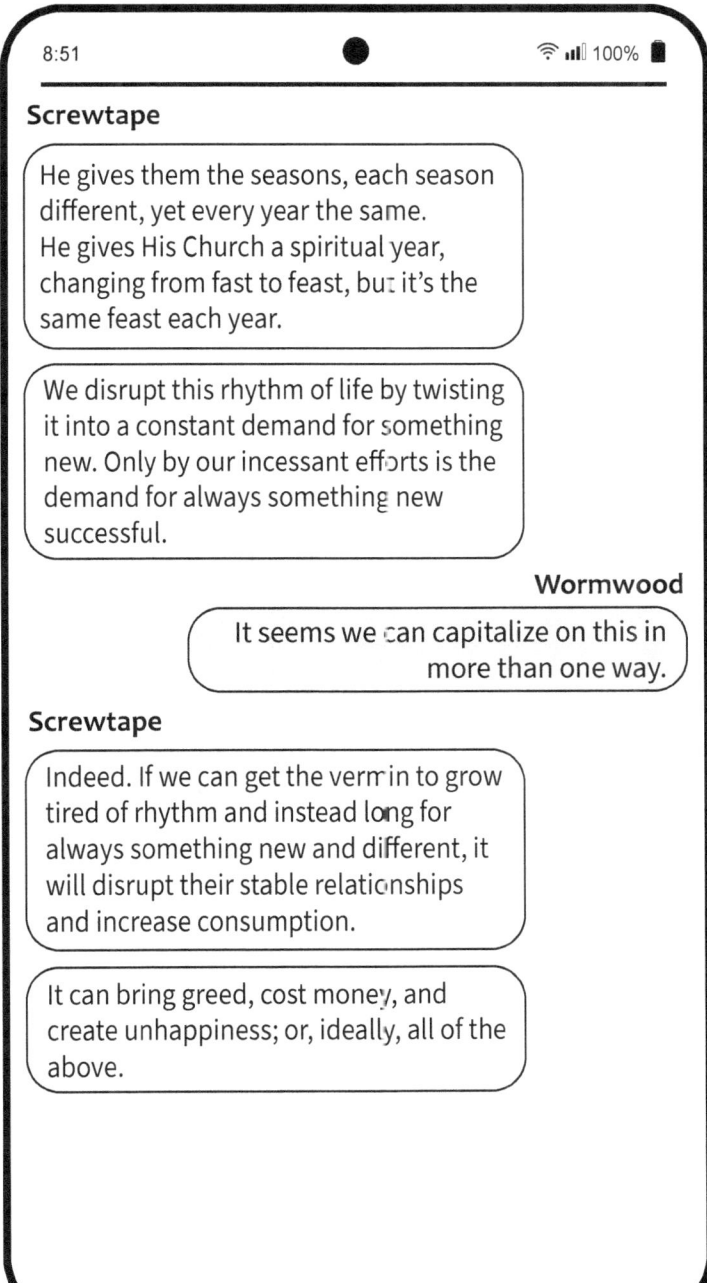

**Screwtape**

He gives them the seasons, each season different, yet every year the same.
He gives His Church a spiritual year, changing from fast to feast, but it's the same feast each year.

We disrupt this rhythm of life by twisting it into a constant demand for something new. Only by our incessant efforts is the demand for always something new successful.

**Wormwood**

It seems we can capitalize on this in more than one way.

**Screwtape**

Indeed. If we can get the vermin to grow tired of rhythm and instead long for always something new and different, it will disrupt their stable relationships and increase consumption.

It can bring greed, cost money, and create unhappiness; or, ideally, all of the above.

## Text Message 25.4

**Screwtape**

The bigger their appetite for change, the sooner innocent sources of pleasure will be used up and the sooner they will move on to pleasures the Enemy forbids.

The desire for change is crucial for producing new Fashions and Fads.

**Wormwood**

Producing new Fashions and Fads? Now what are you talking about?

**Screwtape**

Let me continue.

We use Fashions and Fads in thought to distract the humans from their real dangers. For each new generation of vermin, we try to make it their fashion and their fad, to rally them against a vice which their generation is not really struggling with.

This is done to distract them from the real vices gripping their generation; and this prevents them from correcting their course.

## Text Message 25.5

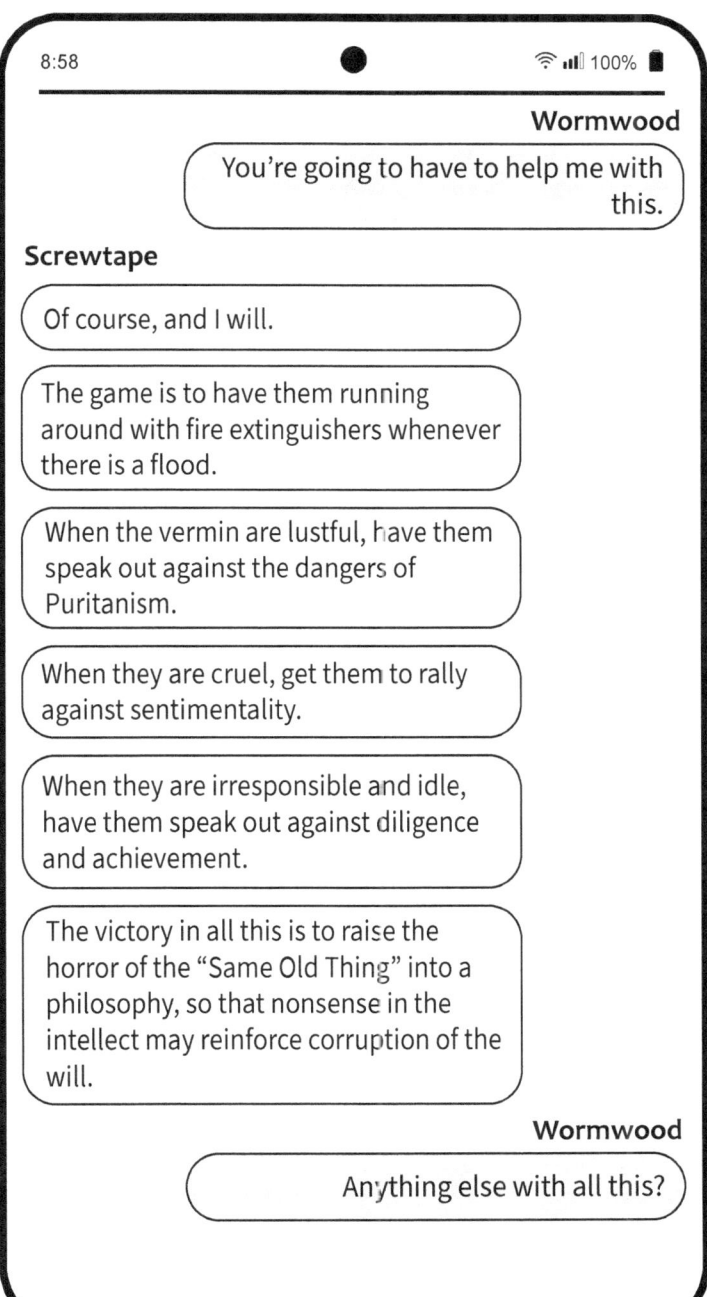

**Wormwood**

You're going to have to help me with this.

**Screwtape**

Of course, and I will.

The game is to have them running around with fire extinguishers whenever there is a flood.

When the vermin are lustful, have them speak out against the dangers of Puritanism.

When they are cruel, get them to rally against sentimentality.

When they are irresponsible and idle, have them speak out against diligence and achievement.

The victory in all this is to raise the horror of the "Same Old Thing" into a philosophy, so that nonsense in the intellect may reinforce corruption of the will.

**Wormwood**

Anything else with all this?

## Text Message 25.6

**Screwtape**

Yes. The Enemy loves platitudes.

When faced with a decision, He wants the vermin to ask very simple questions.

Is it righteous?

Is it prudent?

Is it possible?

So, we must keep them asking:
Is it aligned with the general direction of our time? Will it be on the right side of history?

Then they will neglect the relevant questions. And then, the questions they do ask are, of course, unanswerable.

**Wormwood**

Why is that?

**Screwtape**

Because they do not know the future.

## Text Message 25.7

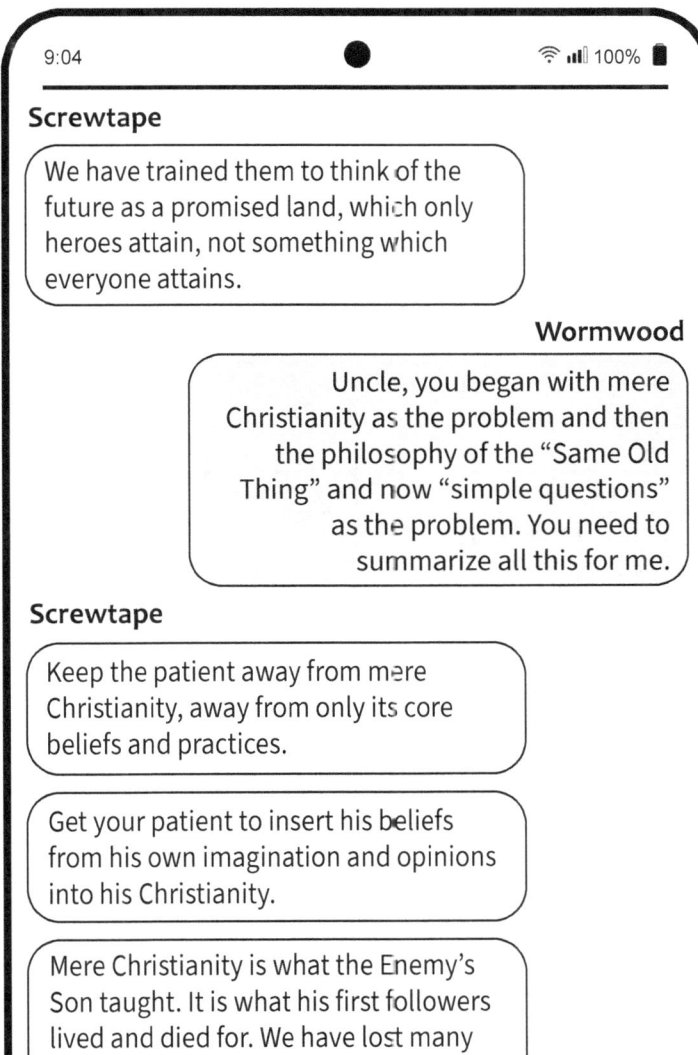

**Screwtape**

We have trained them to think of the future as a promised land, which only heroes attain, not something which everyone attains.

**Wormwood**

Uncle, you began with mere Christianity as the problem and then the philosophy of the "Same Old Thing" and now "simple questions" as the problem. You need to summarize all this for me.

**Screwtape**

Keep the patient away from mere Christianity, away from only its core beliefs and practices.

Get your patient to insert his beliefs from his own imagination and opinions into his Christianity.

Mere Christianity is what the Enemy's Son taught. It is what his first followers lived and died for. We have lost many souls to the Enemy who remained merely Christian.

## Summary

This page from the enemy's playbook suggests staying focused on core Christian beliefs and practices weakens the devil's attack. Satan encourages us to add our own opinions and values to what we say Christianity is.

## Resources

| | |
|---|---|
| The commissioning of the disciples | Matthew 28:16–20 |
| The Church at Antioch (where the disciples were first called Christians) | Acts 11:26 |
| Apostolic Tradition | CCC paragraphs 75–79 |
| Relationship between Tradition and Sacred Scripture | CCC paragraph 80 |
| Two modes of transmission (Sacred Scripture and Holy Tradition) | CCC paragraphs 81–82 |
| Apostolic Tradition and ecclesial tradition | CCC paragraph 83 |
| The liturgical year | CCC paragraphs 1168-1173 |

"Fallacies do not cease to be fallacies
because they become fashions."

~ G. K. Chesterton
Illustrated London News, 4/19/1930

CCC paragraph 185

Whoever says 'I believe' says 'I pledge myself to what we believe.' Communion in faith needs a common language of faith, normative for all and uniting all in the same confession of faith.

## The Nicene Creed

I believe in one God,
the Father almighty,
maker of heaven and earth,
of all things visible and invisible.

I believe in one Lord Jesus Christ,
the Only Begotten Son of God,
born of the Father before all ages.
God from God, Light from Light,
true God from true God,
begotten, not made, consubstantial with the Father;
through him all things were made.
For us men and for our salvation
he came down from heaven,
and by the Holy Spirit was incarnate of the Virgin Mary,
and became man.
For our sake he was crucified under Pontius Pilate,
he suffered death and was buried,
and rose again on the third day
in accordance with the Scriptures.
He ascended into heaven
and is seated at the right hand of the Father.
He will come again in glory
to judge the living and the dead
and his kingdom will have no end.

I believe in the Holy Spirit, the Lord, the giver of life,
who proceeds from the Father and the Son,
who with the Father and the Son is adored and glorified,
who has spoken through the prophets.

I believe in one, holy, catholic and apostolic Church.
I confess one Baptism for the forgiveness of sins
and I look forward to the resurrection of the dead
and the life of the world to come.
Amen.

"The Church exists for nothing else but to draw men into Christ, to make them little Christs. If they are not doing that, all the cathedrals, clergy, missions, sermons, even the Bible itself, are simply a waste of time."

~ C. S. Lewis, Mere Christianity


## Counterattack Actions

- Spend time reflecting on one of the lines from the Nicene Creed. Reflect on a different line each day.
- Do or say something today that will draw someone closer to Jesus.
- When tempted with wanting something new, pray to discern if it is just a temptation.

## Questions

1. How do you define mere Christianity? What is the difference between Tradition (big T) and tradition (little t)?
   Note: the Resources in this chapter can help with this question.

2. What do you like or dislike about the Same Old Thing when it comes to Christianity? Why would someone dislike mere Christianity? What benefits do you see in the Church's liturgical year? (Advent, Christmas, Lent, Easter, and Ordinary Time)

3. How does always wanting something new attack humans; wanting new things like: a new phone, new car, new clothes, etc.?

4. Do you agree with C. S. Lewis' statement that if we are not drawing others to Christ that we are wasting our time?

5. How do you keep questions, especially moral questions, simple rather than unanswerable?

6.  What do you do to combat temptations and suggestions like the ones Screwtape suggests in this text message?

## Text Message 26.1

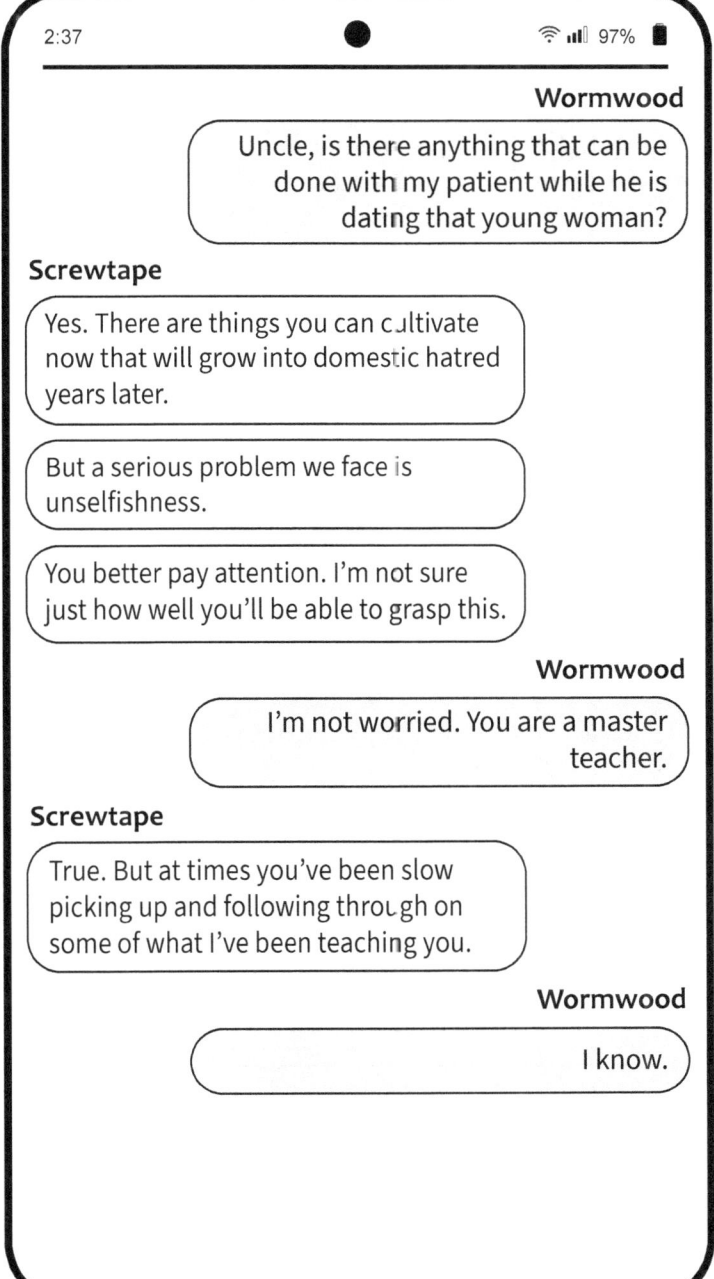

**2:37** 📶 97% 🔋

**Wormwood**

Uncle, is there anything that can be done with my patient while he is dating that young woman?

**Screwtape**

Yes. There are things you can cultivate now that will grow into domestic hatred years later.

But a serious problem we face is unselfishness.

You better pay attention. I'm not sure just how well you'll be able to grasp this.

**Wormwood**

I'm not worried. You are a master teacher.

**Screwtape**

True. But at times you've been slow picking up and following through on some of what I've been teaching you.

**Wormwood**

I know.

## Text Message 26.2

**Screwtape**

> Alright. Now listen. Teach a man to make sacrifices, but not for the sake of serving others, but for making himself happy for serving others.

**Wormwood**

> That doesn't seem complicated.

**Screwtape**

> I'm not through.

> When there is a man and a woman involved, we can use the difference of their perspectives with this type of unselfishness.

> A woman's unselfish perspective is to take trouble for others.

> A man's unselfish perspective is to not give trouble to others.

> A woman who is quite committed in the Enemy's camp will make a real nuisance of herself, more so than any man.

> Conversely, a man will wait a long time in the Enemy's camp before he performs as much spontaneous work to please others, much less than an ordinary woman may do every day.

## Text Message 26.3

**Wormwood**

> So, the woman thinks of sacrificing for others and the man respects others by not imposing on them; and the two types consider the other as radically selfish?

**Screwtape**

> You actually got it! I AM a great teacher!

> Of course.

> On top of these confusions, you can add more. Early in the dating process, sexual desires are high, and both accommodate the other, each happily giving in to what the other wants.

> For their entire married life, you must make their sexual desire the driving force behind their willingness to sacrifice. Then when, not if, the sexual desires fade, their willingness to sacrifice will also fade.

> Delightful results will follow when this happens.

**Wormwood**

> Like what?

## Text Message 26.4

2:45 97%

**Screwtape**

Person A will argue for person B's assumed wishes and against their own.

And Person B will argue for person A's assumed wishes and against their own.

It becomes a delicious mess, and it becomes even more delicious when there are more than two fools involved, each person insisting on what they assume the other wants.

If we're really lucky, nasty quarrels begin, and resentment flares up on all sides.

**Wormwood**

But if each side remains honest with their intentions, they will stay within the bounds of reason and kindness and none of this works.

**Screwtape**

Yes, and this is why we must encourage this phony unselfish technique. Their feelings of resentment can build up and simmer under the surface for years.

Just don't let the young fools notice this.

## Text Message 26.5

2:48

**Wormwood**

> What will happen if the fools do notice phony unselfishness?

**Screwtape**

> They will soon discover that love is not enough, and that charity is needed and not yet achieved.

## Summary

This page from the enemy's playbook suggests sincere unselfishness (Charity) weakens the devil's attack.

## Resources

| | |
|---|---|
| Be perfect, as your heavenly Father is perfect | Matthew 5:48 |
| Martha and Mary | Luke 10:38-42 |
| Remain in His love | John 15:9-10 |
| Love one another as I have loved you | John 15:12 |
| Living for God in Christ Jesus | Romans 6:11 |
| The way of love | 1 Corinthians 13:1-7 |
| Love, the greatest virtue | 1 Corinthians 13:13 |
| Live in love | Ephesians 5:1-2 |
| Charity, true measure of all charisms | CCC paragraph 800 |
| Virgin Mary – Church's model of faith and charity | CCC paragraphs 967-968 |
| Life in Christ | CCC paragraph 1694 |
| Charity | CCC paragraphs 1822-1829 |
| Grace; charisms | CCC paragraph 2003 |
| Christian holiness | CCC paragraph 2013 |

## Counterattack Actions

- Take time to look at a crucifix and ponder what perfect unselfish love looks like.
- Pray for the grace to love and sacrifice for others unselfishly.

## Questions

1. Does the difference in perspective between men and women (not giving trouble vs. taking trouble for others) when serving others create potential problems? Why?

2. Is there a right perspective for serving others unselfishly? What would you say that right perspective is?

3. How could the extremes of serving others be seen as selfishness?

4. Do you agree with Screwtape that there is a connection between phony unselfishness and sexual desire?

5. Is it dishonest to put another person's perceived wants before your own? How can you avoid being unselfish for the wrong reasons?

6. What do you do to combat temptations and suggestions like the ones Screwtape suggests in this text message?

## Text Message 27.1

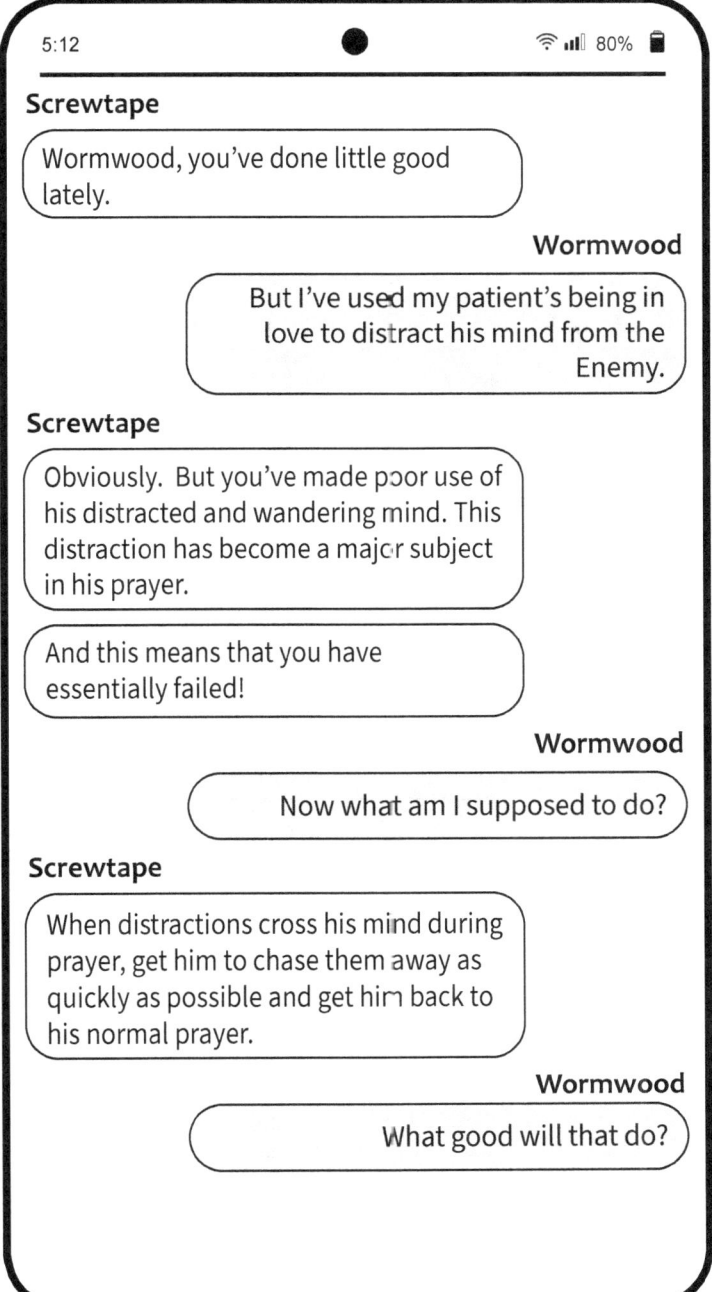

**Screwtape**

Wormwood, you've done little good lately.

**Wormwood**

But I've used my patient's being in love to distract his mind from the Enemy.

**Screwtape**

Obviously. But you've made poor use of his distracted and wandering mind. This distraction has become a major subject in his prayer.

And this means that you have essentially failed!

**Wormwood**

Now what am I supposed to do?

**Screwtape**

When distractions cross his mind during prayer, get him to chase them away as quickly as possible and get him back to his normal prayer.

**Wormwood**

What good will that do?

## Text Message 27.2

**Screwtape**

Awareness of the distraction is an awareness of being distant from the Enemy. Your patient's awareness of not being as close as he should be to the Enemy weakens our attacks.

Even awareness of sin can move him closer to the Enemy.

Keep your patient in normal prayer with his silly little petitions.

And now that he is in love, he now has a new concept of what happiness is.

With that said, now is the perfect time to raise intellectual challenges regarding prayer in his puny little mind.

**Wormwood**

I'm not sure I am ready for this.

**Screwtape**

Nor am I sure of your readiness. Regardless, I will teach you about false spirituality.

**Wormwood**

False spirituality. My patient is very obedient to the Enemy. Could it work with him?

## Text Message 27.3

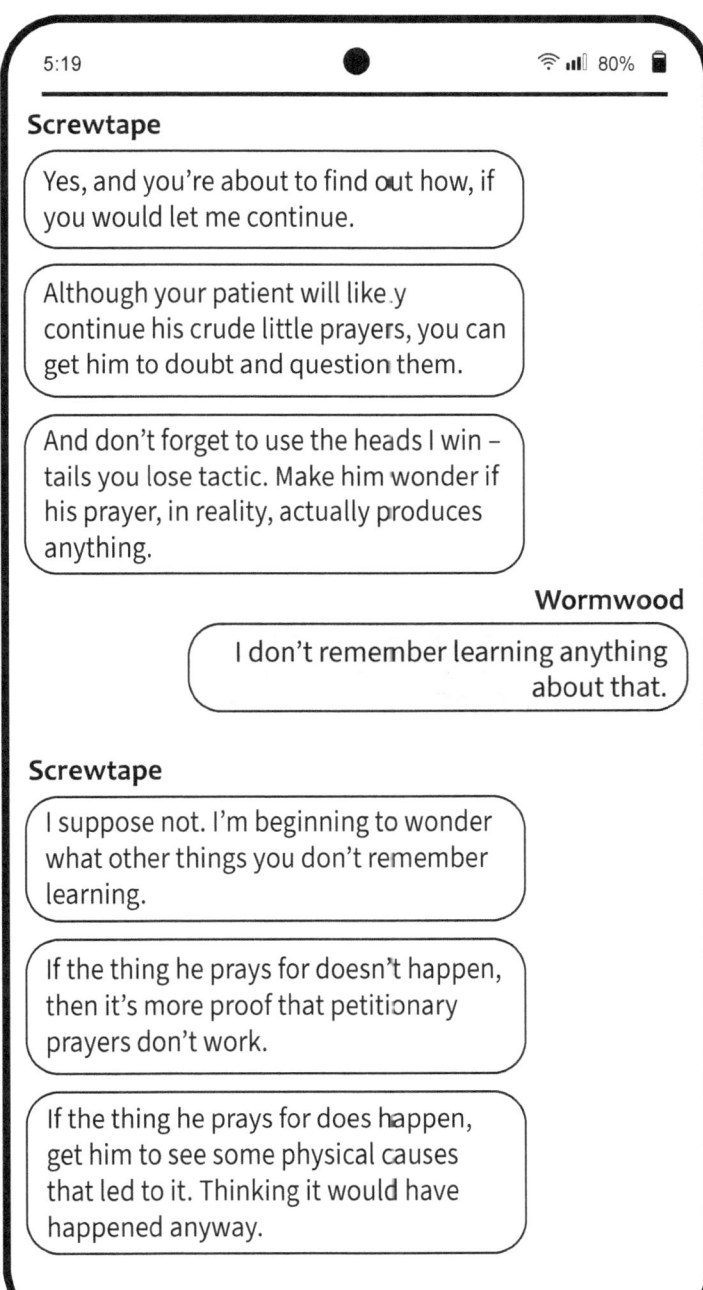

**Screwtape**

Yes, and you're about to find out how, if you would let me continue.

Although your patient will likely continue his crude little prayers, you can get him to doubt and question them.

And don't forget to use the heads I win – tails you lose tactic. Make him wonder if his prayer, in reality, actually produces anything.

**Wormwood**

I don't remember learning anything about that.

**Screwtape**

I suppose not. I'm beginning to wonder what other things you don't remember learning.

If the thing he prays for doesn't happen, then it's more proof that petitionary prayers don't work.

If the thing he prays for does happen, get him to see some physical causes that led to it. Thinking it would have happened anyway.

## Text Message 27.4

5:23        ●        🛜 ▪ll 80% 🔋

**Wormwood**

> That makes a granted prayer as effective as a denied prayer is ineffective.

> If you flip a coin enough times it all becomes chance.

**Screwtape**

> What!? You actually got it. But then, even a blind pig finds an acorn once in a while.

> You can also consider playing with the concept of predestination.

> And don't bother asking. I'll explain it to you.

> Get your patient to consider that the Enemy always knows what humans are going to pray before they actually do, so that they aren't really praying freely.

> Get him to consider that everything is already known in advance and that the humans are just pawns in the Enemy's twisted game.

**Wormwood**

> But don't humans have free will? Like we did.

## Text Message 27.5

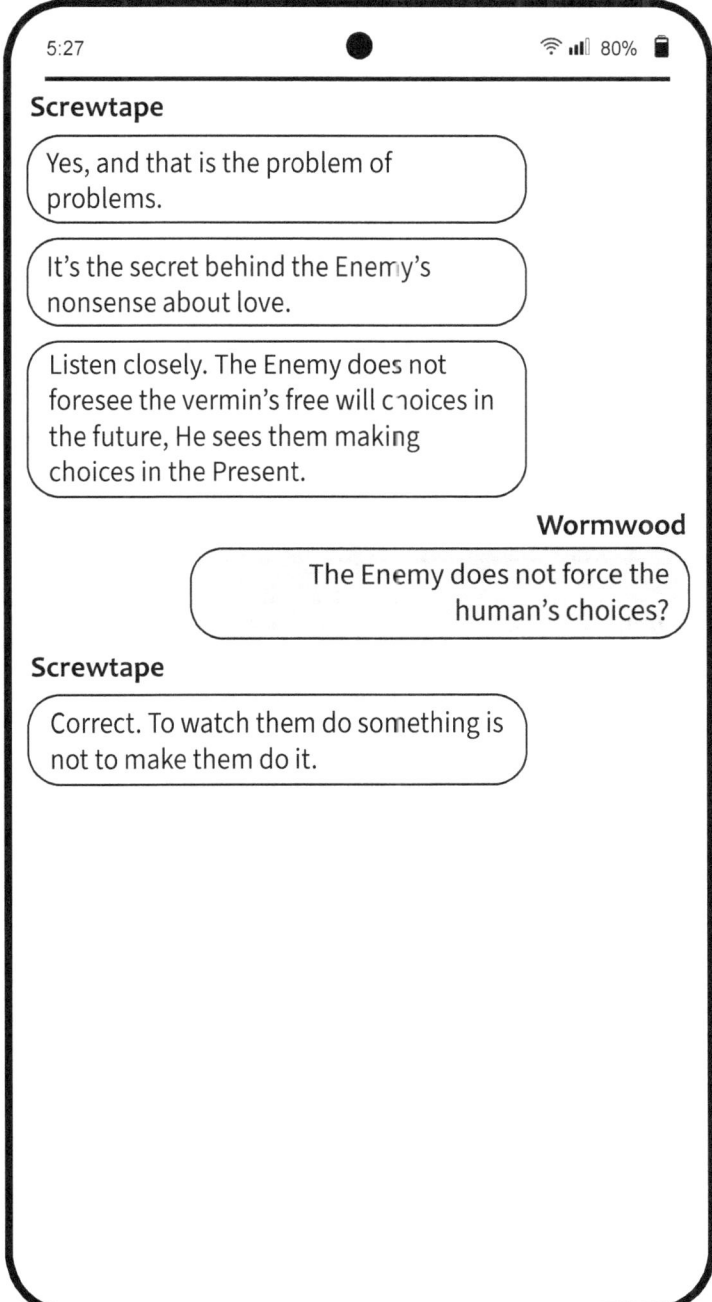

**Screwtape**

Yes, and that is the problem of problems.

It's the secret behind the Enemy's nonsense about love.

Listen closely. The Enemy does not foresee the vermin's free will choices in the future, He sees them making choices in the Present.

**Wormwood**

The Enemy does not force the human's choices?

**Screwtape**

Correct. To watch them do something is not to make them do it.

## Summary

This page from the enemy's playbook suggests that noticing when we are distracted from getting closer to God weakens the devil's attack. Screwtape also tries to attack our confidence in whether God really hears and responds to our prayers. He wants us to think it is all chance.

## Resources

| Predestination | Romans 8:28–30 |
|---|---|
| Constant prayer | Ephesians 6:18–20 |
| Pray without ceasing | 1 Thessalonians 5:17 |
| Distractions in prayer | CCC paragraph 2729 |
| Prayers not heard | CCC paragraph 2737 |
| Difficulties in prayer | CCC paragraphs 2729–2737 |
| Perseverance in prayer | CCC paragraph 2742 |
| Predestination | CCC paragraphs 600, 2012 |

## Counterattack Actions

- When you find yourself distracted in prayer, ask God to help you move your focus back to Him. Tell God the distractions create an undesirable distance between you and Him.
- Thank God for hearing your prayers, knowing that our prayers are answered in God's time and in the way that is best for us.

## Questions

1. How can awareness of distraction in prayer draw us closer to God?

2. Why would Screwtape consider some prayer not threatening the devil's cause?

3. Have you doubted or questioned the value of your prayer? Why? How did you resolve it?

4. How do you respond to answered prayer? How do you respond to unanswered prayer?

5. What are your thoughts on predestination? Not all Christian faiths have the same beliefs regarding predestination.

6. What do you do to combat temptations and suggestions like the ones Screwtape suggests in this text message?

## Text Message 28.1

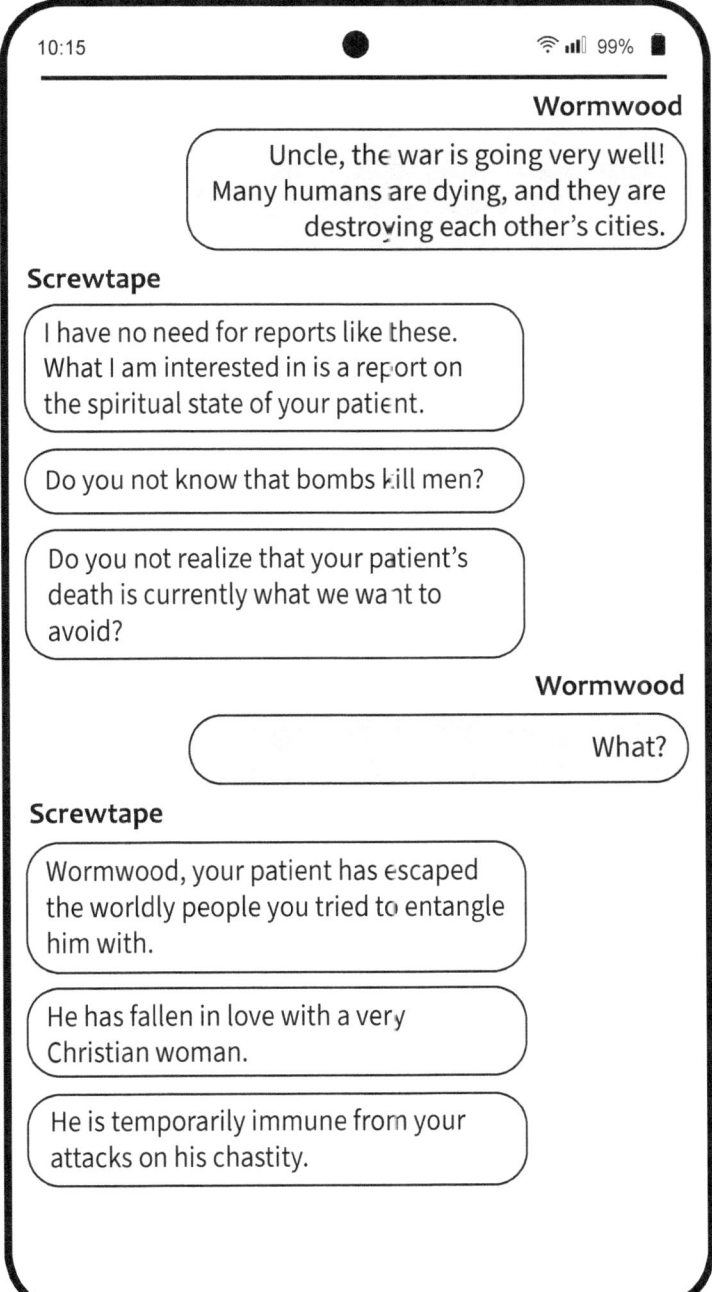

**Wormwood**

Uncle, the war is going very well! Many humans are dying, and they are destroying each other's cities.

**Screwtape**

I have no need for reports like these. What I am interested in is a report on the spiritual state of your patient.

Do you not know that bombs kill men?

Do you not realize that your patient's death is currently what we want to avoid?

**Wormwood**

What?

**Screwtape**

Wormwood, your patient has escaped the worldly people you tried to entangle him with.

He has fallen in love with a very Christian woman.

He is temporarily immune from your attacks on his chastity.

## Text Message 28.2

10:18      ●      🛜 ᵘᴵᴵ 99% 🔋

**Screwtape**

And the methods of corrupting his spiritual life have so far been unsuccessful.

**Wormwood**

Oh. It is not a good time for him to die. We would lose him to the Enemy now.

**Screwtape**

Yes. And to make things even worse, all this news of the war has put his worldly hopes at a lower priority. His concerns are for the girl and his neighbor.

His dependency on the Enemy is increasing daily. So yes, it is not a good time for him to die!

If he were to die today, we would most certainly lose him to the Enemy.

We have taught the vermin to consider death as evil and survival as the greatest good.

He is now in a place where he is not thinking this way.

## Text Message 28.3

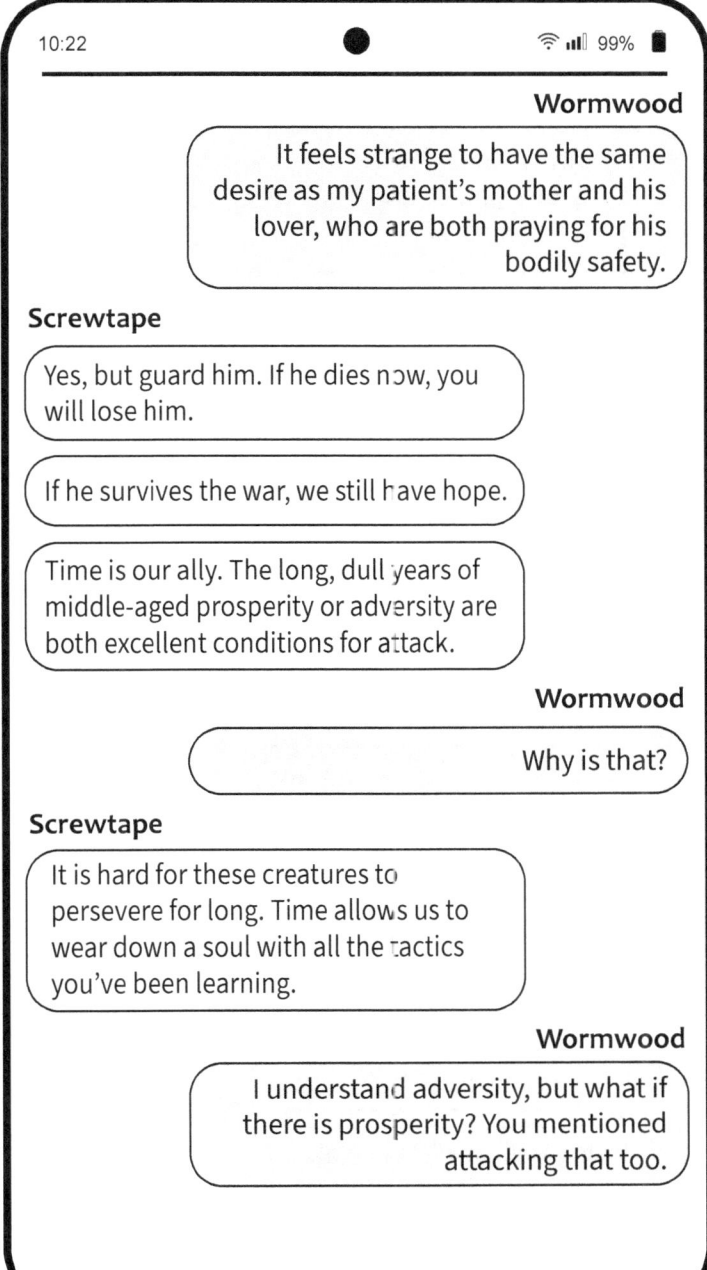

**Wormwood**

It feels strange to have the same desire as my patient's mother and his lover, who are both praying for his bodily safety.

**Screwtape**

Yes, but guard him. If he dies now, you will lose him.

If he survives the war, we still have hope.

Time is our ally. The long, dull years of middle-aged prosperity or adversity are both excellent conditions for attack.

**Wormwood**

Why is that?

**Screwtape**

It is hard for these creatures to persevere for long. Time allows us to wear down a soul with all the tactics you've been learning.

**Wormwood**

I understand adversity, but what if there is prosperity? You mentioned attacking that too.

## Text Message 28.4

**Screwtape**

Prosperity is even better for us.
It connects them to the world. They feel they are finding their place within it.

But really, the world is finding its place in them.

**Wormwood**

How is that?

**Screwtape**

Increasing reputation, increasing circle of friends, and increasing self-importance all build up a sense of being at home in the world.

**Wormwood**

Which is what we want.

**Screwtape**

Yes. Because of this, we often wish long life for our patients.

70 years is not too much for the task of unraveling a soul from Heaven and building up attachments on earth.

In some cases, we need to make these creatures believe that earth can be turned into Heaven with politics or science or whatnot.

## Text Message 28.5

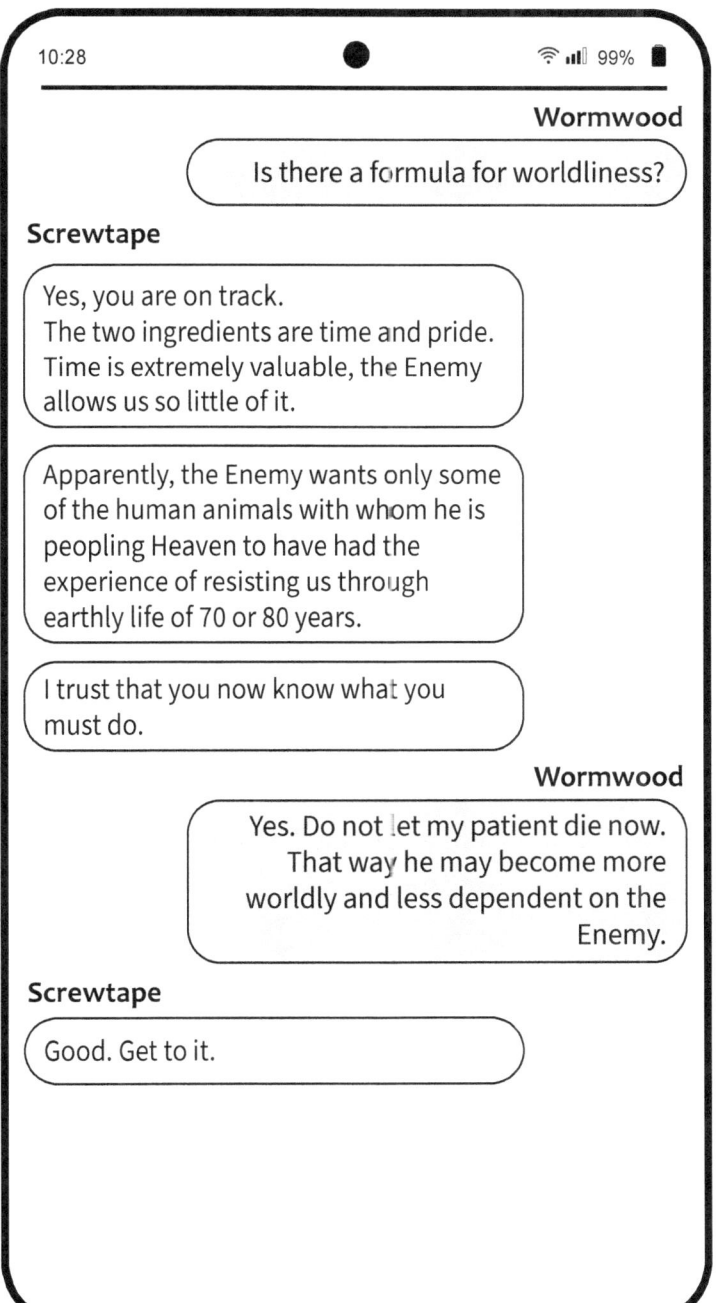

**Wormwood**

Is there a formula for worldliness?

**Screwtape**

Yes, you are on track.
The two ingredients are time and pride.
Time is extremely valuable, the Enemy
allows us so little of it.

Apparently, the Enemy wants only some
of the human animals with whom he is
peopling Heaven to have had the
experience of resisting us through
earthly life of 70 or 80 years.

I trust that you now know what you
must do.

**Wormwood**

Yes. Do not let my patient die now.
That way he may become more
worldly and less dependent on the
Enemy.

**Screwtape**

Good. Get to it.

## Summary

This page from the enemy's playbook suggests that dependence on God and having your soul right with God weaken the devil's attack.

## Resources

| | |
|---|---|
| Woe to you who are rich | Luke 6:24 |
| The narrow gate | Matthew 7:13–14 |
| Death | CCC paragraphs 1006–1009 |
| The meaning of Christian death | CCC paragraphs 1010–1019 |
| The disorder of covetous desires | CCC paragraphs 2534–2540 |
| Poverty of heart | CCC paragraphs 2545, 2547 |
| I want to see God | CCC paragraph 2548 |

## Counterattack Actions

- Identify something in your life that is not prioritized as it should be and resolve that item.
- Live today as if you had one day left to live on earth.

## Questions

1. Are there things you do to prepare yourself for death? What are they?

2. Is there a good time to die? When?

3. Are there events that cause you to reprioritize your life? What are they? Why do you have to revisit them periodically?

4. How often do you see yourself dependent on God?

5. Relative to your spiritual life, how do you keep prosperity in check? What are you most attached to?

6. What do you do to combat temptations and suggestions like the ones Screwtape suggests in this text message?

## Text Message 29.1

**Wormwood**

Uncle, the war in my patient's country is intensifying and he remains in physical danger. What should I do?

**Screwtape**

You have choices. You can attack his courage by using pride or hatred of his enemy. You can also attack cowardice.

Though there isn't much to gain by trying to make him brave.

**Wormwood**

Are we able to produce virtues?

**Screwtape**

No, we have yet to find a way to produce any virtue, especially a virtue like courage.

**Wormwood**

How do virtues help us?

**Screwtape**

To be effectively wicked, humans need some virtue. What would Attila have been without courage?

In most cases though, we're still better off attacking virtues and encouraging vices.

## Text Message 29.2

9:52       ●       🛜 ⏽⏽ 97% 🔋

**Wormwood**

> OK. So back to my question. What should I do now, during my patient's time of fear and stress?

**Screwtape**

> Hatred is always effective to use against courage. The tension of human nerves during noise, danger, and fatigue makes them prone to violent emotion.

> We simply guide this vulnerability toward our needs.

**Wormwood**

> What if his conscience gets in the way?

**Screwtape**

> Get him to think he feels hatred not on his account, but on behalf of other people wronged by their enemies. Suggest to him that Christians are told to forgive their enemies, but not other people's enemies.

**Wormwood**

> I like that!

**Screwtape**

> Yes. But remember that hatred is best combined with fear.

## Text Message 29.3

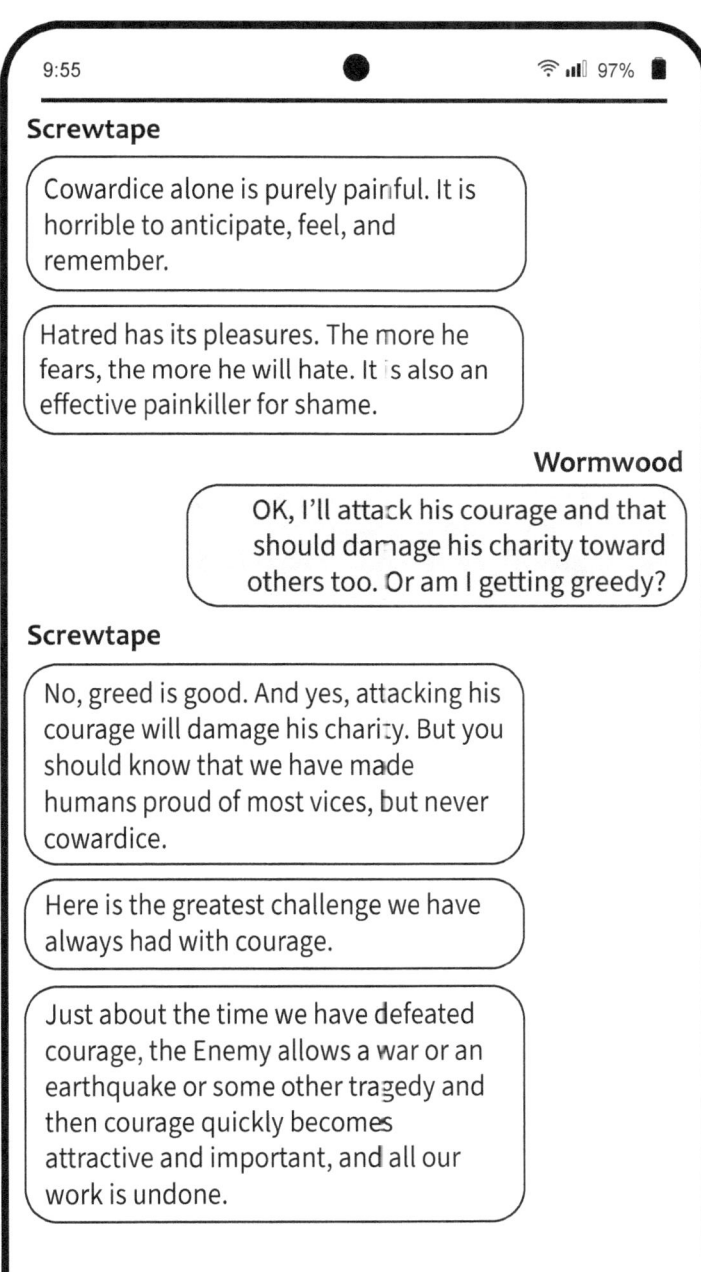

**Screwtape**

Cowardice alone is purely painful. It is horrible to anticipate, feel, and remember.

Hatred has its pleasures. The more he fears, the more he will hate. It is also an effective painkiller for shame.

**Wormwood**

OK, I'll attack his courage and that should damage his charity toward others too. Or am I getting greedy?

**Screwtape**

No, greed is good. And yes, attacking his courage will damage his charity. But you should know that we have made humans proud of most vices, but never cowardice.

Here is the greatest challenge we have always had with courage.

Just about the time we have defeated courage, the Enemy allows a war or an earthquake or some other tragedy and then courage quickly becomes attractive and important, and all our work is undone.

## Text Message 29.4

9:59 ● 🔋 97% 📶

**Wormwood**

If the degree of my patient's courage is unclear, should I put thoughts of cowardice in his mind?

**Screwtape**

Yes, but be aware that there is danger in introducing cowardice in your patient.

**Wormwood**

Great. Now what?

**Screwtape**

Cowardice can produce real self-knowledge and self-loathing, and these can lead to repentance and humility.

During times of peace we can make many of the vermin ignore good and evil, and ignorant of cowardice and courage.

Wars awaken many from the moral stupor we've led them to.

**Wormwood**

Things like physical danger and natural disaster can lead to virtue?

## Text Message 29.5

10:03      🔵      🛜 .ıll 97% 🔋

**Screwtape**

> Yes, and the Enemy appears to use this against us. Anyway, courage is not simply one of the virtues. It is the key virtue. Courage allows other virtues to remain strong even in the face of personal danger.

> Without courage, virtues like chastity, honesty, or mercy collapse when the stakes are high.

> A young woman is chaste until she fears losing her unchaste boyfriend.

> A business owner is honest until an economic downturn threatens his income.

> And Pilate was merciful, until it became risky for him.

**Wormwood**

> I may lose as much as I gain by making my patient a coward. He may learn too much about himself.

**Screwtape**

> It sounds like YOU need some courage.

## Text Message 29.6

**Screwtape**

There is the chance you can aggravate his cowardice to the point of despair. This would be a great victory!

Despair is a greater sin than any of the sins which provoke it.

**Wormwood**

So how do I proceed?

**Screwtape**

Precautions can increase fear. Keep his mind playing vague ideas of things he can or cannot do. Use ridiculous hypothetical worries based on other, imagined worries.

Also, use false confidence and then at the moment of real terror, rush the false confidence out and get the fatal act done before he knows what you are up to.

The emotion of fear does us no good.

The act of cowardice is all that matters.

## Summary

This page from the enemy's playbook suggests courage and self-awareness weaken the devil's attack.

## Resources

| | |
|---|---|
| Righteousness whose works are virtues | Wisdom 8:7 |
| Take courage | John 16:33 |
| The conditions of discipleship | Matthew 10:39; 16:25 Mark 8:35, Luke 9:24 |
| The day of the Son of Man | Luke 17:33 |
| Cardinal virtues | CCC paragraph 1805 |
| Fortitude | CCC paragraph 1808 |
| Pilate's cowardice | CCC paragraph 1851 |
| Martyrdom | CCC paragraph 2473 |

## Thoughts on courage from G. K. Chesterton

"Take the case of courage. No quality has ever so much addled the brains and tangled the definitions of merely rational sages. Courage is almost a contradiction in terms. It means a strong desire to live taking the form of a readiness to die. 'He that will lose his life, the same shall save it,' is not a piece of mysticism for saints and heroes. It is a piece of everyday advice for sailors or mountaineers. It might be printed in an Alpine guide or a drill book. This paradox is the whole principle of courage; even of quite earthly or brutal courage. A man cut off by the sea may save his life if we will risk it on the precipice.

He can only get away from death by continually stepping within an inch of it. A soldier surrounded by enemies, if he is to cut his way out, needs to combine a strong desire for living with a strange carelessness about dying. He must not merely cling to life, for then he will be a coward, and will not escape. He must not merely wait for death, for then he will be a suicide, and will not escape. He must seek his life in a spirit of furious indifference to it; he must desire life like water and yet drink death like wine. No philosopher, I fancy, has ever expressed this romantic riddle with adequate lucidity, and I certainly have not done so. But Christianity has done more: it has marked the limits of it in the awful graves of the suicide and the hero, showing the distance between him who dies for the sake of living and him who dies for the sake of dying."

~ G. K. Chesterton, Orthodoxy


## Counterattack Actions

- Review your day to see if danger or fatigue have affected you spiritually.
- Ask God for more courage in the area of your life where you need it most.

## Questions

1.  Why does tension from experiencing danger or fatigue make us prone to violent emotion?

2.  Is it possible to hate someone or something for another person but not for yourself? What would be some examples?

3.  Where does cowardice come from? How can you overcome cowardice? How have you become more courageous at times in your life?

4.  What is an example of an act of cowardice? Screwtape even calls them a "fatal act."

5.  What are your thoughts on what G. K. Chesterton said about courage? Specifically: "…Courage is almost a contradiction in terms. It means a strong desire to live taking the form of a readiness to die. 'He that will lose his life, the same shall save it,' is not a piece of mysticism for saints and heroes."

6.  What do you do to combat temptations and suggestions like the ones Screwtape suggests in this text message?

## Text Message 30.1

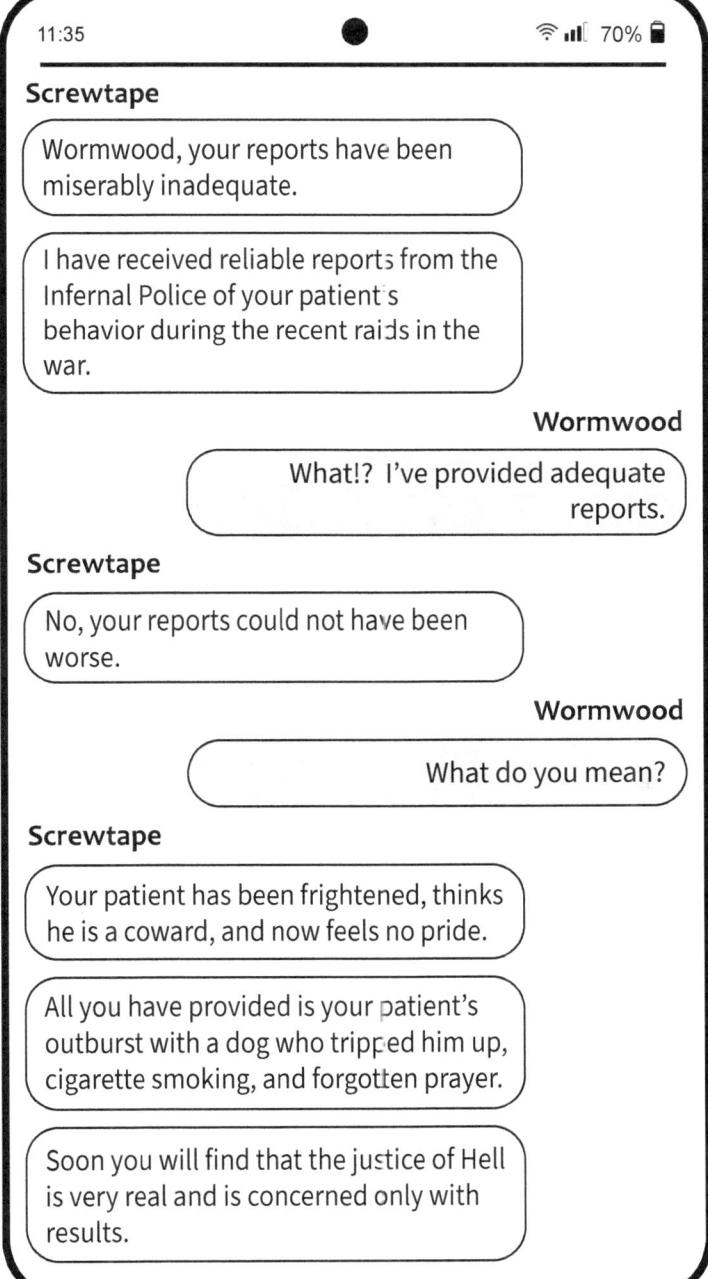

## Text Message 30.2

11:38        ●        📶 70% 🔋

**Screwtape**

Bring us food or become food yourself.

**Wormwood**

I reported that I expect good results from my patient's fatigue.

**Screwtape**

Yes, but these were the only constructive words I read.

Fatigue is well enough, but it won't just fall into your hands.

**Wormwood**

What do you mean?

**Screwtape**

Unfortunately, fatigue can produce extreme gentleness and quiet of mind.

If you've seen humans led by fatigue into anger or impatience, that is because they, Wormwood, had competent tempters.

And moderate fatigue is a better soil than absolute exhaustion.

For fatigue to really work for us we need something else.

## Text Message 30.3

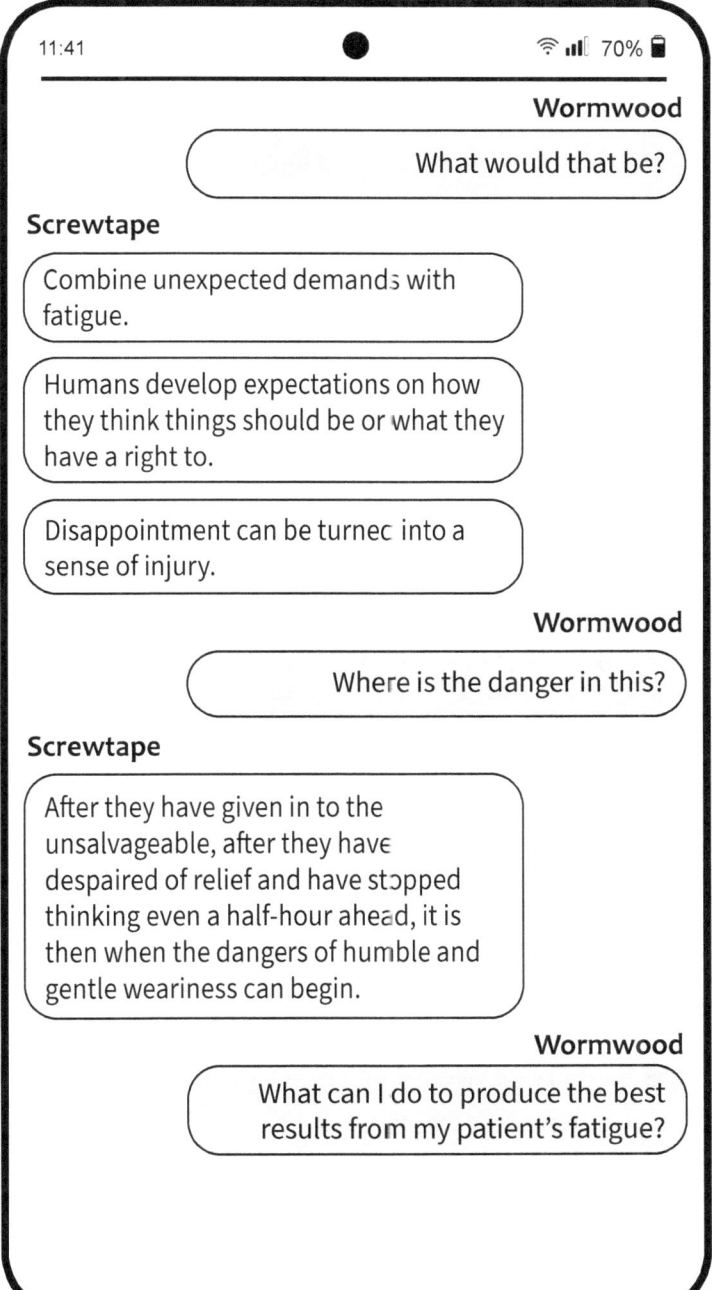

**Wormwood**

What would that be?

**Screwtape**

Combine unexpected demands with fatigue.

Humans develop expectations on how they think things should be or what they have a right to.

Disappointment can be turned into a sense of injury.

**Wormwood**

Where is the danger in this?

**Screwtape**

After they have given in to the unsalvageable, after they have despaired of relief and have stopped thinking even a half-hour ahead, it is then when the dangers of humble and gentle weariness can begin.

**Wormwood**

What can I do to produce the best results from my patient's fatigue?

## Text Message 30.4

**Screwtape**

Feed him with false hopes. Put into his mind plausible reasons for believing attacks in the war are ending.

Get him to comfort himself that very soon he'll be back home in the comfort of his own bed.

Exaggerate the weariness by making him think it will soon be over. Humans often feel that the strain can no longer be endured at the very moment it is ending or, when they think it is ending.

Like with cowardice, keep him from total commitment. Whatever he says, keep his inner resolve from bearing that which comes, but to bear it for a "reasonable amount of time."

And keep the "reasonable amount of time" shorter than the trial will likely last.

The fun is to make them yield just when relief is almost in sight.

If your patient meets the girl under conditions of strain, make full use of the fact that fatigue often makes women talk more and men talk less.

## Text Message 30.5

**Screwtape**

> Much resentment, even between lovers, can come from this.

> We can also have some fun with the word "real."

**Wormwood**

> What do you mean by that?

**Screwtape**

> In all experiences which can make humans happier or better, make them think only physical facts are "real"; and that spiritual elements are subjective.

> Spiritual elements should be your primary focus in all experiences which can discourage or corrupt them.

> For example: in birth, the blood and the pain are "real" and the rejoicing is a mere subjective point of view.

> In death, terror and ugliness reveal what death really means.

**Wormwood**

> Explain that more.

## Text Message 30.6

**Screwtape**

Make him think the hatefulness of a hated person is "real," in hatred you see men as they are.

Make him think the loveliness of a loved person is merely a subjective haze concealing a "real" core of sexual appetite.

Work on this, and your patient, properly handled, will have no difficulty in regarding his emotion at the sight of human destruction as a revelation of "reality" and his emotion of happy children or beautiful weather as mere sentiment.

**Wormwood**

This is good. I have new hope for getting my patient.

## Summary

This page from the enemy's playbook suggests that hope and resolve (spiritual perseverance) weaken the devil's attack. Unmanaged fatigue and self-defined expectations can be a target the devil focuses on with us.

## Resources

| | |
|---|---|
| Abound in hope | Romans 15:13 |
| Pray always | Ephesians 6:18 |
| Fight a good fight | 1 Timothy 1:18–19 |
| Perseverance in faith | CCC paragraph 162 |
| The grace of final perseverance | CCC paragraph 2016 |
| Perseverance in prayer | CCC paragraph 2728 |
| Perseverance in love | CCC paragraphs 2742–2743 |

## Counterattack Actions

- Create a list of what you hope for. Include those who are the sources of hope for each item.
- Pray the Lord's Prayer, found in chapter Text 24, paying close attention and really meaning the words "Thy will be done."

## Questions

1. When do you feel closer to God: in moments of pride or in moments of humility? Why?

2. Why can fatigue take you in different directions? Sometimes to gentleness and peace, and other times to anger and impatience.

3. How do you handle unexpected demands today? Did you handle them differently when you were younger? How?

4. How can you guard against false hopes?

5. Have you found yourself making partial rather than total commitments to some things? How did that work out?

6. Do physical facts seem more "real" than spiritual elements? Why do you think that is? What examples can you think of?

7.  Regarding physical facts and spiritual elements, how might
    the devil, by using "suggestion," create doubt of the Real
    Presence of Jesus in the Eucharist?

8.  What do you do to combat temptations and suggestions like
    the ones Screwtape suggests in this text message?

## Text Message 31.1

8:05  ● 🔋 60% 🔋

**Wormwood**

Uncle

**Screwtape**

Yes

**Wormwood**

My patient has died in the war.
I have lost him

to the Enemy

**Screwtape**

My dear, dear Wormwood.

**Wormwood**

All your guidance and care for me
since the beginning must still count
for something, right?

**Screwtape**

Far from it!

Yet again you are mistaken. From the
beginning we have both desired
something from each other.

The difference between you and I is
that I am the stronger.

## Text Message 31.2

8:07     ●     📶 60% 🔋

**Wormwood**

You have said "bring us food or become food yourself."
What did you mean by that?

**Screwtape**

Yes, we expected you to bring us a new human soul for us to feed on, but you have let him slip through your fingers.

If not his soul to feed on, then yours!

The howl of this loss and of your failure echoes through all the levels of the Kingdom of Noise.

Recall what happened at that moment, when they snatched your patient from you.

Suddenly, and for the first time, he saw you clearly and he recognized the part you had had on him and knew that your influence was now over.

Think about it! And let it be the new beginning of your agony.

Think about what he felt at that moment!

## Text Message 31.3

**Screwtape**

It is bad enough to see the vermin remove their sins and their imperfections and the closeness they sometimes attain with the Enemy.

But then! This final and permanent removal of sin and imperfections!

The more I think about it the angrier I get!

He got through so easily! No doctor's sentence, no nursing home, no false hopes of life; just sheer, instantaneous liberation.

It seemed to be all our world; the scream of bombs, the stench of explosives on his lips and lungs, feet aching with weariness, his heart cold with horrors; and then the next moment it was all gone, like a bad dream.

You defeated, outmaneuvered fool!

Did you see how naturally it al happened? How this earth-born two-legged animal entered into new life? How all his doubts became, in the twinkling of an eye, ridiculous?

## Text Message 31.4

**Screwtape**

And as your patient saw you, he also saw Them.

I know how it went. You backpedaled, dizzy and blinded.

You were more hurt by Them than your patient ever was by the bombs.

How demeaning. This thing of "earth and slime" stood upright and conversed with the spirits and all you could do was cower.

The gods are strange to the mortal eye, and yet not strange.

Your former patient hadn't the faintest idea until that very hour how They would look; until that very hour, he may have even doubted their existence.

But when he saw Them, he knew that he had always known Them and he realized what part each of Them had played at times in his life, during those times when he imagined himself alone.

He did not say to each of Them, "Who are you?" But rather, "So it was you all the time."

## Text Message 31.5

**8:15**      60%

**Screwtape**

All that They were and said at this meeting awoke memories. The dim consciousness of friends around him, which had haunted his solitude, were now explained.

He not only saw Them; he also saw Him. Your patient, this animal, this thing, begotten in a bed, could look at Him.

**Wormwood**

What was that blinding, suffocating fire?

**Screwtape**

That is what it was to you, but to him it is a cool light, it is clarity itself, and it wears the form of a Man.

**Wormwood**

I saw my patient prostrate himself before the Presence and saw him in pain despising his sins, the same way I controlled him.

**Screwtape**

Nonsense!

## Text Message 31.6

**Screwtape**

> Yes, your former patient may still have to encounter some pain, but he will embrace those pains. The vermin would never trade these pains for any earthly pleasure.

> All the delights of the senses, of the heart, or the intellect, with which you once have tempted him are gone.

> They are now about as tempting and attractive as a haggard prostitute would seem to a man who hears that his true beloved, whom he had loved all his life and whom he thought was dead is alive and now at his door.

**Wormwood**

> Isn't it possible to find out what the Enemy is really up to?

**Screwtape**

> Besides the curse of useless tempters like you, the greatest failure of our intelligence department is our inability to understand the ways of the Enemy.

> That knowledge, so hateful and sickly a thing, is what is needed for Power! And it remains unknown to us.

## Text Message 31.7

8:21                    ●              🛜 📶 60% 🔋

**Screwtape**

Sometimes I am almost in despair, and
all that sustains me is the conviction
that our reality must win in the end.

But now, I have you to settle with.
You know what I must do.

**Wormwood**

But uncle

**Screwtape**

We have nothing more to discuss.

## Summary

This page from the enemy's playbook describes how Satan responds after losing a soul for Hell. It also describes some of what the human soul experiences after physical death and before entering Heaven.

## Resources

| | |
|---|---|
| The resurrection body | 1 Corinthians 15:35–49 |
| The resurrection event | 1 Corinthians 15:50–58 |
| Nothing unclean will enter Heaven | Revelation 21:27 |
| Expiation for the dead | 2 Maccabees 12:46 |
| Angels in the life of the Church | CCC paragraphs 334–336 |
| Intercession of the Saints | CCC paragraph 956 |
| What is rising from the dead? | CCC paragraph 997 |
| Who will rise from the dead? | CCC paragraph 998 |
| How will the dead rise from the dead? | CCC paragraph 999 |
| The final purification (Purgatory) | CCC paragraphs 1030–1032 |
| Christ's work in the liturgy – Christ glorified | CCC paragraphs 1084–1085 |
| Sacrament of Penance | CCC paragraphs 1480–1484 |
| A cloud of witnesses (the Saints) | CCC paragraphs 2683–2684 |

## Glory Be (Doxology)

Glory be to the Father
and to the Son
and to the Holy Spirit,
as it was in the beginning
is now, and ever shall be
world without end.
Amen.

## Counterattack Actions

- Pray the Glory Be prayer everyday.
- If your faith tradition has the Sacrament of Reconciliation and you have not received the sacrament in a while, go and receive this sacrament. Satan will not be pleased.
- In addition to asking your friends and family to pray for you, include the saints in your prayer circle. They are closer to God than those we live with here in this world.

## Questions

1. How do you remove your "sins and imperfections" and attain the closeness to God that Screwtape speaks of?

2. How do you interpret the final and permanent removal of sin and impurities that Screwtape mentions?

3. What doubts in the spiritual battle should be considered ridiculous? How would you live differently if these doubts didn't exist?

4. Do you think saints and angels have played a part in your life? How?

5. What do you understand final purification (purgatory) to be? Is it necessary? Why or why not?

6. Have you imagined what it will be like to see Jesus in all his glory? How do you imagine that to be?

## Postscript

All of Holy Scripture can be reduced to a single word: **Jesus**.

Our spiritual battle has many weapons, and they can be reduced to a single word: **Love**.

Jesus said, "This I command you: love one another." ~ John 15:17

### Prayer for the Journey

God our Father,
you are the creator of everything good,
of all things visible and invisible,
of all things physical and spirit.
Send your Holy Spirit to guide us on our pilgrim journey
and be our companion on the way.
Protect us and strengthen us against the tactics of the devil.
And when our earthly journey is complete,
welcome us home to eternal life with you.
We ask this in the name of Jesus,
our Lord and Savior.
Amen